ZERBANOO GIFFORD was born in India in 1950 and came to live in England at the age of three. Her father was the founder-President of the World Zoroastrian Organisation. Zerbanoo Gifford was educated at Roedean and the Watford College of Technology. In 1982 she was elected onto Harrow Council and she has twice contested parliamentary seats. She has chaired the Liberal Party's Community Relations Panel and their 1986 Commission looking into ethnic minority involvement in British life. In 1989, she was given the Nehru Centenary Award by the Non-Resident Indian Association.

Having travelled extensively as a writer, politician and tourist, she has contributed to, and been featured in, numerous TV and radio programmes, newspapers and magazines internationally. For her work as editor of a women's magazine, she was nominated for the British Editors' Awards.

She is Co-Chair of the Warwick University Centre for Research in Asian Migration, Adviser on Community Affairs to the leader of the Liberal Democrats, the Rt. Hon Paddy Ashdown MP. A patron of ADiTi – which supports and promotes South Asian Dance – and an adviser to the Princes' Youth Business Trust.

Zerbanoo is married to Richard, an international lawyer, and they have two sons, Mark and Alexander ('Wags').

THE
GOLDEN THREAD

THE GOLDEN THREAD

Asian Experiences of Post-Raj Britain

Zerbanoo Gifford

GRAFTON BOOKS
A Division of the Collins Publishing Group

LONDON GLASGOW
TORONTO SYDNEY AUCKLAND

Grafton Books
A Division of the Collins Publishing Group
8 Grafton Street, London W1X 3LA

First published in hardback
by Pandora Press 1990

This edition published by Grafton Books 1990

A CIP catalogue record for this book is
available from the British Library

ISBN 0–246–13863–7

Printed and bound in Great Britain

With thanks to
Mark, Wags, Ian, Alison
and Richard of course.

The proceeds of the
Golden Thread are
donated by the author
to *Warwick University*'s
Centre for Research
in Asian Migration.

The establishment of the Centre
for Research in Asian Migration
at Warwick University marks the
beginning of a new chapter in
the field of academic research in
Britain. The aim of the Centre
is to put on record the hitherto
unknown and often ignored facts
relating to the contributions, past
as well as present, made by Asian
people to countries in which they
have settled.

The Golden Thread is dedicated to "Bapai",
Zerbanoo Gifford's paternal grandmother,
Gover Rustom Irani (1901-1984), out of love for her
and because she symbolises all that is best in Asian
womanhood: selflessness, wisdom and beauty.

Contents

List of illustrations

Preface

Zerbanoo means 'golden lady', a name inherited from my maternal grandmother. In the East naming is an important custom by which the family can keep those they love amongst them. My sister, Genie, and brothers, Rustom and Naswan, were also named after relatives and through this we have a special affinity to our ancestors. In many ways I can be compared with my maternal grandmother, Zerbanoo; I share her zest for life, as well as having inherited some of her physical characteristics. Despite these similarities, I always felt a stronger bond to my father's mother, who had looked after me when I was young and whom everyone saw as the pillar and strength of the family. Although my grandmother, Bapai, was married at 14, bore twelve children and was widowed at 36, she knew the importance of real education. This was a lesson also passed on to me by my mother, Kitty, one of the last four pupils to study personally under the famous educationist, Madame Montessori. Like the female figures in my own history, I too prize education as a way to the enlightenment and enrichment of character. Education, from the Latin meaning to draw out, is therefore one of the golden threads of this book and is a catalyst to the changing attitudes at today's cultural crossroads.

So little seems to be known about Asian women in Britain that this book is an attempt to educate by example and add a little to a growing body of scholarship on Asian migration. With the aim of fostering present enthusiasm and the hope of inspiring further interest in this subject, all my proceeds from the book will be donated to Warwick University and the Centre for Research in Asian Migration which is being established there. The book is dedicated to my grandmother, Bapai, because of my love for her and because she symbolises all that is best in Asian womanhood: selflessness, wisdom and beauty. She, more than anybody, would have appreciated the need for an international centre to research and document the rôle of Asians and

Asian women in the diaspora. One book could not possibly include all the women who merit mention or all the information collected, but at least now a start has been made to gather material together, and all relevant papers and photographs will be given to Warwick University for their archives and further research.

Maybe it is appropriate that a 'Golden Lady' should be the golden thread which ties together the lives of the women within this book. I find that all people have the capacity to intrigue and their life stories can be riveting. When young, I would sit with my mother on trains and study the people opposite us, trying to decide where they were born, their background and what deeds they were hiding. An upbringing in our family hotel gave me a quick eye and nurtured my natural human curiosity, gifts which I have used to build a natural network of friends from all walks of life.

I had access to a cross-section of Asian women, and took the opportunity to show their diversity and talents. Indeed, although I have given all of the women the name 'Asian', as their families originally came from the Indian subcontinent, I felt it was important that they came from different places, generations, cultures and backgrounds. To the majority of British people, Asian women are simply seen as different from themselves but the same as each other. Few realise the wealth of journeying all over the world which has characterised Asian peoples' lives, or the differing life styles and ambitions which they hold. The heritages which they bring to Britain are often tri-cultural, infused with European, African, or West Indian cultures. Many have not lived in either India or Pakistan but have chosen to settle in Britain, their other motherland, instead. By revealing the range of Asian womanhood, their stories undermine the stereotypes and popular mythologies to offer the more complex and exciting realities of their lives. The challenge to draw the many characters of Asian womanhood together has taken much time and energy, but the quality of their lives and successes has made it a satisfying and enriching task. I felt that the time was right for such a book.

I experienced great enjoyment in meeting the women, and my sons still amusingly recall how I returned home each time with the feeling that today I had met the most wonderful woman in the world. I felt frustrated that other people did not even know of these women and could not share my excitement. Certainly, most of the women within this book have been privileged in some way. Some by their family's social position, others by the care and education given to them, but many only by their own strength of character and determination to create a better life.

This book is intended to be a celebration of their lives, a testament to the contributions which they have made to many aspects of British life which seem to be unnoticed. The lack of public acknowledgement shown to some of these women made them feel unsure about their achievements. Unlike some of their male counterparts they are not in *Who's Who*, but once the mirror of their own lives was held up to them, they realised their worth and began to fill out their own reflections.

This book is meant to be one of life and not of letters. It lets Asian women speak for themselves and offers them the opportunity freely to voice their beliefs and experiences, one which few had been given before. By telling their stories in their own words, the language of the book conveys an essence of their personalities. The biographies at the end of the book are designed to give a fuller picture of each woman and provide an insight into the way in which their backgrounds have shaped their lives, expectations and beliefs.

Women clearly have the starring rôles in this book, in contrast to most literature in which they are simply the props in a male-dominated script. The significance and attention given to the women made the many golden threads of Asian womanhood visible to themselves too, and enabled each woman to learn about and rediscover others, often weaving an Eastern design of interconnection and interdependence. The book tells of Asian women whose lives have become forgotten stories of success and offers them not as lost rôle models but as lost beads on the necklace of enlightenment for all women.

Women are the link to the future, leading to new generations, not only of children, but of creative ideas. Nevertheless, I believe that we should be looking towards an inclusive society rather than an exclusive one, and so I have included some male views too. The token man must never be forgotten. This book tells of the high value which Asian women place upon relationships, unravelling compelling stories which bind together women and men. However, in exploring Asian women's relationships with men, it discloses their attitudes to themselves as women.

Sex, religion and politics are the most interesting areas of life and all are revealed here in order to trace the golden threads which lead us to fulfilment, enlightenment and our ultimate destiny in life. The quality of the spiritual yarn is balanced by the substance of the earthly flax. The book tells of life for Asians living in Britain today, the realities behind the promise of Britain 'The Motherland' and the experiences of immigration and integration into British society.

When Asians first travelled to Britain they held on to their suitcases, collecting souvenirs to take home with them and thereby creating the myth of return. Now the second generation, born in Britain, is clearly here to stay and it is up to them to claim their just place and voice within British society. The British must also acknowledge that there will be no 'return of the native' and that the presence of those who were seen just as workers, a transient and convenient population, is now a permanent fixture. Although there are many differences between India and Britain, between Asian and British people, there is also a special bond that can never be denied.

The differences between cultures need not breed conflict. The perspective of the British through Asian eyes, which this book offers, acknowledges points of contrast, but is also a positive and humorous account which shows how others' cultures can be appreciated and enjoyed. Many Asians living in Britain feel affection for the British way of life. Social antagonism and resentment is usually created by attempts to defy differences between peoples and to impose uniformity. Instead differences between the English and the Asians should be harnessed creatively and used to lead Britain into the New Post-Raj Era.

The positive attitude of the Beatles, that 'things are getting better all the time', had a universal appeal which captivated the world. In truth the 'good old days' were rarely so and the myth of a golden age of innocence should be replaced by the reality of an age of wisdom, moderation and shared joy – a true golden age.

This is my story, but the book has many stories, each with several layers of meaning open to interpretation by the reader. Stories are an important form of education as they are easily remembered and so can pass their message onto others. The first story of the book tells of a queen whose refusal to be overborne by her king, when coupled with her love and understanding for this man, enabled her to offer him the ultimate knowledge of self-realization.

1

For the Love of an Asian Woman

In the seventeenth century, the Taj Mahal, one of the wonders of the world, was created for the love of an Asian woman. Although the Taj Mahal is dedicated to a woman, Mumtaz, it tells a male history, that of her devoted husband, Emperor Shah Jahan. However, this king, like many other royal men of power, was possessed by a dual passion for architecture and horticulture. The first offers the irresistible temptation of immortality and the second confirms the ultimate significance of life itself.

Shah Jahan's famed rose gardens have not survived to tell their own tale, but they do offer us the female plot. Like so many other stories, it has been passed down to us through the guardians of many generations and is part of an oral tradition which, like the golden thread, joins our past to the present, weaving into our own lives the wisdom of our ancestors.

The story tells how this Mogul king once chastised his beloved Queen Mumtaz for complaining about the discomforts which she felt during her fourteen endless pregnancies. He informed her that most of his female subjects happily gave birth in the fields, unattended by doctors and servants. Mumtaz was incensed at his lack of compassion and determined to make him understand her situation. She went to his head mali, the chief gardener, and ordered him to cease watering, pruning and weeding the king's precious roses.

As the weeks passed, Shah Jahan noticed that all was not well in the gardens; his roses were losing their colour and fragrance, they were wilting, even dying. Bewildered, he asked his wife for her advice. She informed him that his subjects' roses happily grew in the wild, unattended by a mali, blessed only by the sun and rain sent by Allah. The king's immediate reaction was one of fury and, characteristic of absolute male supremacy, his first thought was of a separation! However, Shah Jahan soon realised that for anything or anybody to flourish and bring great joy, nurturing and care are essential.

A rose, the archetypal icon of English beauty, may seem an unlikely metaphor for Asian womanhood, but the *gulab*, the rose, is prized as highly in Agra as in Surrey and in many ways offers a valid symbol of Asian womanhood. Indeed, the range of women to be found within these pages constitutes a garden of infinite variety and complexity. There are the buds of youth, the flowers in full bloom and the subtle fragrance of maturity.

Some are pressed roses, preserved between the pages of history by the legacy of their remarkable achievements. Many are hybrids; women whose bi- and tri-cultural heritages have imbued them with the strengths of diversity. Selecting the best from their many cultures they are the prized flowers, holding the potential to be the strongest strains, with their quality of survival matched by their originality. Many have undoubtedly been cultivated but, far from justifying elitism, this care challenges accepted stereotypes by uniting the antitheses of nature and nurture.

A few are wild roses, neither exotic nor rare, blossoming despite adversity; these women are to be found where they are least expected. Even the women who have suffered have transformed their hardship, perfuming the hand which crushes them, gaining strength like roses that are pruned.

Their unique qualities as individuals defy stereotyping and name-calling, confirming that these roses do indeed smell as sweet by any other name. However, perhaps the most important tale they tell is of growth and change. Certainly the most successful ones have adapted to their new climate, putting down strong roots in a foreign soil, giving forth a multitude of flowers whose colours enrich the landscape for all. Some have been unable to achieve this, finding the British soil too shallow or hostile to sustain their growth and yet they have their own radiance.

The rose, like the lives of these women, inspires us. Their stories mock the pseudo-simplicity of stereotypes which make no attempt to embrace the complexity and contradictions of real life. Breaking free of these images which only define in order to confine, they challenge the fundamental status quo and, by their own honesty, dismiss any notion of the 'typical' or 'true' Asian woman. They do not seek to impose an alternative exclusive view; they do not need to. Like the rose which spontaneously discloses its glories, their qualities will emerge naturally.

At this very moment this new rose garden is coming into full bloom, offering a rainbow vision which spans the spectra of race, religion, culture, caste and class. Sharing the common root stock of Asia and the soil of Britain, these women reveal a multiplicity of new varieties. Cajoled by the charisma of colonialism, they have come from all parts of Africa, the Middle East, Europe, the Far East, Australasia and the Americas, as well as the Indian subcontinent. They have grafted themselves onto British society with varying degrees of success and the stories of their lives provide us with a vital vision of history: a mirror with the power to reflect their identities and those of others.

2

The Muse in the Mirror

Shattering the looking glass of vanity, in which the eye gazes only for admiration, these stories have given me a new and far more interesting mirror through which to see my whole self. It is a mirror which, in reflecting other Asian women's lives, has made me feel more confident about my own.

Our shared stories brought humour and joy, transforming the sterile technique of interviewing into the genuine forming of friendships. Confiding and conferring, we all agreed that the British 'compliment', 'You can't be Indian, you're not like the rest', was the gravest insult of all. As Mishti Chatterji, the publisher, pointed out, 'So many times people have said to me, "But you're so English!" It is supposed to be taken as a compliment, if you were Indian you couldn't possibly be as nice as you are.' By rejecting the false flattery of being considered the exception, we all realised that we had so much in common. No longer isolated from each other, we began to feel the strength of the golden thread which unites us in a shared history, knowledge and vision. The Asian women within these pages have come to realise their own value inside British society and also the worth of others, about whom they knew so little. Maybe the experiences and emotions which are revealed by their voices will mirror the other fascinating Asian women, which time and space have sadly prevented from being included.

Indeed, it is the golden thread of womanhood which emerges as the strongest link between us, stronger even than that of race. The stories of these women will add a new dimension to every woman's reflections on herself. On the day when Benazir Bhutto held history in a woman's hand, as the first woman Prime Minister of Pakistan, this mirror was shown to me by another remarkable woman, Barbara Rogers, the editor of *Everywoman*. She perceived that I was well placed to write about Asian womanhood as my work in community politics, women's magazines and my interest in history meant that I had access to the many different faces mirrored within it. Barbara offered me her moment of vision and inspiration, and stressed that, as an Asian woman, I should give it a voice. Her intuitive understanding enabled her to see that I was in a position to empathise, while she could only sympathise; I could share their experiences, while she could only try to understand them.

Motivated by Barbara's words and Benazir's momentous deeds, I dashed from a TV programme which blatantly trivialised Asian women's rôle in political life to interview Palestinian publisher Naim Attallah about his epic book, *Women*. I was disappointed by his picture of exceptional women, which was almost entirely Western, and decided to end the ignorance which resulted in Asian women constantly being overlooked. I knew that the moment was right for such a book.

Belonging to the same generation as Benazir, who had just exploded the mythologies of female submission, I too sensed the potential for change within British society and a flux in attitudes and beliefs which needed to be seized upon. It is now evident that entering a new decade humanity is undergoing a global reassessment of ideological and political values. Like the rose bud which must open, society can resist change no longer.

In Britain, the cultural watershed of the 'Salman Rushdie Affair' has provided a biased and partial crash-course in Islam. By suddenly making the real numbers of Asians within this land visible, it has divulged the face of Islamic terror and not that of its beauty.

For me it is the time of a personal watershed as celebrating my 40th birthday brings me to a crucial crossroad in my life. Forty is undoubtedly a number with enormous symbolic significance: the forty years in the wilderness for the Jews and the forty days there for Jesus, the forty days of the flood and forty days for the womb to regain its position after giving birth. All of these offer a time for reflection and renewal. It is a time to leave the longing for fame and glamour in the past, to accept the present with new wisdom and beauty, and look forward to a future with more time to explore one's own identity. Rather than offering a reflection of grief and disappointment at fading beauty, age can offer a mirror of inner radiance and experience which the glories of youth can seldom match.

Certain that I was fulfilling my destiny, I approached Philippa Brewster at Pandora Press, as Barbara had assured me that she would be interested in handling my project. I was not disappointed. She

responded wonderfully, presenting me through Pandora the last gift
to leave her box, the hope of enlightenment. Luckily for me, this was
the first book of its kind and so I could set my own precedents, and
Philippa gave me all the creative space and freedom necessary.

Our first thought was of an autobiography, but we realised that
this was an insular quest. A book about a single Asian woman may
have confirmed the belief that she was different from the rest,
whether exceptional or eccentric. Yet what emerged was in a way
an autobiography, a collective one and therefore a more honest one.
It reflects not only an image of ourselves, but also the way in which
contact with each other has enabled us to evolve and understand
ourselves. Our lives are all interwoven by the golden thread.

As Asian women it is important for us to take our destiny into
our own hands. It is easy to blame others for our invisibility, but
it is more important to claim for ourselves space within the picture
frame of British society. By allowing people to speak in their own
voices, I hope that the characters on the pages will fully reveal
their characters within. With a sense of daring and commitment,
these pages actually tell all that was told. They are not designed to
confirm one point of view, but to present the reader with a variety
of perspectives and viewpoints which reflect the experiences of a
range of Asian womanhood.

In order to give a true reflection of the multiplicity of their mirror
images, the vulgar tabloid sensationalism which has created among
the English the 'cult of the victim Mumtaz', where Asian women
are seen only as oppressed within their communities, had to be
rejected. The more betraying kind of image of Asian womanhood
which is offered by some Asian writers, who tell only what they
know will satisfy the curiosity and complacency of Western society,
was also spurned. Yet others have allowed themselves to become
mouthpieces for pressure groups and, by worshipping at the 'shrine
of the unknown victim', have advocated only sympathy and pity for
Asian women. It is a pathos which we can live without.

Feminist journalist Gloria Steinem wrote in one of her articles
that, 'Michael Caine is only attracted to subservient women, and
he's now found one', meaning his wife, Shakira. Shakira has her
own flourishing business and a happy marriage, despite living amidst
the lurid life of show business, accomplishments of which any
person could be proud. To infer that she is a nameless 'doormat'
is hurtful as well as untrue, yet Shakira's reaction was simply to
think how sad it was to think like that. So often it appears that

women who claim to be fighting to liberate others become substitute authorities, judging by their own criteria the 'true rôle' of woman. Shakira's choice to value her husband and daughter ahead of her own ambitions was not a means by which to deny herself personal satisfaction, but one through which to gain it. The blind spots of certain Western feminists might make them unable to perceive that fulfilment can be gained through the giving of self, as well as through the promotion of self.

In the past they have focused on their rightful contempt for chauvinism but have unconsciously created their own breed of female victims. There is now a new feminist agenda which looks at the situation from a woman's point of view and does not judge her only as an appendage to a man. When I interviewed Shakira I felt in tune with her philosophy of life, we shared an understanding of being eldest daughters responsible for our brothers and sisters, the pull that London held for us, the importance of family life and the magnetism of the Englishman. I was not as interested in why Michael Caine was attracted to Shakira, that seemed obvious, but rather in what drew her to the English character. Gloria Steinem may be convinced that Michael is a chauvinist, but at least he showed good taste in marrying Shakira.

As a feminist, I was conscious that there was very little written about the cross-section of Asian women's experiences in the West and took the challenge of meeting them and letting them tell their remarkable stories. The many faced looking glass of this book has created something of particular value to me, it has shown me many faces which have merged together to give a single reflection. Sharing my beliefs in *Kismet*, one's destiny, with the renowned writer Bapsi Sidhwa, I remarked that astrologers had predicted I would have a daughter. I saw this as an aspect of my destiny which I had managed to cheat, as I do not have the energy to have another child. Bapsi pointed out that writing a book is a creative process which, in many ways, mirrors the procreative one. Certainly there is the excitement of conception followed by the period of gestation as the ideas and materials begin to grow. Then there is the agony of giving birth, the pains of punctuality and perfection. After the birth, there is the joy of receiving congratulations, which are eagerly awaited, and the defence against the criticism which is not! Finally there is the sense of fulfilment in watching your child change your own life and those of others.

Maybe then my daughter, who was always predicted to be artistic, is coming to life through this book. Bearing the stories of so many outstanding women, she is undoubtedly a female child. Yet as Eastern philosophy teaches us, each creation holds a balance of male and female within it and so the book mirrors this too. The men recorded in this book are able to give us a different vision in their reflections upon Asian womanhood and life in Britain today.

Men may have won the toss throughout history, but that was because they printed counterfeit coins with the king's head on both sides. Such coins used to give them the surety of success, but now women have revealed their true nature. It is up to women to stamp their identity back on to the coinage, but not to repeat the fraudulence of men by producing a female replica with a double queen. It is only when the two faces exist as complimentary to each other that there will be an opportunity for equal success and joint progress.

Like a choir, the voices in this book compliment each other in their diversity. Some are superb soloists, while others provide the mellow background music, but they are all joined by the golden thread which runs through every symphony. Only a few of their possible harmonies can be heard within the space of this book, but they offer a challenge and an opportunity to many who will focus on a single octave and explore its subtle melodies. It is the collective voice of this book which imparts its strength and wisdom. Like a Greek chorus that sets the stage of history, these women's lives tell a collective truth which is eternal and which will outlive and outshine the individual stars within the drama of life.

3

Talking to Mirrors

Throughout history stories have been a constant source of fascination and inspiration. Their ability to entertain while educating us has made them a source of delight as well as of knowledge. They help us to remember the lives of our ancestors and to achieve an understanding of our own. Stories hold a special power to change attitudes because, unlike laws and commandments, they do not resist change themselves. Like a golden bracelet which offers a more interesting history with each charm added to it, a story continues to evolve and is enriched by the new details and insights which each narrator brings. By engraving my own initials upon a Middle Eastern story, I have allowed the female figure to enter the male plot and tell her own tale of life. The story reveals that life offers us many different rôles and that there are varying ways in which we can change the beliefs and lives of others.

It tells of two people walking by the shore who decided to inscribe their philosophies for others to behold. The man took a chisel and engraved his words on the face of the rock. The woman took a stick and wrote her words upon the sand. As the tide rose, the sea gently erased the words on the sand, but did not touch those carved in the rock. The man, proud of his actions, gazed for a long time upon his own words: 'I am he who is.' He then turned and, noticing the woman's words were washed away, asked her what her message had been. She replied, 'This I wrote: I am but a drop of this great ocean.'

In his desire to triumph over anonymity, the man failed to realise that his immortal words were also immutable. The chisel may have left an impressive inscription, but it could only be seen by those who passed by, and would never alter its meaning to embrace the changes which time brings. The woman's words reached beyond the monoliths of personal testimony and taken by the sea, they bore themselves and their wisdom to every shore.

Most movements to challenge the injustice, inertia and the status quo of power structures have been inspired by remarkable individuals whose timely visions captured the collective imagination of their societies, and whose achievements have now been engraved into the tablets of fame. Yet, as the woman in our story reveals, great changes can also come from small ripples within the sea of society. It was an unknown black woman, Rosa Parks, who ignited the fire of the American Civil Rights movement with a simple gesture of defiance. In 1955, physically exhausted after a long day at work, she refused to leave her place at the front of a bus and take the back seat which was deemed by American society to be her position in life. She confronted the racial injustice of America's Deep South which was so evident and yet had been accepted for so long, and by her refusal to be pushed around any longer, inspired others to follow her example. The Civil Rights movement made the world aware that racial injustice survived in America and shamed a whole people into taking long awaited action to confront racial arrogance.

In many countries laws have changed people's actions. Both the unwritten and written laws of racial discrimination are now beginning to be abolished. The blatant racism which the British displayed in the China of old, with signs reading 'No Dogs or Chinese' placed at the entrance to the Shanghai Park, and the euphemistic words 'Right Of Admission Reserved' which were displayed outside many public places in colonial East Africa, have both disappeared along with British imperial power. In Britain too, the tacit colour bars of the 1950s that operated in hotels and restaurants have all but faded.

However, laws which stop people implementing their bigotry cannot stop them from still adhering to it. All too often, laws prohibit a negative action without fostering a positive substitute. Like the stone tablets of the Ten Commandments, words chiselled into the pillars of the law only engrave the words 'Thou Shalt Not' into our memories.

Societies can only fundamentally change when the community embraces the spirit of the law. There must be a change in political will and a raising of consciousness for attitudes to evolve along with actions. English history has recorded that it was their saintly white politicians and poets who were the great abolitionists. In fact, there were two sides to the story and it was the slaves who, like the suffragettes and now the peoples of Eastern Europe, claimed their own right to freedom. English history gives an equally whitewashed version of Indian Independence. A questioner at a political meeting once asked why I did not support the Labour Party, 'After all they had given India its freedom, hadn't they?' I had to inform him that Independence had not been a gift bestowed upon the Indian peoples by any of His or Her Majesty's Governments. It had been a long battle in which millions of Indians had died or been imprisoned and, thus, Independence became inevitable.

At the end of the twentieth century progress has given us sophisticated communication and travel links, offering a global vision which should make such a naïve and biased version of events less likely. However, this progress has also brought us to the age of the nuclear and ecological apocalypse. Humanity is being forced to change its attitudes as its final hope for survival. A global questioning is beginning and the ancient values of the East are being hailed as the new values of the West. To the East, the West was always the model of success. Their own scientists, writers, artists and musicians were not visible, as they were drawn by the magnetism of technology and financial security in the West. For those of us living in Britain, we often only valued Eastern culture when it came to us through the filter of the West. Asha Phillips, the child psychotherapist, was one of the many who came to appreciate classical Indian music through the Beatles' discovery of the compelling music of Ravi Shankar!

Now the mirror is being turned around and the West is looking to the East for inspiration and wisdom. Like the sun which rises in the East and sets in the West, those philosophies which originated in the East are now achieving fulfilment in the West. Their gurus, mystics and holy men have always had the insight and humility to realise that science, although greatly important, was not supremely so. To them it offered only the proof of eternal truth and not the discovery of it. They recognised that science, like all other forms of knowledge, has its limitations.

This wisdom is also one which has been kept alive by stories. Jyoti Munsiff, lawyer and Shell Oil executive, told me of the time Abdul'baha, the son of the founder of her Baha'i faith, spoke to a scientist who stated, 'I don't believe in anything I can't prove myself.' 'Is that so?' asked Abdul'baha. 'If you have a lake, with two rivers flowing into it, can you prove from which river a drop of water came?' 'Oh yes, if we analyse the water, we can tell that,' came the reply, and they went on reflecting about all the different kinds of water and how you might prove where they came from.

The scientist was feeling very satisfied at being able to prove all the various origins, until he was asked, 'When you analyse a tear-drop, how do you know whether it was a tear of sadness or of joy?' Yet, of course, that is the most important distinction of all.

As we begin to understand the importance of issues which science can never resolve, we are balancing our fervour for technology with our concern for the quality of life. The recent trend towards ecology is, in fact, only a change in attitudes and not a creation of new beliefs. Within the ancient Persian religion of Zoroastrianism, the preservation of the purity of the elements is a central ethic. Thought to be the first prophetic and monotheistic religion, Zoroastrianism is also considered to be the first environment friendly one! Yet it is only in the light of the advancement of science that the Zoroastrian bible, the *Avesta*, has become known as the first anti-pollution code.

The Western world is now being forced to recognise its mistakes and to finally change its attitudes. In its quest for El Dorado, the mythic land of gold and God, Western civilisation has turned the golden autumn of the green world into an eternal winter. A true golden age can only be achieved when people acknowledge the golden thread which links us to our elements, and our lands and people to each other.

As a Zoroastrian, I was brought up with a creation story that emphasises the intimate link between nature and human nature. For us, the genesis of humanity is an organic process in which man and woman grow together from a single seed. Our golden age was always a green one. Unlike Adam and Eve who were expelled from the garden of Eden for daring to taste the apple of supreme knowledge which enabled them to know good from evil; for us Zoroastrians, it is an individual duty to make this distinction. Neither did Zoroastrians ever suffer the God of the Old Testament's dubious blessing to man, 'Be fruitful and increase, fill the earth and subdue it, rule over the fish in the sea, the birds of heaven, and every living thing that moves upon the earth', which in turn has promoted a lack of care for our environment, over-population and a need to dominate. Indeed, by following these words, the soil from which we grow has become polluted and made the apples of both the tree of life and of knowledge turn sour.

However, if the Bible failed to offer us the lessons needed to preserve the planet, then maybe the other great influence upon the English, Shakespeare, did. Indeed, it is these two sources of knowledge which are seen as essential to man's survival by the English, and the British Broadcasting Corporation's *Desert Island Discs* radio programme makes them mandatory reading for every shipwrecked soul! Long after the British legal system permitted other religious books into the court room, the BBC still presumes that civilised man, stripped of all luxuries on a desert island, should not be deprived of the essential reading of the King James' Authorised Version of the Bible and the complete works of William Shakespeare.

It is probably Shakespeare who, through the centuries, has shown the world the subtleties of the British mind. Sita Narasimhan, an accomplished academic at Cambridge, recalled an amusing event around 1942, when she was part of a little cell of revolutionaries in India who were discussing how to rid their country of the British. It was suggested that bombs be thrown at British military bases, as they were the most vulnerable at that period in the Second World War. Sita could never forget a provincial school teacher, a maths teacher at that, suddenly becoming very vehement and agitated, jumping around and shouting, 'We can't throw bombs at the British, we can't throw bombs at the British, they gave us Shakespeare!'

Yet there was method in this maths teacher's madness, for in preserving the reputation of Shakespeare, he knew he was preserving a mind through which the English psyche could always be studied. Shakespeare, like every English gentleman who has followed him, prided himself on being able to appreciate both sides of the story, but this quality of fair-mindedness still has the ability to expose other people's weaknesses. He exploited a powerful stigma of his time in *Richard III*, where the historical king's disability is heightened to reinforce the depraved and grotesque deeds of the character. We know throughout *Othello* that it is Iago who is spiritually evil, but it is Othello himself who performs the ultimate evil of committing murder. Shakespeare instinctively understood the vulnerability of the black man loving 'not wisely but too well'. In *The Merchant of Venice*, the merciless baiting of Shylock moves the audience to sympathise with the Jew but, finally unable to answer Portia's hypocritical call for Christian mercy, Shylock is left looking a pathetic usurer. In truth, it is Shylock who has been used by Elizabethan Venetian 'Yuppies'. In all of these plays Shakespeare played up to the underlying prejudices and materialism of his, and our, society.

In *The Tempest*, Shakespeare offers us his prophetic vision of colonisation. It is a tale which has often been retold within West Indian literature. Writers from this region have revealed and restored Caliban's status as the native ruler and the betrayed slave, in order to review their own history. For Asians, *The Tempest* is prophetic in other ways for, although also usurped by imperialist power, Asians are not engaged in a search for their roots, having never been subjected to the cruelty of real slavery where one's identity was whipped away. Yet Caliban as the 'natural man', in tune with the elements of the isle, but tricked into submission by the science of Prospero, does offer a mirror for Asians. The East has been cheated by the con tricks of science and technology into breaking the golden thread between humanity and the planet, a breach which has perverted not only its spirituality but also its land.

Caliban offers another mirror of colonial betrayal to the Asian people because, like them, he showed love to his future master. Unaware of Prospero's greed for wealth and power, Caliban wanted to impress and please the man who was then his friend, 'and then I lov'd thee and show'd thee all the qualities of the isle.' Likewise, the Indians, not realising that the British were only after their jewels and their land, offered them magnificent hospitality, both sincere and ostentatious.

If Caliban's emotions mirror those of the Indian people, then his words also do. In telling Prospero, 'You taught me language; and my profit on't is I know how to curse', he foretold one consequence of the introduction of the English language into India. The British brought words which offered the Indians the opportunity to curse, as well as to praise, their new rulers.

Although cursing is seen as somewhat comical in the West, it is taken very seriously in the East, where people realise that evil vibrations directed against them do have real consequences. Many years ago, the royal family of Princess Usha Devi Rathore was cursed by a sage who was insulted when one of her ancestors, the Maharaja of Burdwan, drunkenly challenged him to perform a miracle. The mystic cursed the Burdwan line by pronouncing that no sons would be born to the Maharajas for seven generations and, when finally one was born, he would be the last to hold the title. The curse came true. Every ruler had to adopt his sister's son as their own until Usha's maternal grandfather was born. He did indeed live to see his princely title abolished by Mrs Indira Gandhi, the Indian Prime Minister, and her then Attorney General who, by a strange twist of the golden thread, was the father of Labour politician Rita Austin, who also appears in these pages.

In 1919, when General Dyer ordered his troops to open fire on the Sikhs who were peacefully demonstrating in their sacred city of Amritsar, Kim Hollis' grandfather witnessed the Sikhs curse the British in revenge. Mr Salariya, a barrister, like Kim who is now head of her own legal chambers in Gray's Inn, had attempted to use his diplomatic skills to prevent this senseless slaughter of hundreds. Universally considered to be a turning point in the struggle for Indian Independence, the massacre is a key scene in the film *Gandhi*. Yet maybe the moment of this curse is an unacknowledged, but equally significant, incident in British history. The curse foretold how the Sikhs would revenge themselves on the British by colonisation in reverse. Indeed, many Sikhs have now settled in Britain, but thankfully they have not repeated the horror of the brutality acted upon them.

It is fascinating that in astrological terms India and Britain have surprisingly similar national birth-charts. On 15 August 1947, at the midnight hour, modern India was born and the resulting planetary aspects curiously complement that of Britain's birth in 1801 with the Act of Union. The relationship between these two countries has also affected Britain's *Karma*, the spiritual mirror for the quality of a nation's deeds. The law of karma is simply that every action provokes a reaction. You cannot escape this natural law; you might do something destructive, and believe you have got away with it, but you cannot. Fortunately, karma is changeable and good deeds in the present can compensate for those of the past. The curse on the Maharajas lasted for seven generations and it has now been seven decades since the curse of the Sikhs. As in all philosophies, the period of purgatory offers the time of purification.

In only ever telling one side of the story, British history has failed to produce a mirror in which to examine its own strengths and weaknesses honestly. To any self-obsessed culture, the reflection from another's glass is feared, for it offers not only the beauty spots but also the blemishes. While this book is primarily a mirror to reveal the complex images of Asian womanhood, it is also one to invert the line of reflection and to show the British their faces the way we see them. In contrast to much previously published material, which continues only to curse and to criticise, the women in this book free themselves from the negative effects of cursing. Like Caliban, they have realised that it is best to 'be wise hereafter and seek for grace', for in blessing they are able to break the monologue of moans and create a face which smiles into a mirror, pleasing both its beholders and itself.

Kusoom Vadgama, author and ophthalmic optician, is casting her own blessing upon Britain by her magnificent task of researching and recording the many contributions Indians have made in Britain before Indian Independence, easily as many as Britain gave in India. Her book, *India in Britain*, was inspired by realising that most of this was undocumented; while on the other hand, 'What the British did in India during the Raj has been recorded down to the last sneeze of the most insignificant memsahib in Simla.'

Kusoom had to laugh with me about the irony of some British achievements in India. 'For, in improving the communication system in India, the British made it possible for Mahatma Gandhi's civil disobedience movement to be known instantly throughout the land.' This reminded me of my favourite scene in the film *Monty Python's Life of Brian* when the occupied Jews continuously complain, 'What have the Romans ever done for us?' There then followed a very long list of Roman achievements in first century Palestine. Likewise many have questioned what the British did for India. In fact, they left the railway system, telecommunications, national newspapers, an education system, a civil service bureaucracy, unified laws, parliamentary democracy, cricket, the English language and literature, and, not least, stocking the streams of Kashmir with trout.

The women I interviewed recognise the past comedy of errors in the relationship between Britain and India. Aware of their histories, they celebrate the opportunities for present and future fulfilment and provide a mirror of example and inspiration, not one of dogma and doom.

Sometimes, the arrival in a new land can free one from the restrictions of the old. While all the women in the book feel an affinity to and pride in their Asian roots, for a few Britain held the promise of a haven from the taboos of Asian tradition. For some it gave freedom from the most visible and voiced taboo of many societies: the constant pressure to be married.

However, in Asian culture, a widow is even more inauspicious than a single woman. Shrouded by taboo, they are prohibited from attending any auspicious occasion, including weddings. When community worker Vasuben Shah's husband Ramnik died, shortly after their arrival in Britain from Kenya, she broke the tradition of depending solely on his family and the taboos against female independence. She has kept to the cultural code which discourages remarriage because of her love and devotion to Ramnik's memory, but she has courageously continued to lead a fulfilled life for herself, her children and the wider British community through her voluntary work for the Citizens' Advice Bureau, mother-tongue teaching and skills in sign language.

Bidge Jugnauth's life offers the supreme example of triumph over taboos. Born to a low caste family in Mauritius, she was brought up in an environment where the severe patriarchal rule wielded by her father cramped her own life and that of her mother. She was judged by local Hindu society in her Mauritian village as unworthy even to teach Hindi to the local children. Escaping to England to train as a nurse, the climatic and cultural shock of an indifferent society induced a physical breakdown. When Bidge was told she had a disabling disease, she must have felt that whoever dealt the cards of life had given her a raw deal, branded by the prejudice of low caste, gender, disability and race, and yet it was at this point that life turned up the king of hearts, her future husband.

'It was love at first sight. He was so handsome I couldn't resist him. I thought of the times I'd been hurt before, and was afraid that it would happen again, but he was very persistent. I told him that my family were from a low caste, but that didn't deter him. "Caste doesn't matter to me, as far as I am concerned there are only two castes, men and women." I told him I came from a very poor family. "So what," he said, "I'm a nurse, you're a nurse." Everything I told him he had an answer for.

'Finally I said to him, "There is one thing, and if you knew you would run away." He said, "Try me." I took a deep breath and said, "I'll end up in a wheelchair one day." He said, "If you can love me from a wheelchair, I can love you in one," and those words I can never forget.' Like Vasuben Shah, Bidge has derived her strength from two sources. A relationship with the man she loves and, as Bidge herself says, a real feminism, 'which is an attitude to yourself, whether you feel you are worth it.'

However, often it is not the fear of breaking free of the personal strait-jackets which a culture or a tradition places upon women that causes them to remain silent. In Asian culture the courage to encounter individual hostility is always tempered by the belief that in doing so you may bring shame on your whole community. *Izzat* dictates that one must preserve the family and community name at all costs and consequently, silence is considered a virtue. Yet, it is only by confronting and calmly voicing our refusal to conform that we can finally break the restrictions and confound the belief that they will bring shame on those we love.

There is a poem by one of Pakistan's most prized women poets, Zehra Nigar, which powerfully expresses this feeling of fear. Since a translation into English from the Urdu could not convey the beauty of her words, I will simply retell the essence of their meaning. There was a young girl who, as a child, played in a garden where there was a tree with many nails in it. Believing that the tree must be suffering immense pain, she always wanted to remove the nails, but was told that if she did so a ghost would be released and would burn her house down. The time came when she could no longer bear the sight of this tree being slowly crucified and so decided to pull out the nails. She approached the tree, but at the very last moment stopped herself. She could bear the thought of enduring pain herself, but what she ultimately lacked was the courage to chance the fire which might harm not only herself, but also her family.

It is important to realise that by confronting the taboos and cruel beliefs which hold so many women in a constant state of anxiety and terror, it is possible to stop your own suffering and, by example, break the fears which create it. By refusing to be held back by the restraining beliefs of society, these women have created their own lives and the histories of others.

4

The Stained Glass Mirror of History

The British have always prided themselves on the fact that their history is to be trusted. British male subjectivity has long been regarded as the objective view. In fact history, like the language which communicates it, can never be neutral and is inevitably coloured by the bias of its author. As a Sufi story tells, one angle of vision can only give one side of the story.

There was once a Dewan, a prime minister, who tried to explain to his king that the advice he received from his courtiers was often contrary to the wishes of his people. The king, however, found this hard to believe as he felt sure that everyone saw things the same way as him. The Dewan realised that to the king only seeing was believing and so decided to give him visible proof. As the king was celebrating his birthday the following week, the Dewan arranged for a magnificent parade before all the people. On the day, the king and his court were seated on one side of the street and his people on the other, while the army marched down the middle.

After the army had passed by, the wily Minister asked the king and his courtiers to tell him the colour of the soldiers' uniforms. 'Why, blue of course,' replied the king without hesitation. He then asked the same question of the crowd who, equally confident, replied that the uniforms had been red. All but the Dewan were puzzled and everyone was convinced that the colour they saw was the correct one.

In fact, they were all correct. The soldiers had been told by the Dewan to wear new uniforms, blue on the right, red on the left. From one side of the street, only half the uniform could be seen, but everyone had assumed that both sides were the same.

Similarly, until recently, history has been seen only from one point of view: that of men in power. By telling only the consequences of their power, history has neglected to remember the great contributions made by women. Apart from Queens, mistresses and Florence Nightingale, the lives of many women have become forgotten stories of success.

Those forgotten or misrepresented by 'his-story' are not only the Asian women who have come to Britain, but also the British women who went to India. The predominant image of women who settled in India during the time of the Raj is of trifling and ineffectual socialites who made no lasting contribution to society. Perhaps the lives of some of the memsahibs did confirm this, but for others the journey to India was infused with a sense of service, and many assumed significant rôles in the social and academic education of Indian women.

Sita Narasimhan, Cambridge academic, fondly remembers the absolutely invaluable lessons taught her by Lady Clutterbuck, wife of the Tutor in Residence to the Crown Prince of Kashmir. 'She taught me my manners, and I had my first taste of thinly cut cucumber sandwiches for tea sitting in her garden in Kashmir. She taught me deportment by example. I was somehow taken into her bosom and intuitively learnt how to hold myself in jodhpurs, how you got off a horse.'

Penal reformer Roshan Horabin remembers her English governess with amusement, 'Miss Jenny used to read to me from the Bible when I was naughty. This had the curious consequence that, despite being a Muslim, I won all the scripture prizes at my Anglican school!'

Princess Usha Devi Rathore remembers her schooling in Bombay at the Walsingham House School For Girls, formerly the palace of the Maharaja of Kutch. Her English headmistress, Mrs Adcock, was the 'spitting image of Margaret Rutherford' and ran a frightfully proper school for all the girls of the top families in Bombay. 'I still remember sliding down the banisters and landing at the feet of a pair of pillar legs, tweed skirt and there was Mrs Adcock towering over me and saying, "Rathore, that's a very interesting way to travel down the stairs. Now we'll go up and try it again."'

Antiquarian Yasmin Hosain feels that her old English teacher, Margaret, deserves praise for the somewhat different lessons in progressive ideas and for instilling confidence in her. 'A tribute to her is essential because she was the one who inculcated many ideas of freedom, progress and liberalism among the Pakistani women studying under her, leaving a lasting impression. Margaret really emphasised the women novelists, whether Jane Austen or Virginia Woolf, and tried to show Pakistani women that their possibilities were tremendous and that they should not be fettered and shackled by ideas that were long outdated. Margaret taught me for two years, then suggested that I should come out to Cambridge to continue my studies and was instrumental in helping me enter Newnham College in 1957. I think she must have persuaded many fathers and brothers to allow their daughters and sisters to continue their education.'

Yet another Margaret needs a special tribute as she has a special place in my affections. While Yasmin's Margaret travelled to Pathan to educate her 'gals', I went to Roedean, near Brighton, to be educated by mine. As my housemistress, Margaret Pickering's large-heartedness and wisdom shaped my adolescence. History was my favourite subject at school, but as I have now discovered the understanding of history depends on where, when and who educated you. Educated in Britain, I naturally spoke of the 1857 uprising as the Indian Mutiny as did Roshan Horabin, who received the same sort of British education in India, pre-1947 Independence, as I did at Roedean in the 1960s. It came as a surprise to me when Princess Usha Devi spoke about India's First War of Independence and Rozina Visram, author and educationist, called it the Indian National Rising.

Journalist Amit Roy also detected a bias in his education when he came to Britain. 'You will find that many educated Indians are more familiar with the Bible and the classical authors than the average Briton. Now to me being British means being familiar with British history and all the great things about Britain like literature, music, religion.' Yet while Asians were busy studying the great English classics, the British did not reciprocate this learning with an appreciation of Asian culture, as lecturer Dr David Dabydeen points out, 'It is a mark of greatness on our part that we are so well versed in Shakespeare. But the British don't know any Bengali poets!'

The knowledge and facts deemed to be important depend upon the ruling powers in one's own history, as history naturally depends on who's writing it and what they choose to emphasise. Rozina Visram herself has attempted to shift the emphasis in her book *Ayahs, Lascars and Princes*, in order to recapture the significant rôles which ordinary Asians played within British society which had been utterly overlooked in the educational curricula of modern British schools.

Another woman who has redressed the imbalance of the past is Kusoom Vadgama. When Kusoom addressed the boys of Harrow School, a particularly significant place as it was the old school of the first Prime Minister of India, Pandit Nehru, I listened with interest to her historical knowledge which made the buried become visible by pointing out the many contributions which Indians had made to Britain pre-1947. The Harrow boys were equally bewitched by Kusoom's gift for bringing history to life and I shall never forget the 'thank you' speech given by a Harrovian. He amused everyone by saying how grateful he was to Kusoom for informing him that there were over 900 words of Hindustani in the English language, because he had never realised that he knew more Hindustani than he did French!

Indeed, imagine the echoes of surprise that would reverberate through the acres of suburbia if householders were to realise that their British lives had their linguistic origins in Northern India. Can't you just see Charlotte now, in her 'dungarees' living her 'cushy' life, peeping from behind her 'chintz' curtains, taking baby out of the 'cot' and wrapping her darling in a 'shawl'? Later, sipping 'punch' with friends and discussing the 'thugs' that 'loot' their 'bungalows', before retiring, sporting 'pyjamas'.

More surprising still is the fact that the great dragon-slaying St George, patron saint and moral epitome of England, is not actually an English knight. An academic friend entertained me with his delightful story of a reunion dinner. He was sitting next to an old friend who proudly told him that the next day was St George's day. He allowed him to continue and then quietly said, 'You obviously like Lebanese people very much.' The friend looked bemused and retorted, 'What has that got to do with it?' 'Well,' came the reply, 'St George was Lebanese wasn't he? If he turned up at Heathrow today, the immigration chap probably would not let him in. St Andrew came from Yemen and he would not have been admitted under *any* circumstances.'

While current opinion seems to suggest that the British do not know how to market themselves, this is a misnomer. They are the masters of subliminal messages. Throughout the world, the English gentleman is most respected and revered, a knight in shining white armour. He symbolises good manners, justice and is seen as preserving women's honour. Like his character, his publicity is subtly understated, outshining the vulgarity of the Casanovas and Don Juans who lack real virility. No wonder everyone thinks an English gentleman is the next best thing to God.

It is hardly surprising then, that the English stole St George for their patron saint as he championed the people and rescued the damsel in distress. They have immortalised his deeds and hidden his history. For the English, it is character, and not origins, which holds ultimate importance. Indeed the British Royal family has a well-known international heritage, but is still the mirror in which the whole British nation gazes for example.

For Asians, the Royal family holds a special history of affection. Prince Charles is for many in Britain a latter day St George who champions their cause; breaking political silence, he praises Asian enterprise and endeavour. As an influential pioneer, Prince Charles has been a catalyst to speed up the changing of attitudes. His pronouncements declaring the importance of the balance of nature, including holistic medicine, vegetarianism and ecology, are coupled with his action in implementing Mahatma Gandhi's words that one must care for 'the last, the lowest and the lost'. The Prince's positive example has given Eastern ideals and peoples a rightful prominence in British life.

Although there is no direct English equivalent for the Indian word *Khandaan*, its meaning is very clear: one's family and breeding. It is Prince Charles' khandaan that marks him out as a future king. His mother, the Queen, also loves the people of her Commonwealth, as did her great-great-grandmother before her, Queen Victoria. Many Indians were bewildered when the British Prime Minister Disraeli, without referral to them, pronounced Queen Victoria 'Empress of India' in 1877, but in her own way Queen Victoria had a deep fondness for all things Indian, and treasured this title above all others.

Queen Victoria's most famous Indian servant was Abdul Karim, the 'munshi', or teacher, who gave her lessons in Hindustani and who, against the wishes of her advisers, she promoted to be her Indian Secretary. When Queen Victoria died in 1901, all documents relating to the munshi's period of service were burnt. What does survive to tell the tale is a modern one-man drama, written by Farrukh Dhondy and performed by the internationally acclaimed actor Zia Mohyeddin. The munshi comes back to life as Zia re-creates the passion and prejudice that surrounded the extraordinary life of this Indian servant in the royal household of the Empress of India.

One of the first Indian women to be embraced by English society was the Princess Gouramma. She was sent to England at the age of 11 to receive a Christian education and in 1852 was baptised by the Archbishop of Canterbury at Buckingham Palace. She was given the name 'Victoria' after the Queen, who was one of her godparents. Queen Victoria's exceptional longevity was not passed on to her god-daughter, who died of consumption five years after her marriage with Colonel John Campbell in 1865, leaving one daughter.

Queen Victoria's Golden and Diamond Jubilees, in 1887 and 1897 respectively, were attended by almost every Indian Prince, Maharaja and Nawab. The strong affinity between the British aristocracy and Indian nobility was a truly golden thread which still unites them. The visiting Maharajas and Maharanis provided the most spectacular display of wealth and power ever witnessed by the British popular press. The glare of their diamonds left the gentlemen of the press blinded and unable to appreciate the rainbow of Asian womanhood which was already beginning to colour British society. They established a tradition in British journalism that identified Asian women as either princesses or, at the other extreme, as ayahs or servants.

Indeed, there were many more of the latter, as once the British had begun to colonise India in the eighteenth century they lost no time in using native Indians as domestic servants, because they were cheap and dispensable. Many ayahs, women servants, were brought back to England with returning families, but were offered no security or reward for their hard work on the arduous journey. A few were retained, perhaps as ladies' maids or nannies, but the rest were no longer needed, or wanted. Consequently Indian servants were often left, like human excess baggage, on the quayside thousands of miles from home. Nothing was done by the British government to save these once respected and respectable women from the twin evils of begging or the workhouse. It was presumed that the Indian people should pay for the abandoned women's return journeys. However, realising that this was impractical, the benevolent face of British liberalism smiled upon a few of them, when a group of missionaries set up a home in East London, to provide a safe refuge and act as a Victorian 'Job Centre' for the unemployed Indian servants.

Even today, the women I interviewed spoke about how they have been made to fit into the opposing extremes of these two models. Mishti Chatterji, who now runs her own publishing house, remembers being treated like a princess at her English public school, where she was the first Indian pupil. Sita Narasimhan also recalls being given special treatment at Cambridge. Even though it was 1947 and Britain was still under a state of rationing, she was spoiled by a 'bedder' who cleaned for her every day. It was presumed she was a princess as she wore only silk saris and had a double-barrelled name.

In contrast, headmistress Shirley Daniel was subjected to the indignities of being treated as a servant. When she arrived at her new school in Kensington, she was given a supply teacher's timetable and told to go and sit in the English and history classes. When she refused, stating that she had a permanent contract as a maths and science teacher and not as a child minder, the headmistress went 'absolutely bananas', shouting, 'What rubbish, you people are only supply teachers and you won't be given a set timetable.' Shirley's refusal to accept such mindless stereotyping and her proven talent for teaching maths and science became evident, as within six months she was appointed deputy head of her department.

Throughout history and especially today, the strengths of individuals continue to overcome the labelling which seeks to bottle them. The mediawallas who only allow themselves to tell of Asian women as dazzling princesses or downtrodden doormats, either full of Eastern promise or full of the smells of curry, betray their own intelligence and the British public. In truth, women are more complex and entertaining and, no longer willing to be misrepresented, they are now reclaiming the powerful female figures within their own histories.

5

Reflections of Female Heroism

Perhaps the most cherished reflections offered to me by the mirror of this book have been those of the female figures of my own heritage. I sometimes think that Asian women must have discovered the secret of invisibility. They have been travelling to Britain for hundreds of years, and the success stories of their lives have made a lasting impact upon both Indian and British society, yet they fail to appear in the history books. Many of them have remained pressed flowers, hidden between the pages of old and heavy books, carefully preserved, but sadly forgotten. Finally, women are lifting the huge encyclopaedias of male heroism to rediscover these roses. As the stories of their lives begin to reappear, they return brilliance to the peeling gold leaf on the picture frame of British history.

I can now perceive that the mirror offered to me by British history was a two-way one; like those used to observe us in airports, it appeared to give an honest reflection, but was actually concealing the glory of certain figures who stood behind it. Now that this opaque glass has been shattered and the past achievements of women have been revealed, history is a mirror to behold with admiration and as a model of inspiration.

The stories of Zoroastrian women's lives are of particular significance for all, as it was the tenets of their religion and the beliefs of their community which made them the natural pioneers of female emancipation. The traditional Asian customs of polygamy, child marriage and prohibition of widow remarriage were never assumed by the Zoroastrian Parsi community, who quietly encouraged women to achieve success. The religious teachings of Zoroaster emphasised the importance of *Humata, Hukhta, Huvarashta* (good thoughts, good words and good deeds) within this life, and thereby fostered a social conscience among its adherents. Unlike the majority of societies which have sought to keep women's lives private, to be disclosed only in diaries after their death, Zoroastrian women were among the first to go through the doors to public and political life. Coming from the most progressive sector of Asian society, these women had a head start over others, but it was an advantage which they used to benefit all society by their commitment to female liberation. Their cultural and religious backgrounds gave them a spirit of adventure and a sense of service which, like golden threads, have bound their lives together in a web of exceptional achievement.

Britain, seen as the land of learning, was a powerful magnet to many Zoroastrian Parsi families who realised that the promise of education was also the promise of advancement. My own parents, like many others, were drawn to England by its reputation for justice and knowledge. Indeed as early as 1842, a Zoroastrian Parsi girl, aged only 9, was sent to England for her schooling. At that time, educating women was highly unusual and subjecting such a young girl to the rigours of the journey and life thousands of miles away caused much opposition. Her family's courage and foresight were rewarded. This little girl grew up to become Mrs Dossibai Cowasjee Jehangir Jassawalla, the acclaimed and highly respected social reformer. Her work for the advancement of the status of women in India was recognised by the whole nation and overseas her work was praised by Queen Victoria and the Pope.

Dossibai was the first of a very brilliant group of Indian women who came to receive a British education, returning to be of service to their fellow Indians. The first Asian woman to study law at an English university was Cornelia Sorabji, the daughter of the Rev. Sorabji Khursedji, a convert from Zoroastrianism. For Cornelia this accomplishment was only one of her many firsts; she was also the first female graduate of the Deccan College in Poona. If she had been a man, her success in India would have made her eligible for a scholarship to study in England. However, being a woman, it was only after a special fund had been set up by English friends, including the irrepressible Florence Nightingale, that she could afford to make the journey in 1889. Her time was not wasted, as she had spent her five years of waiting as the first woman professor at the all-male Gujarat College in Ahmedabad.

Once in Britain, Cornelia often felt patronised by her tutors. The profound ignorance of many people, both students and colleagues, was a constant source of exasperation and, occasionally, amusement to her. Although she was allowed to sit the exams, alone in a room away from all the male students, it nevertheless needed an appeal to the Vice-Chancellor before she was awarded the degree to which she was entitled.

The legal profession took longer still to accept women, and refused to promote Cornelia above the low rank of 'legal adviser'. She practised in both England and India and was honoured with the Kaiser-i-Hind gold medal in 1909 for her work in the field of social reform, especially for providing legal assistance to women in purdah, widows, wives and orphans. Finally called to the Bar in 1923, Cornelia retired to England in 1929, and died there in 1954. She has been the example to follow for many other Indian women; indeed, a modern day comparison is Jyoti Munsiff, whose great-grandfather was the first Indian to be made a magistrate. Jyoti herself had to wait until she was 21, then the age of majority, before she could enrol as Britain's youngest ever solicitor.

In the medical field, Dr Dossibai Patel, also a Zoroastrian, is recorded in 1910 as being the first woman Licentiate of the Royal College of Physicians. Dr Roeinton Khambatta still recalls her impressive figure in a white sari, asking medical students the most searching questions at the Cama and Albless Hospital in Bombay. Known throughout India, Dossibai was admired for her pioneering work in gynaecology.

At Cambridge, author Piloo Nanavutty, another Parsi, was a Blake scholar who went on to become the principal of Janki Devi College, Delhi, where she continued the education of women in India. Amy Rustomjee, yet another Parsi, also went to Girton College, Cambridge, in 1922 and used the knowledge she gained there to develop the educational system in Bombay. As well as holding responsible positions as Inspector of Schools and a Chief Examiner, she did much to encourage the uptake of education by all ages and classes, especially among women. Her work was recognised by her appointment in 1956 as the first Asian Vice-President of the International Federation of University Women.

Many more Zoroastrian women had come to Britain for education, including India's first female architect, Perin Jamsetjee Mistri, who went to secondary school in Croydon before returning to India to qualify, eventually becoming a partner in her father's firm of architects. By the mid 1930s there were over 100 Indian women students at British universities. These women picked subjects that would be of use to their country; subjects like medicine, education and science which were in tune with their sense of purpose and commitment to the society of their day.

Of all these women, it is Mrs Cama, the compassionate revolutionary, who is my heroine and whose life I feel is linked to my own by the golden threads of womanhood, religion and politics. Bhikhaiji Cama was born to a wealthy Zoroastrian Parsi family in Bombay in 1861, a particularly auspicious year which also saw the birth of Tagore, the Nobel Prize-winning bard, and of Motilal Nehru, the father of India's first Prime Minister, Pandit Nehru. Bhikhaiji's life offers the ultimate example of social commitment and explodes the blinkered class mythology that only working-class heroes can be of true worth to the cause of the masses. Mrs Cama's strength of will and independence of spirit came from her own interpretation of the spiritual teachings of Zoroastrianism, which encourages its followers to take positive steps through good thoughts, words and deeds. To her, religion was an inspiration as well as a faith and it remained a steadfast belief throughout her life. Unlike many other religions which discourage political involvement, Zoroastrianism gave Bhikhaiji the incentive to enter both journalism and politics, in the belief that through these she could fight all forms of social evil with language and action.

At school, Mrs Cama dedicated herself to mastering European languages, a fitting and prophetic pursuit for a young lady whose life was to make a great impact throughout the world. She first left India in 1902 and came to Britain for medical treatment. Anxious to ensure her daughter's comfort, Bhikhaiji's mother had packed some of the family's jewels for the journey. Bhikhaiji sold the jewels, not to make her life more luxurious, but rather to fund the revolutionary activities which she was intent on promoting.

Bhikhaiji Cama's political career, like my own, evolved from an initial desire to improve the quality of women's lives. Indeed, far from wishing to be an honorary man, Mrs Cama fully realised the potential that being a woman offered her and even exploited the curiosity which surrounds women's dress to make political statements. Asserting her independence of choice, she shocked her own Parsi community by being one of the first Indian women to wear a frock. Yet in Europe she was seen in a sari in order to stress her Indian identity, as she understood that even the subtlest of gestures could convey a powerful message.

In a sense, I too have continued this tradition, for although I wear mainly Western clothes for the convenience and practicality they offer in a hectic life, I wear a sari on formal and public occasions to convey my solidarity with other Asian women and the special feeling of pride and contentment in being Asian. Asian women are proud of the sari, as it is one of the few national dresses to be retained within everyday life and it is not merely a novelty piece to be taken out of the wardrobe only for national holidays and ethnic dances. For all women in politics, dress offers them a chance to be noticed against the dismally drab shades of grey presented by their male colleagues.

However, Bhikhaiji Cama's interest in the improvement of women's lives was not divorced from her political will and, like modern female revolutionaries, she believed that freedom from foreign power would inevitably lead to the emancipation of women and men alike. Her ability to challenge the status quo should be an inspiration to all women. Mrs Cama had an energy and self-will which even led her to break the decorum of British gentility by playing cricket, most unusual for a woman of her time, and with a straight bat at that. By a curious twist of fate, cricket was also my favourite sport and at school I learnt how to play the game and have never been able to assume the 'female' rôle of happy spectator since.

While Mrs Cama's political goals continued to aspire to greatness, her vision of India unified and independent did not blind her to the importance of each individual within it. Earlier, in 1896, when the plague swept through Bombay, she was moved spontaneously to take up hospital work. Disregarding the expectations of her social position and the real risk to her own health, as a vaccine had not then been developed, Bhikhaiji donned a white apron and, acting like a Florence Nightingale of India, nursed the sick. Certainly, it was the impulsive nature of her character which led her to make many radical gestures which a logical appraisal would have strongly counselled against.

The most dramatic and defiant of these gestures came in 1907 when, at the Second International Socialist Congress in Stuttgart, Germany, Mrs Cama rose from the audience and made history as the first person outside of the homeland to unfurl the Indian national flag. Although women have often been the motifs and mascots of freedom fighting movements, like the figure-heads on the ships of male glory, they have rarely been seen, as Bhikhaiji was, to be the live actress upon the stage of history and not the mannequin used to represent it. Yet by the time Mrs Cama raised the flag, her vehement criticism of British imperial policy had already forced her to flee Britain for France, where she continued to be given safe exile despite British demands for her extradition. During the First

World War, however, she was interred at Bordeaux as the French authorities no longer felt themselves able to refuse the requests of their allies completely.

The British ultimately managed to weaken the body and spirit of this fiery and formidable woman, by continuing their oppressive rule over her beloved India and, moreover, by refusing her permission to return there. When Bhikhaiji Cama was finally granted her wish to end her life on home soil, it was only on the condition that she cease all political activity. She returned to her native Bombay in 1936, and died there that very August. Like so many great reformers, she never lived to see the new age, the new India, to which she had devoted so much of herself. As the words of Bhikhaiji's epitaph powerfully convey, it was her religion which had given her the spirit of personal independence, and this spirit which had given her the vision of national independence. She weaved a golden thread between her own life and that of her motherland in the belief that 'Resistance to tyranny is obedience to God'.

It seemed particularly fateful and fitting that when I arrived in India on a family holiday in 1989, I turned on the television only to behold Mrs Cama's face. Forty-two years after the Independence for which she had fought was finally achieved, the Indian Government were acknowledging her contribution by placing her portrait in their Parliament, the Lok Sahba. The unveiling of her portrait revealed the physical and spiritual beauty which graced her life and the position which it had now achieved reflected her proper status as an international voice and architect of modern India.

The Asian women in this book represent many different communities and religions and accordingly they all have heroines of their own, women whose histories they recall with particular affection as models of inspiration. Nevertheless, Sarojini Chattopadhyay, who later became Mrs Naidu, was a favourite of so many from different backgrounds. In 1896, while Bhikhaiji Cama was tending the plague victims in Bombay, Sarojini Chattopadhyay was carving out her own niche in history at Girton College, Cambridge.

Attia Hosain, author and broadcaster, remembers her as 'a friend of my parents, I grew up listening to her. Apart from her political status, she had grandeur as a leader amongst men and women of every kind. She was a woman with a voice that was divine, as if from a nightingale. She had a wonderful memory and a love for all the gossip, she would sit and tell me the stories. "Come and meet Mickey Mouse," she said, meaning Mahatma Gandhi. When I was ill, she'd bring a poem she had written for me, as if she had nothing else to do. She was so complete, nothing was beneath her. She was from a very intellectual background, she symbolised for me the best of Indian womanhood, the fight for Independence.'

For Community Relations officer Rita Austin, Mrs Naidu was also 'an absolutely fantastic woman, another Bengali, a heroine for me. Feet on the ground, very practical, very proper, gorgeous, and an acerbic sense of humour. She displayed to the Indian Nationalist movement all the traditional women's skills. She bandaged the men when they got hit over the head in a baton charge. She ensured that Gandhi had enough to eat. She joked to the Indian National Congress that it cost them a hundred times more to keep Gandhi in his homespun cloth, so why didn't he wear ordinary cloth like anybody else?! She was close to where the power was, she knew she was powerful and she used her power. She was the first woman to be appointed a State Governor in India. But she was very laid back with it, very modest. You never saw her head unveiled, even in the most terrifying circumstances, her sari was always on her head.'

While the younger generation of the time grew up admiring women like Sarojini, as schoolgirls they too wanted to become involved in the struggle for Indian Independence and made small, but significant, gestures of defiance. Still at school, author Kusoom Vadgama read about the Indian Freedom Fighters in the newspapers and bitterly regretted being stranded in Nairobi. She carried on the fight for Indian Independence in whatever way she could. 'A neighbour had a dog, and didn't know what to call it. The best way to insult the British was to call the dog "Churchill" because we hated Winston Churchill. This was a small way of overcoming my frustration. There were few ways you could contribute to any form of national spirit.'

It was the time of Subhash Chandra Bose's Indian National Army and Kusoom still recalls with spirit her personal stand for her heroine, Captain Lakxmi, captain of the Women's Section of Bose's army. 'One of the Indian National Army's slogans was "*Jai Hind*" ("Long Live India"). Our English Headmistress, Mrs Lincoln, told us not to use this phrase, because it was used by a traitor. I didn't know what the word "traitor" meant, so I looked up the meaning, and thought that "betraying one's country" was a bit much. As head of house I went to school the next morning and told the other girls before assembly not to say, "Good morning, Mrs

Lincoln," but "*Jai Hind*, Mrs Lincoln!" When the time came, the others chickened out and I was the only one who shouted it out. Total silence. Mrs Lincoln never quite recovered.'

In India, actress Madhur Jaffrey's father, Raj Bans Bahadur, was very involved in the struggle for Independence. She remembers how anyone could be involved in the protests against British occupation. 'Whenever the National Anthem was played, we marched out; my father would lead and the rest of us would follow. It was a minor protest to show that India was our country and we wanted to rule it ourselves, although we supported Britain's fight against fascism.'

Another remarkable woman, Lady Bomanji, was known affectionately as the 'Heroine of Harrogate' for her heroic selflessness during the Second World War in Britain's fight to retain its independence from Nazi Germany. She had come to Britain in the 1920s as the young bride of a shipping magnate and fell in love with England. She had had a 'sound British education', one of only two girls among 300 boys at Deccan College in Poona. Her husband had fallen in love with her through a portrait he had seen at an exhibition and travelled across India to propose to this beautiful young lady. This love story is an historic version of Shakira Caine's, which also tells of love at first sight, although this time it was a coffee advertisement which presented her striking face to her future husband, actor Michael Caine, and set him on his romantic quest.

At the outbreak of the Second World War Lady Bomanji, who had by that time settled in England with her husband, put her Windsor mansion and her two Rolls Royces at the disposal of her adopted country, where she chose to stay despite the promise of safety in India. It was suggested that she allow certain titled people to join her at her Harrogate home, in order to escape the worst of the bombing in London. Lady Bomanji replied that she would be delighted to help, but that her priority was to ensure that the working people whose homes had been bombed had the first choice – after all, the rich and titled could afford hotels.

Lady Bomanji's spirit of generosity typified the well-known saying, 'Parsi thy name is charity', which she continued to translate into good deeds even during peace time. Among the many causes of which she was President, her most acclaimed titles were President of the Friends of Harrogate and President of the Yorkshire branch of the Save The Children fund. Her loving daughter, Mehroo Jehangir, recalls a Paris taxi driver telling 'Mummie Darling', as she was known to everyone, that 'if they had had more gracious people like your Ladyship in France, the French revolution would never have happened!' Lady Bomanji was awarded the Honorary Freedom of the Borough of Harrogate in 1984, the city's Centenary Year. This remarkable woman, who by then was known as 'The Lady in the Sari', the unofficial 'Lady Harrogate', died in 1986. Five services had to be held to accommodate all the people who wished to attend her funeral and the local florists were unable to cope with the demand for tributes.

However, it was not just Indians settled in the country who helped the 'Motherland', Britain. At least 1,200 Indian nurses came to Europe to help Britain in the First World War with over 3,500 other medics and over 1,300,000 troops, the second largest force after the British, and almost twice that number in the Second World War. This was in addition to the valuable contributions of medical supplies, services and cash which were freely granted. Their skill, determination and resourcefulness was much admired and commented upon by their English allies.

As well as helping Britain in its darkest hours in the fight against fascism, Asian women graced all of Britain's great institutions during this period. The Wimbledon tennis championships saw Leela Row appearing in 1934 and 1935, and Princess Indira of Kapurthala broadcast regularly on the Indian section of the BBC's World Service during the Second World War, concentrating on Parliamentary affairs and debates. She was also a regular contributor to *Woman's Hour* from 1942, again commenting on Parliamentary affairs. Indeed, *Woman's Hour*, unlike much of the media, has always resisted the stereotyping of Asian women and has continued to provide them with a valuable forum. On the day of my birthday, 11 May, I was on *Woman's Hour*, the politician chosen to represent the Liberal/SDP Alliance, with Janet Fookes, Conservative MP for Plymouth Drake, and Gwyneth Dunwoody, Labour MP for Crewe and Nantwich. We were discussing the vital rôles which women play within politics, when, by a strange twist of coincidence, the programme announced that the 1987 General Election had been called.

An even more historic announcement was made on the birthday of Mandarin Chinese expert Freni Talati's mother. The family, who were the only Indians living in the diplomatic quarter of Peking, were celebrating when the radio, silent in their own house, declared the entry of Japan into the Second World War. An auspicious family day foretold a disastrous event, as in 1941 the tragedies of war affected Freni's family. For Freni herself, still a visibly frail woman today, her heroine was thankfully never far away and her mother's activities in the camp to which they were subsequently taken offer a story of great courage and endurance. The camp was even more claustrophobic than we are often led to believe, as Freni says, 'In the television series *Tenko*, they could wander out of the compound, we couldn't do that. We weren't given any rice either, we had to cater for ourselves.' Food was a precious and rare delight, 'in camp we literally dreamt of food.' Yet, out of the two thousand people within its walls, Freni's mother was one of the few elected to cook, as she could be trusted not to steal the food. Her honesty was a testimony to the traditional virtues of the Zoroastrians, who the other communities would always entrust with their money when travelling away from their villages.

Although Freni's family had been wealthy before the war, this remarkable woman knew that new circumstances called for new action. 'Some people who had been very well off outside became extremely selfish and unhelpful inside the camp,' but Freni's mother willingly gave up everything of material value which she possessed. 'About once a month you could buy an egg. That would cost you £1, in 1940s money. I remember my mother selling her gold wedding ring to buy an egg for the family.' Thankfully, Freni survived to tell the tale of their experiences, although they were in the last camp to be liberated and its effects claimed both her parents' lives soon afterwards.

Another extraordinary woman who showed extreme courage throughout the war sadly did not survive to tell her own story. Noor-un-Nisa Inayat Khan was born in Moscow in 1914. Her mother was an American and her father was the leader of the Sufi religion in Europe, and a descendant of Tipu Sultan, the Tiger of Mysore. The family moved around Europe and spent long periods in both England and France, where Noor took a degree at the Sorbonne, and then worked as a writer for *Le Figaro*. The family moved back to England in 1940 to escape the Nazi occupation, and Noor joined the Women's Auxiliary Air Force and was one of the first group of women to be trained as wireless operators.

Within a few years 'Nora', as she was then nicknamed, was recruited by the Special Operations Executive; her French education was invaluable to the French section of this branch of Military Intelligence. She was left in no doubt by the War Office of the dangerous nature of her task, for wireless operators were the most vulnerable to detection and arrest. Her training, under the aegis of

FANY (Women's Transport First Aid Service Nursing Yeomanry), included lessons on explosives, field tactics and what to do if captured.

With the code name 'Madeleine', Noor was the first woman wireless operator to infiltrate into France; arriving in Paris in June 1943, she posed as a mother's help. Hers was the most perilous posting in France and raids by the Gestapo followed, as did an SS ambush. Nevertheless, Noor refused a chance of returning to Britain, as she was unwilling to deprive the Paris Resistance of its only wireless operator, and so remained as the only British officer in the area.

Noor was eventually arrested by the Germans in October 1943 and held in the Gestapo HQ, where she was interrogated. She was never broken and even tried to escape twice. Regarded as a particularly dangerous agent by the Germans, she was transferred to a prison in Germany and was kept handcuffed in her cell for almost a year. Although she had been given a 'suicide pill' when she first embarked upon her mission, she was unable to use it and was executed at Dachau on 12 September 1944. After the war she was posthumously awarded both the George Cross, the highest civilian award from Britain, and the Croix de Guerre with Gold Star from France.

A modern-day heroine who has also shown bravery in the face of grave peril is Frene Ginwala. I first saw Frene on TV when I was woken by my mother one night who told me to switch on the news as there was a Parsi woman wearing a sari, talking on behalf of the African National Congress. There is only one word to describe Frene: 'magnificent'. While others use their talents to improve life for themselves, Frene is using her gifts to help create a non-racist South Africa and, when justice finally triumphs, she will be in their history books as one of the women who have helped change their world.

The fact that South Africa has an Asian population is often overlooked, yet Frene's ancestry is rooted in southern Africa, where there are two distinctive groups of Asians. About 90% came as cane cutters, indentured labourers, the successors to slaves in the British Empire. After these came a very small number of traders, teachers, accountants – the semi-professionals who were needed to service the community. In a sense, Frene has followed their lead, serving her community in its most significant struggle. 'I was anxious to do something that would allow me time to be involved in politics, but

I had to earn a living, and therefore decided to come to England to study law.'

After qualifying, Frene presumed that the South African government would confiscate her passport when she returned home and therefore she took advantage of what she thought would be her last opportunity to travel around Africa. The knowledge which she gleaned from this trip turned out to be invaluable to her future rôle in her country's political life, a story which she tells in her own words. 'I was just a junior member of the African National Congress, but the leadership asked me to help get someone out of the country. They had decided to establish an external mission, out of the reach of the Pretoria regime. The problem was that the nearest *free* part of Africa was Ethiopia, but how could we get there? All of Central Africa was run by Europeans, and they would send you back to South Africa if you were caught. About the only time the white regimes in Africa would co-operate with each other was when dealing with black people wanting freedom. I suggested that if we got to what is now Tanzania, we would not be sent back. I knew that the nationalists in Tanganyika, as it was then, were respected by the British and I was sure that, if we got there, they had enough political muscle to persuade the British rulers not to send us back.

'So, not knowing what it would lead to, I agreed to help.' On the night of 21 March 1960 the Sharpeville massacre occurred. It should have been another auspicious day, as the Zoroastrian New Year, but it held a tragic history for South Africans. 'I was doing a lot of freelance journalism at the time and was interviewing Dr Naicker, the leader of the Indians in South Africa, when the phone rang. It was for me, and it was Walter Sisulu, the Secretary General of the ANC. He suggested I go and see my parents. That might have sounded innocent to the police tapping the phone, but as my parents were in Mozambique, it was the order to set the plan in motion. I was the one person in the ANC who still had a passport. While I was there the ANC was banned, and the person I had offered to help had to escape in a hurry. It wasn't easy, but we got him out. Only then did I discover that it was Oliver Tambo, the President of the ANC.'

Frene's story reminded me of the film *Cry Freedom* and of the liberal editor Donald Woods' escape from South Africa in the late 1970s. I had met Donald Woods at a Liberal Party Assembly in 1985, when we had both spoken in the debate in favour of sanctions.

I am positive that one day Frene will feature in a film about Oliver Tambo's life and his escape from South Africa, as a thrilling and valiant heroine, even though she does not regard herself as such.

Frene's actions led to her exile from South Africa. Still in her twenties, she set up a magazine, *Spearhead*, in Tanganyika and became its editor. A car accident in which she was badly injured led her to Britain again, this time for bone grafts to her legs. Around the same time, internal Tanganyikan politics led to her deportation. Once in England, she decided to go to Oxford and study for a doctorate. Fate intervened in the shape of a message from newly independent Tanzania: President Nyrere was nationalising the newspapers, would she edit them? Like all successful people, she said 'yes' first, then sweated about her lack of experience later. 'I had no daily newspaper experience at all, and it was hurriedly arranged for me to work for a week on the *Times of Zambia*, really just sitting in on editorial conferences. If you had an Identikit picture of who would not be the editor of a national newspaper, you would have come up with a foreign woman, an Asian, a well-known left liberationist, i.e. me! I had a terrible time. . .Well, it was very exciting, but very straining.'

After several years, Frene returned to Oxford to finish off her doctorate. She thought about going back into law in Britain, but decided to work full time for the ANC in London instead. The ANC is a South African political party that was banned in 1963 and so was illegal there until the ban was lifted in 1990. Although supported by Anti-Apartheid movements throughout the world, the party itself consists only of South Africans fighting for the liberation of their country. Sometimes, though, people do not see Frene as South African. 'When I get up at international meetings, people get a shock: an Asian woman representing the ANC! But the ANC doesn't think it in any way strange, they're sending Frene, they're not sending an Asian woman.'

I hope that Frene, as a modern-day heroine, will be able to offer the women of her nation the equality that Mrs Cama had hoped to offer to the women of India. 'We have a unique opportunity in South Africa; we will be starting from the ground up, building a new society. We pledge to eliminate racism. Now it has been accepted that sexism can be just as limiting, we have the chance to eliminate both. The ANC issues constitutional guide-lines as to what will happen in a free South Africa. I'm trying to ensure we don't just have a clause in the constitution saying that there will be sexual equality. That's not enough, because it gets left at that, with the most discriminated against groups in society having to fight for their rights. It is going to be the positive obligation of the state to eliminate racism and I want to ensure that there is an obligation of the state to eliminate sexism as well.'

For Frene Ginwala, like Freni Talati, a change in circumstances has given her a new vision of the world which shatters the narcissism of political complacency. 'My father always drummed into us how privileged we were: you had to think of those who were not as privileged as yourself, whether we had three meals a day or one, at least we had a meal, some people didn't have anything.' These words reminded me of my own mother's favourite saying, 'I cried that I had no shoes until I saw a man who had no feet'. Such philosophy puts everything into perspective.

'We all get depressed at different times, but when you're depressed you think of the people, especially the women in South Africa, who are suffering *incredible* difficulties. So I talk to myself, and say, "Frene, you have no right to be depressed! Look what's happening to others, you're well-off, you're comfortable, you're warm, you've got three meals, you don't have the police hammering at your door." Given what I am – me, my ideas, psyche – there's nothing else that I can do. I have really thought about it when I get depressed. This happens periodically, there are personal problems, political problems, problems in the ANC, problems of women, all of us get depressed. Then I say, "God, I'm going to walk out." I've sat down and seriously thought about it. In all seriousness, there. . . is. . . nothing. . .else. . .I. . .can. . .do. . . – *and be me.*

'If you take a wall, if you bang your head against it, yes, your head gets battered. But, ultimately, you weaken the wall, and the next person who comes along probably shoves it over with their little finger. But you contributed to that, you've got to see it in that sense. I am a South African, and *no one* is going to tell me I'm not.'

The present regime in South Africa must feel like the people in Jericho, waiting for their walls to tumble. They must know that, with people like Frene outside, it is only a matter of time before the people of South Africa are able to reclaim their homeland.

Frene Ginwala's story is especially significant because it has never been adequately recorded, unlike that of another popular heroine who was also interested and active in politics from her student days. Famous even then as the daughter of Jawaharlal Nehru, as Mrs Indira Gandhi, the wife of Parsi politician Feroz Gandhi and no relation to the Mahatma, she became the first of the two Prime Ministers to have been educated at Somerville College, Oxford, the other being a Miss Margaret Roberts, now Mrs Thatcher.

In many ways these two female leaders provide an interesting mirror for each other, for although they share the same Oxford education, their political and personal lives led them down very different paths. Mrs Thatcher and Mrs Gandhi are both seen as heroines to a certain group of Asian women. Like every good English – and Indian – girl, Mrs Thatcher has evidently read her Jane Austen. The 1980s will be remembered as her decade. She captured the patriotism and xenophobia of the British people to make England a land of 'Pride and Prejudice'. However, as her policies begin to affect the welfare and well-being of the lives of many ordinary people, the nation is realising that maybe these two attitudes are no longer the best for Britain. Moving into the 1990s, I hope that the government and its leader will not forget the wisdom of Jane Austen, but will rather use it to lead Britain into a decade of 'Sense and Sensibility'.

Like the lives of many of the women in this book, those of Mrs Thatcher and Mrs Gandhi are linked by several golden threads leading to success. Both of them experienced the isolation of being a woman at the pinnacle of political life and this gave them a respect and understanding of each other. However, the comparisons between Mrs Thatcher and Mrs Gandhi reach beyond a feeling of solidarity, which exists between all women who enter the predominantly masculine profession of politics. Indeed, these two female figures both enjoyed the position of being 'queen bees', the sole women surrounded and indulged by an all-male hive of workers.

Both Mrs Thatcher and Mrs Gandhi were innate politicians, women with immense energy and a physical and mental stamina which enabled them to thrive on power. Their determination and undying belief in themselves gave them the vision and courage to grasp their political destinies and turn the tables on the male politicians who tried to use them as temporary stopgaps. These are qualities which they continued to reveal even during the lowest points in their careers, bouncing back like Indian rubber balls to reclaim their positions of power.

Like many of the successful women in this book, both women shared the golden thread of an adoration of their fathers. While

Mrs Thatcher's father did offer her the example of his own political achievements as an Alderman in Grantham, this was in no way comparable to the paternal image of the charismatic leader, Pandit Nehru, with which Indira grew up. This difference is a very important one. Mrs Thatcher was very clearly an outsider enlisted by the family of British politics like a nanny, while Mrs Gandhi, with her ancestry, was a natural choice for the 'mother of Indian politics'. Unlike Mrs Gandhi who was from the élite of Indian society, Mrs Thatcher was not born into the upper classes, but like the nanny, was engaged to nurture their interests.

Indeed, Margaret Thatcher's style of rule has been much like that of a nanny who impresses her authority and status upon her charges; while Indira Gandhi had the natural authority of the mother. As the nanny, Mrs Thatcher has had to do the dirty work of her political family, while Mrs Gandhi was more able to collect affection from hers. Indira could accept and forgive the weaknesses of her people, because she recognised that they were inherited and could perceive them in herself; whereas for Margaret, the weakness is the frailty of her own power, knowing that the nanny can be dismissed.

Yet, while many in Britain do see Mrs Thatcher as the Victorian nanny somewhat strict and harsh in nature, to some she is the Mary Poppins figure providing the spoonful of sugar to help the medicine go down. During her political rule, Mrs Thatcher has become famous for her act of 'handbagging', but her handbag, like that of Mary Poppins, has been a bottomless bag of tricks. Each time her charges have shown signs of being discontented, bored or tearful she has plucked out a treat in order to distract their attention away from their injury or hardship.

Mrs Thatcher has yet to reach into her handbag to reveal that in many areas of British life it is the Asian people's tireless work, enterprise and honesty which has been the spoonful of sugar to sweeten the coming to terms with post-Raj Britain.

6

The Sweetening of Britain

Bapai, my grandmother, taught me my prayers, and much else. From her I learnt about myself and my heritage.

She told me the story of how our ancestors, the Zoroastrian Parsis, came to settle in India. Around the year AD 785, seven boats of Parsis set sail from their Persian homeland, probably the first boat people. Their land had been conquered by the followers of the new Islamic religion and they were escaping from the religious persecution which followed. Fate decreed that they landed at Sanjan, a small fishing village in Gujarat on the west coast of India.

On arrival, they were taken in front of Raja Jadhva Rana, the local ruler. This wise king explained to the immigrants that his country was too crowded and there was no room for new settlers. As a demonstration, he took a bowl and filled it with milk until it was so full that not even one more drop could be added. The Zoroastrian High Priest, being an even older and wiser man, called for a little sugar. He carefully put the sugar into the bowl, where it dissolved without spilling any of the milk. 'Perhaps your land is full, but we will enrich it with our presence, without displacing any of your people or your customs.'

This simple action and reasoned words so impressed the king and his assembled subjects that he asked these strangers what they would need. He was told that they required only the freedom to bring up their children according to their own traditions, the freedom of worship, and enough land to feed themselves. They did not want to be a burden on their new homeland.

The Gujarati ruler Raja Jadhva Rana had the foresight to allow the Zoroastrian refugees to settle in his land. He offered them a home, but he also delivered certain conditions, which they duly respected. The first of these was that the people from Pars (Persia), the Parsis, as they were to be called, must wear the local Gujarati costume: for the women, the sari and for the men, the fainto, a black hat shaped like a cow's hoof in veneration of the Hindu sacred animal. This was a condition which benefited both communities, as it was a mark of respect for the local Hindu religion and also a way to make the new settlers less conspicuous.

The second condition was that they must learn Gujarati as their main language so that they would be able to take part in the life of their adopted country. Without the knowledge of the local language they would have become isolated, second-class citizens, unable to communicate their needs effectively. Nevertheless, they could, and did, retain their own language and customs as well.

Thirdly, the Raja requested them to explain the religion and traditions for which they had suffered so much, and for which they were willing to start a new life in a far off country. The king's genuine interest in his new subjects meant that the education process was mutual; from listening to the lives of the Parsis, the king and his community were able to understand and to appreciate the different qualities and experiences which they brought and benefit from them.

History has shown that the Zoroastrians were true to their word and did enrich the whole of India. In return, the Indian peoples welcomed them. Neither one lost their culture and both benefited from each other's way of life. The Zoroastrian Parsis were given a sense of belonging in India and, consequently, they contributed in excess of their numbers. Many Indians have Parsis to thank for their schools, both for boys and girls, their trade unions, scientific institutes, national flag, city water supply, airlines, banks, hospitals, to mention but a few. It was a Parsi who saved the life of Mahatma Gandhi when a mob tried to lynch him in South Africa. Parsis even founded the first Indian cricket club, and the first Indian to sit in the British House of Commons was a Zoroastrian Parsi, Dadabhai Naoraji, who won his seat for Finsbury Central as a Liberal in 1892.

Throughout their history, the British have also been much admired for the way that they have allowed refugees and successive waves of immigrants to settle in Britain. Yet, while these peoples have been offered a haven, they have seldom been given a home. It may be a surprise to the British that it is the Asian people who are the real experts on immigration. Indeed, it is their expertise which keeps this fact hidden, for the people who made India their home were successfully integrated. Successive waves of conquerors have ruled Hindustan and, in time, have been absorbed by them. In contrast, she has never deliberately had a history of foreign conquest and Indians only ever emigrated in numbers during the time of the British Empire, when they were enticed to its many different lands by the promise of a better life. As the consequences of this migration have unfolded, Britain, with its great public relations campaign of promises and patriotism, has become the 'motherland' to which many Asian people have returned. Maybe it is time that the British take lessons from Indian history and the Raja Jadhva Rana's example in order to achieve successful integration. At present, the hallmark of the Indian ruler, much curiosity tempered with some caution, has been reversed by British immigration policy to generate little interest and much fear. While the immigrants coming to Britain do not have to comply with any conditions, neither do they inspire curiosity or a warm welcome.

Much of the blame for this lies with the policy-makers in Britain and their lack of foresight. If they had thought to inspire the British people's innate sense of fair play, compassion and adventure, instead of pampering to a minority's fears and prejudices, Britain would now be cherishing its new citizens instead of resenting their right to be here. Having beguiled the Asian peoples to all corners of the world for their imperial purposes, the British remain ignorant of their origins and experiences, even when they land upon their shores.

In fact, the only people to ask the new arrivals why they have come to Britain and where they have come from are the immigration officers. Yet, for those interested to hear, all these people have different stories to tell; stories of the many different countries they have come from and of the varied reasons for their journeys.

Lack of knowledge has led to the Asian population being perceived as a threat and a drain upon the nation's resources. However, in truth this is a view created by the British mentality which judges all others by its own standards. To the British, travel was a feast in which they consumed the wealth of other nations, milking India of its jewels and exploiting the West Indies for its sugar. In contrast, the peoples who are now returning to Britain are seeking only to sow the crops of their own success and not to reap those of others.

In many ways the trading history between India and Britain has been re-established by the current exchange of knowledge and skills. The unfounded and absurd belief that Asian people only come to Britain to claim social security is further ridiculed by the calculation which the Harrovian, who thanked Kusoom Vadgama after her eye-opening lecture at Harrow School, so diligently made.

Bhikhaiji Cama (1861-1936), the "compassionate revolutionary"

Lady Bomanji (d. 1986), affectionately known as the 'Heroine of Harrogate' for her selflessness during the Second World War

Cornelia Sorabji, the first Asian woman to study law at an English university

Sarojini Naidu (1879-1949) is seen with Mahatma Gandhi and the Aga Khan at London's Ritz Hotel at the time of the Round Table Conference 1930

*Noor-un-Nisa Inayat Khan
(1914-1944), posthumously
awarded both the George Cross,
Britain's highest civilian award,
and France's Croix de Guerre with
Gold Star*

*Princess Indira of Kapurthala,
affectionately known as the
'Radio Princess' for her BBC
broadcasts from London during
the Second World War*

Sehri Saklatvala, aged five, with her MP father, Shapurji Saklatvala on his 50th birthday

Attia Hosain, author and actress

Yasmin Hosain being introduced to Queen Elizabeth II, while studying at Cambridge

Jyoti Munsiff as a young girl, meeting India's first Prime Minister Pandit Nehru

Piloo Nanavutty (fifth from right, first seated row) *at Girton College, Cambridge, 1933*

Jeya Wilson, President of the world famous Oxford Union Debating Society in 1985

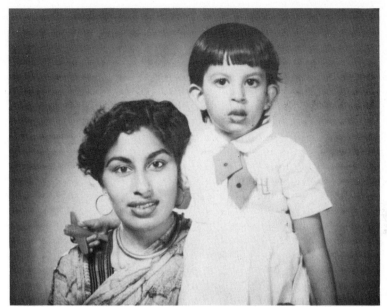

Princess Usha Devi Rathore (right) *with her mother, Varuna Devi of Burdwan*

Pushpa Bijlani being crowned a beauty queen by the Maharaja of Baroda

Nasreen Munni Kabir interviewing actor Dilip Kumar for 'Movie Mahal'

Nasreen Rehman (right) *with her guru Pandit Ravi Shankar* (centre)

'Madam, even if every single Indian signed on for income support, the money they would receive would not even pay back the interest on the gifts given so freely to Britain by the Indian peoples during the two World Wars.' Certainly, it is important to appreciate the balance between giving and receiving which defines the relation between India and Britain.

Some of the women in this book came to England to be educated. For teacher Pramila Le Hunte this meant a degree at Cambridge and for Jeya Wilson it was postgraduate study at Oxford, where she became president of the Oxford Union debating society. For Rita Austin, English education was a Catholic school in St Albans, while for Princess Usha Devi it offered an escape from traditional 'feminine' education and the promise of art college. 'My parents wanted to send me to a finishing school in Switzerland. I convinced them that that was totally archaic, what I wanted to do was study television production and art.' Yet, those coming to learn are balanced by those invited to teach. Aban Bana came to Britain on request, to help found the North London Rudolf Steiner School, famous for its progressive and caring approach to learning. Also Hena Mukherjee came back to Britain to work at the Commonwealth Secretariat as the chief project officer for their education programme.

Other women came to Britain for its medical facilities: both Vasuben Shah and Aruna Paul travelled in order to seek cures for their children. Frene Ginwala came for surgery after a car accident. Nevertheless, while these came to be nursed, others came to nurse. Both Saro Hutton from Malaya and Bidge Jugnauth from Mauritius landed on British shores to begin their nurses' training.

Many of the women came to seek refuge in Britain. Frene Ginwala and the parents of artist Sharon Lutchman sought asylum in Britain as political intolerance made it impossible for them to stay in their homeland of South Africa. Ella Vala was one among an entire Asian population to be expelled from Uganda under Amin, and antiquarian bookseller Yasmin Hosain and international dancer Nahid Siddiqui both left Pakistan as the change in political and moral attitudes precipitated by General Zia's rule in Pakistan made their lives virtually unbearable.

Yet for some, the motivation to visit Britain was not nearly as serious, urgent or conventional. Shakira Caine first visited Britain for the Miss World competition as Miss Guyana and won third prize. Most incredible of all were the expectations of Princess Usha who saw Britain as the 'party paradise' and mathematician and astrologer Shakuntala Devi to whom England was part of 'one big playground'!

Too often the diversity of origin and motivation which immigrant people represent is lost within Britain, as their visible difference hits a cultural panic button that simultaneously switches off interest and switches on fear. This is not because the English simply aim to be hostile, it is because they do not know how to make people feel instantly welcome. Many people complain that Asian people have made little attempt to embrace the English way of life and have simply created 'little Indias' of their own, like Southall in West London. The irony of this is that creating a microcosm of one's own country in a new land is a lesson best taught by the British. What are 'Snooty Ooti' in South India or Simla further north, if not little Surreys? Indeed, wherever the British colonised, they created miniature English counties, but they are still surprised when it happens in Britain. For any people, moving to a new and different environment is daunting and seeking the warm heart of the mother-land, only to be given the cold shoulder, is an experience bound to cause retreat and insular security. It is up to all communities to respect, value and learn about their neighbours' cultures, but this can only be achieved through a common commitment and genuine communication. One of the fundamental bars to the latter is the lack of a universally spoken, common language. While it is only right that each language of a people is retained and promoted, it is imperative to have a public language so that every person has an equal chance to articulate their rights and needs within the society.

For some of the women in this book, language problems arose when their families moved from England back to India. Radio presenter and educational video producer Rani Sharma's family was 'called back' to India by her grandfather when she was 5. 'I only really spoke English, and it took me some time to pick up the Indian languages.' Staying in Jullunder for six years, Rani was being taught in Hindi, so when the family returned to Leeds she had forgotten all her English. 'That was quite a problem, but it didn't take me long to relearn. There weren't many Asian kids around, we were the only ones in the school, so we were always being invited out for tea.'

Research psychologist Pireeni Sundaralingam travelled back to Sri Lanka for a year when she was 6, after spending most of her young life in Britain, speaking English. 'I was sent to a convent school and I ran away the first day! Everyone was talking and teaching in Tamil and I didn't understand. So I was put into a nursery school at the age of 6. This meant being made to sit in tiny chairs, painfully taught the Tamil alphabet.'

As these women's success stories now reveal, learning another language necessitates no loss, but holds potential for new understanding. As I am not a linguist, the Tower of Babel is the greatest curse to me and, as I was educated in England, I have the characteristic British phobia of other languages, yet language is undeniably crucial in overcoming misunderstandings and problems. History has dictated that in Britain at least, the public language should be English and maybe we are doing those people who grace the British shores an injustice in not encouraging them to learn this language.

Often the biggest surprise for educated Asians arriving in Britain was that others came without speaking English. I am just as surprised that the immigration service of the Home Office lacks sufficient Indian language translators. Headmistress Shirley Daniel was pressed into service when she came back to Britain to take up a teaching post. 'On my plane from India 80% of the Asians couldn't speak English. I had to sit in Heathrow for two hours translating on the day I arrived. The medical officers asked and I agreed, I felt sorry for my companions, I couldn't walk away. But I was scandalised that they let all these people in, where were they going to go? How were they going to survive without knowing English? I couldn't understand it, it was a terrible shock to me.' Shirley's brother is now a consultant heart surgeon in Sweden. The way Swedes integrate immigrants is, she feels, 100% more advanced; they are taught Swedish immediately. If you arrive in Sweden without knowing Swedish, you go to classes until you can ask to leave in Swedish!

Certainly those women who came to Britain without a knowledge of English remember the feelings of frustration at not being able to communicate easily. I clearly remember the irritation at nursery school in London of not being able to understand all that Winnie the Pooh had to say!

Others too found that, without the language, isolation in Britain was almost inevitable. Vina Shukla, now a law student at Cambridge, had a slow start at school, and remembers being 'really frustrated' during the year it took her to learn English. 'I had a friend at school who was trying to explain the rules of a game and when I didn't understand, she went away and played with someone else. I was annoyed about that.'

When model Safira Afzal first came to Britain she could not speak a word of English. 'The very first thing I remember when we attended school was that we had to wear a salwar kamiz and everybody took the mickey out of us. Within a week, my father had bought us some Western clothes and we started speaking very slowly, "Yes" and "No" originally.' Following the example of the Hindu Raja Jadhva Rana, Safira's father realised that once his daughters were less conspicuous they would be treated more fairly. While each culture should be able to retain its individuality, it should also show tolerance and flexibility. Even as a largely monolingual country, Britain holds the potential to be culturally pluralistic, and in many ways is beginning to realise this.

British society is in a state of cultural flux, the nation's life is constantly being enriched by the new insights which others bring to it. Even since my own childhood in the 1950s rapid changes have taken place. I was a natural vegetarian as a child, but when I was at school such a practice was inconvenient. Now my eldest son is a vegetarian and no one thinks it strange. Contrary to popular opinion that it was the 'cranks' who started the vegetarian revolution, it was only made popular and 'un-cranky' by the 1970s' influx of East African Asians who were naturally vegetarians and in no way eccentric 'nutters'. Certainly the food fads of the 1980s have made Asian delicacies a mainstream craving and foreign foods are now seen as exotic and desirable, even sold in supermarkets such as Sainsburys and Marks & Spencers. I can still remember my parents receiving a letter from my school, 'telling them off' for sending me these strange fruits called mangoes and custard apples. If my parents wished to send me fruit, then English apples were acceptable.

Hopefully, as we begin to sample the delights of others' agriculture, we may progress to their culture. All human beings are born with eyes in the front of their head, as a species we are destined to look forward and must now seize our culturally plural destiny. With so many different religious and cultural festivals being celebrated by different communities at different times in the year, there is a great source of celebration and enjoyment still to be tapped. Again remembering back to my school days, I enticed my friends into celebrating *Navroze*, the Persian New Year on 21 March, the first day of spring and a more logical date to welcome the new year. Like all Zoroastrian festivities, Navroze revolves around having a good time. It involves eating the seasonal fruits and vegetables, tasting

Swiss chocolate, sipping wine, sprinkling each other with rose water and being given a silver coin for good luck. Finally a friend holds up the mirror into which one smiles in order to promise to bring joy in the new year. Certainly my Navroze party brought excitement to my Christian and Jewish friends who still recall it today.

The act of coming to a new land is also a cause for celebration and something one never forgets. Yet, when someone is finally allowed to become a British citizen, they receive only an impersonal letter through the post. In America, the mayor of the town gives a party for his new fellow Americans, but the new Americans first had to devote many hours of study at 'citizenship classes' to learn the language, laws and customs of their new homeland, America.

In Britain, those many hours are wasted in queues at the Home Office, or at Consulates abroad, and the time is spent learning only how to wait patiently. While this is a valuable skill for those intending to settle in Britain, it does not equip them for their new life in the same way that the American citizenship or Swedish language classes do. At present, the new arrivals to Britain do not feel that they have been invited to the party because, in truth, there is no party being thrown.

7

Nayee Zindagi – 'New Life'

There is an old-wives' tale which says that a woman is never the same after giving birth. While this is true, a great change is also inevitable for a poor unsuspecting baby thrust into a new world. All babies cry to let those present know that they have arrived. Although it is said that the prophet Zoroaster laughed when he came into the world. The legend states that he was all-knowing and was to bring great joy to all mankind.

Today, the instinctive knowledge of thousands of years has been usurped by the 'birth best sellers' which tell of the 'right' way to give birth. Recent rediscoveries include the importance of relaxation and deep breathing for the mother, the presence of both parents and the immediate physical bonds of cuddling and breast-feeding the child. Both ancient and modern knowledge reveals that the less traumatic the birth is, the better adjusted the child and parents will be.

When I gave birth to my first child, Mark, the doctors, although aware of the likelihood of complications, were unprepared for the amount of blood I would lose during the delivery. All I remember is passing out and the nurse bringing my baby to me. I said that he looked like a wise old man, and indeed, Mark has grown up to be very wise. A religious guru, who did not know the story of Mark's birth, later told me that his even-tempered and relaxed attitude to life was a result of his birth, which gave him an awareness of the close affinity between life and death. Mark does not believe a word of it.

To most Asian immigrants, England is still subconsciously their motherland and the entry into the new world of the UK is also affected by the labour of passing through immigration. If this experience is unpleasant, then subsequent relations can be strained, with unnecessary difficulties arising. Among the women within this book, those who confronted initial difficulties were clearly distressed and have found it less easy to think of Britain as a true motherland.

Geeta Dave is the wife of my local newsagent and a family friend. She arrived in Britain one December as a young bride with her husband, only to face 'the coldest weather I'd ever known' and to discover that the immigration officials could be just as cold. Her husband had a British passport and she had a visa to enter with him, 'but they wouldn't let me go with him. I was whisked away in a police car. I was only 20, and for my first night in London I was alone, without my husband. It was my first time alone, in India you're always with people. I spoke a little English and I understood what was said to me, but I couldn't say much back. They gave me some food, but they didn't understand that I couldn't eat meat or eggs, so I couldn't eat any of it. Then they put me in a room to sleep with two other people, *men*. That was my main worry, but the officers said it was pressure of space and I might be able to go back to the airport in the morning. In the morning everything was cleared up, but that first night I shall never forget.'

Nurse and television presenter Bidge Jugnauth also spent her first night in Britain at the airport, although this time it was because a train strike and a shortage of money prevented her from travelling on. Bidge's first night was a lesson in British male/female relations. 'I had led a very sheltered life in Mauritius, I was only 21, and now I was witnessing couples kissing and cuddling. I thought, "My God, first the bad weather, then the train strike and now this. . .This is definitely hell."'

However, some visitors are not even allowed into Britain long enough to be shocked. Actress Sneh Gupta was on a flight from East Africa to Germany which made a transit stop in London. She decided to spend a day visiting an uncle whom she had never met, but when she arrived at Heathrow airport she was stopped by immigration. 'My bags were checked, my tickets were checked and double checked and I was interrogated for about seven hours. My mother had given me a box of cooking spices and they wanted to know which one of them was the hashish. They wouldn't believe I was actually going off to Germany the next day, even when Lufthansa confirmed it. My uncle was allowed to see me for just ten minutes.

'Then two police officers took me to a refugee camp, obviously put up for the Ugandan Asians as there were still a couple of families there and they were very kind. I was so naïve at the time that I couldn't understand why the immigration officers wouldn't believe me. Nothing worked with these guys. You pleaded with them, you said sorry to them, you were angry with them, but no emotion had any effect, they simply took you to the camp. The next day they came and picked me up. I just smiled, what did they think I was going to do, run away? Instead of taking me to the departure lounge they took me right to my seat on the plane. I didn't get my passport back until the plane was half-way to Germany.'

Ella Vala did come to Britain from Uganda and the immigration authorities had made some effort to ensure that she and her fellow refugees felt at home, but still the experience of leaving the womb of Africa was not easy. 'When we arrived, we were vaccinated then given a pile of Oxfam clothes, then we queued for meals. I'll never eat egg curry again, it tasted so horrible there.' The British were trying to be thoughtful by providing Indian vegetarian meals, but unfortunately, when egg curry is served every day it becomes less appealing.

Lawyer Naseem Khan came to Britain alone in order to study and was only rescued from a traumatic beginning by her Asian extended family, when the British Council failed to meet her at the airport. 'Fortunately, some friends of a relative of a friend of my father were picking up some jewellery from the airport and they met me instead. They took me somewhere, miles away. I stayed the night there, then began ringing other friends of the family.'

Although these stories of unfortunate arrivals offer cautionary tales, in fact there is enough knowledge and experience today for such traumas to be unnecessary. With care and preparation, bringing a new baby into the world and a new citizen into Britain can be a pleasurable experience for all. When I gave birth to my second son, Alexander, better known as Wags, the doctors had learnt from experience and were well prepared. It was the happiest day of my life, a complete party and I feel certain that Wags' confident attitude to life has been determined by his easy passage into it. In 1986, when I chaired a Commission to investigate the involvement of ethnic minorities within British life, the findings emphasised that, above all else, it was the lack of a genuine welcome which disturbed and alienated the immigrants arriving in Britain. The experiences of the women within this book have confirmed this, but they have also proved that a positive beginning leads to a happier end.

In complete contrast to Geeta Dave and Sneh Gupta's experiences, Rose Barreto, a legal secretary, found her immigration officer to be anything but cold. 'I think he must have fancied me. The first thing I said to him was, "Please don't send me back on the next plane, whatever you do!" "Well, if your papers are in order, there's no reason why we should." Not only did he then see me through immigration, but he went with me to collect my luggage. Now that's unheard of! A week later, he phoned me to say he was visiting Manchester to watch a football game and was I interested in going? I still have one of his letters, asking if I was all right in this country.'

Penal reformer Roshan Horabin also had an unusual welcome to British shores when she came with her husband Ivan, a British naval officer and son of a Liberal MP and Chief Whip. They arrived in Britain in 1946, on a ship with 1,800 naval officers and only eight other officers' wives. Roshan was pregnant with the first of their three daughters and everyone treated her with great courtesy, taking her for walks around the decks while her husband played bridge. When they docked in Liverpool with the yellow flag to show that someone aboard had typhoid, everyone was kept on board in quarantine. Eventually allowed off, Roshan remembers first meeting her in-laws at lunch at the House of Commons. Her impression of British gentility was confirmed by the attendants there who naturally thought that she, wearing a pink silk sari, was a visiting princess.

Actress Madhur Jaffrey was one woman who took an immediate liking to Britain. Indeed, Britain now seems to have returned these feelings and has certainly taken a great liking to her. Unlike most others, Madhur even liked the British weather. She had been told that it was 'very cold and nasty', yet when she arrived in November she found it was 'not cold, not nasty, but marvellous! The chocolates were wonderful. I was just gaga; I loved it! However, nothing was a great surprise because when falling in love with Laurence Olivier I'd seen every English film and I'd read all the English novels.'

Like Madhur, I too looked forward to coming to Britain. When I was 3, my parents left me, then their only child, with my paternal grandmother, Bapai, in India so that they could go ahead of me and start a new life for us all in Britain. About a year later, I was brought as a Christmas present to my parents by my uncle Gussie, who had lived in Britain since the 1930s. Apparently I behaved very well during the twenty-four hours the flight took then, though a family story tells that this was more because I had been introduced to the joys of Scotch whisky rather than any co-operation on my part.

Wearing my uncle's gloves to keep out the cold, I ran towards my parents, anxious to be taken to Father Christmas in case he had not been told my new address. When I waited up on Christmas Eve to see him, I was horrified when he did not arrive. My mother had to tell me that girls who stayed awake did not deserve visits, but that he had left my presents in our bathroom all the same. This and many other memories – of sleeping in the office so as not to be separated from our television, of repeatedly cherishing the thrill of running up and down escalators, and of accepting telephone bookings for our family hotel, then forgetting to tell my parents who were stunned when a party of schoolchildren arrived from Derbyshire - combined to make me feel right from the start that Britain was exactly where I wanted to be. Now every time I arrive at London airport, I feel I have come home.

Even when one has an easy entry in the new world, life outside the womb is never as warm or comforting and you have to come to terms with its realities, including the famous English weather. To many it was the dramatic change in climate that offered the first shock of the reality of Britain.

Advertising copy-writer Anjali Paul was one of several women who arrived in the middle of the English winter. 'My first impression was very dismal. We got off the plane at Heathrow, it was drizzling with all these grey people walking around on these grey roads. I thought "Oh, no. . ." That feeling actually lasted for a few years. But I've grown accustomed to it now.' Sister Jayanti's first memory is also of the winter weather, this time the December rain: 'I couldn't believe that there could be such greyness during the day. I thought maybe the sun never shone in a place like this.'

Community Relations officer Rita Austin came just after Christmas with her brother and father and her initial impressions were 'quite horrific. I couldn't understand why the sun went away at three o'clock each afternoon, which it does of course in Britain on December 28th. I could not bear the feelings of stockings on my legs and the really rough, prickly and horrible cardigans. It was very cold, damp and miserable. It was the dampness that was the worst.' After that, things improved. The family lived in a hotel just next to Harrods. 'I suppose I must be one of those exceptional people who learn to do their shopping there!'

Bidge Jugnauth had left Mauritius during one of its tropical heatwaves and so the British climate must have seemed particularly appalling to her when she arrived in England on 21 December with a hail storm in progress. 'In immigration they said, "Oh lovely day today". . .I thought, if this is a lovely day, what is a bad one like? The photos I had received from friends in England only showed the lovely country house gardens in sunshine.'

English children's books and comics, available in East Africa, were also common sources of information on Britain, although they too were not always reliable! Actress and theatre producer Sudha Bhuchar had gained her childhood vision of England 'via Enid Blyton, *Five on Kirin Island*, boarding schools and midnight feasts. . .We came here in January, and I couldn't believe the reality.'

The weather and midnight feasts are not the only causes for alarm which face newcomers to Britain, and the picture postcards and children's books which give a false image of England play only a minor rôle in the positive advertising campaign of themselves and their land which the British have exported, along with colonialism, all over the world. For so many Asians arriving on British shores the promised motherland of Britain did not live up to their expectations. The behaviour and values which had characterised the British throughout their Empire had largely been those of the upper classes who retreated into the 'inner sanctum' of their homes and clubs in order to create a sense of mystery and reverence. In fact, the inner sanctums, like those of the clergy, hold no great enigma, but nevertheless instilled a craving for discovery and also for initiation among those excluded. In a sense British culture is at its purest in the ex-colonies, rather than in Britain, for when the British left India the Indians preserved their education system and many other customs and beliefs in a kind of 'time warp'. Consequently, when Indians finally gaze upon their imagined picture of glory they are disappointed; in the Britain of today many of the characteristics of the imperialists have faded and many of the great monuments are now shabby.

The British in India left a vision of England as an ideal place, free from dirt, crime and corruption. In India, Dr Chandra Patel, a founder member of the British Holistic Medical Association, was told the story of somebody from India who had come to Britain, dropped some papers on the road and been arrested. When he paid the fine, he was given a receipt and he threw that down and was arrested again! Yet when Chandra herself arrived in Britain she was 'disillusioned about that, it wasn't so clean, there was litter on the road. The other thing from childhood was the idea that

people were so honest that you could actually leave your luggage
on the road and nobody would take it. As soon as I came, I went to
the market, bought too many potatoes and left them outside a shop
while I went looking for my husband and the car. When I returned
fifteen minutes later, they were gone. I must say, though, that no
one has ever stolen my milk bottles in Britain.'

Lawyer Naseem Khan received a similar culture shock when she
realised that she did not know the 'real' Britain at all. 'I had been
taught that everything good, including justice, manners and fair
play, had come from the English. It was a shock to find that it
was not so. On many occasions, it was the opposite.'

Rita Austin's father, a distinguished lawyer, was also surprised at
how the reality of Britain had changed. His trip in 1950 with Rita
and her brother was the first since the 1930s when he had been a
student at Cambridge. He then made an annual visit to Rita and
her family until he died in 1970. 'He used to complain about what
he saw as the slip in standards, people didn't dress as well as they
used to. He also used to complain about all these foreigners here! He
very much considered himself as a pukka English gentleman, which
he was in many ways. He didn't like the way the pace of life hotted
up, the way *The Times* changed, the rise in the cost of having a suit
made, the way his favourite Dunhill pipe went out of production!'
Rita also remembers her father taking her and her brother around
the sights of London and how he was extremely hurt and insulted
when her brother was not impressed by Big Ben, saying it did
not look half as good as the Capital Cinema clock in Darjeeling.

Many people experienced this 'instant recognition' of the sights
of London and many also found that the magnificent places known
throughout the world from photographs and paintings were no longer
as wonderful. Hena Mukherjee of the Commonwealth Secretariat was
surprised when she arrived from Malaya to see Westminster Abbey in
the rain. 'It was soul destroying. I had always thought of it as a place
where novelists and poets had been buried, almost a monument.
They had cleaned up one part for a royal wedding, but the rest
was filthy and that just stays in my mind. I had a sense of *déjà
vu* because I could recognise everything in London. It was like I
knew all the buildings and almost every street name.'

I too experienced this, for although I was in India and my parents
in Britain, as it turned out both of us went into the hotel business.
They bought a real one in central London, while I became an avid
player of 'Monopoly' with my cousins. This meant that when I

eventually joined them in 1953, I could even name some London streets outside the main tourist areas, like the Old Kent Road. I wanted to see all the sights of London, though even today I have never been to Pentonville. I also received a shock at the reality of these buildings. When I first saw my parents' hotel, I was very surprised that it was not painted red like all the London hotels I had in my 'Monopoly' game.

However, for many, the shock of accommodation was much more serious than my own. The vision of small, cramped houses was a particularly powerful first impression for those Asians arriving from Britain's African ex-colonies. This group offered a special perspective which, without exception, mentioned the lack of colour in Britain; the brightness of the African sunshine especially being missed. Belkis Bhegani, a television researcher, found the journey into London from the airport 'very depressing. It was totally dark, just bleak after the wonderful African sunshine.'

East African Asians typically came from a middle-class background and, coupled with the high standard of living available there, this meant that the quality of the average English house came as a surprise to them. Biochemist Kiran Kumar 'couldn't believe how bad they were, all miserable, grey, tiny backyards. Coming from Kenya, where our houses were beautiful and well laid out with large gardens, I couldn't understand all this fuss about England.' Ella Vala's family arrived at Stansted airport from Uganda and were equally shocked by the notion of a terrace of houses. 'We were driven through Cambridgeshire to an army camp acting as a reception centre for the refugees. All the houses we passed looked the same, joined up to one another.'

When lawyer Naseem Khan came to Britain from Pakistan as a 'very protected 23 year old', she found the state of the rooms available for rent in London a shock. 'They were dark and dingy with old furniture. One place cost £12 including meals, which was expensive then. When I said I wanted it, the landlady said, "You know I can't cook curries?" I had to explain to her that I just ate boiled food, because of a medical problem, amoebic dysentery. But she wasn't interested in renting a room to a Pakistani, even at that price.'

Gurbans Kaur Gill, an SDP councillor and JP, was probably the most disturbed and traumatised by the standard of housing available to immigrants. Gurbans remembers 'never really wanting to come to Britain.' She had a job with her husband in the Punjab, but some of their colleagues wanted to go to England, so it was a 'comradely thing to all go together.' Gurbans had one daughter and was expecting another, so her husband went first, arriving on Christmas Day 1965. By his third letter back home, he wrote that he was returning: 'he couldn't take all the prejudice and the climate. As we had resigned from our jobs in India, my father wrote back saying that he'd better stay in London and I would join him. He still may not like it, but we'd be all together.

'My husband and a friend hired a car and picked me and my eldest daughter up from the airport. On the way back, we stopped in a terraced street, all tatty looking houses. They had been talking about the landlady and I thought they had stopped to let me meet someone. We went in and my husband asked me to go upstairs. I slowly climbed the stairs and saw there were two rooms there. After a few minutes, our friend came up with a mop and started cleaning the rooms. I asked what he was doing, I wanted to go to the really big, lovely house I was expecting. Then he said that this was where we were going to live. "You've got to be kidding! I can't live here!" "Yes, you're very lucky, you don't realise how difficult it is to find somewhere." It was such a shock that I suffered from acute depression, even after my second daughter, Reenu, was born.'

Unable to sleep for months, Gurbans' doctors could not help her, no tablets worked. Eventually they determined that her depression was caused by her living conditions and advised two options: either go back to India or be referred to a psychiatrist. 'I objected to being treated as a stupid peasant. When people told me to "go back home", I told them that my wealth, my opportunities were in Britain. So when the doctors told me the only other option was to go to a psychiatrist, I said no, there wasn't anything wrong with my mind or my body. When I got home, I threw every tranquilliser into the bin and said, "Fair enough, I'll learn to live with it." Since that day, I haven't looked back, because it frightens me too much.'

Certainly, the experience of coming to a new land and the problems which have to be faced often lead to feelings of homesickness and the wish simply to return. Yet for all of the women in this book the spirit of determination and the will to succeed has triumphed over these emotions. As Bidge Jugnauth recalls, 'I wanted to go back and then I thought about all the debts incurred so I could come to Britain. If I went back, it would have been a failure and I don't like failures.'

Often it is the dramatic change in status and the impression of hostility and prejudice which makes people unhappy in Britain. During the time of the British Empire there was a greater solidarity between the upper classes of all races, but when the upper-class Indians arrive in Britain now, they confront a mix of classes which holds no special respect for them. Nevertheless, upper-class Indians still feel themselves to have more in common with the upper-class English than with other Indians, and the rejection by their own class on racial grounds seems especially cruel. Author and actress Attia Hosain, from a privileged Taluqdar feudal landowning family from Lucknow, was surprised when the feudal classes in Britain did not immediately welcome her to their bosom.

A student at Oxford, Pireeni Sundaralingam, also found that moving to Britain meant a change in rôles, coming from what she described as an 'aristocratic family, both sets of grandparents are landowners. My mother was head of a vast household in Sri Lanka, with servants and chauffeurs. In fact she didn't know how to cook until she came to this country. Then her husband was away all day and most nights, she had a small child, me, and suddenly had to learn to cope on her own. My parents were aware of England as being a very different country. They didn't have any language problems, but there was the vast change in their status which they didn't expect. My father has said some quite bitter things about being held back because he's black, things he didn't think about before coming. He now knows he is never going to be the top surgeon in Britain because of his colour.'

However, the shocks which arise from such a class mentality also extend to other sectors in the society. For people from India, there was the surprise of seeing working-class *Indians* in Britain. Yoga teacher Princess Usha Devi Rathore recalled seeing 'Punjabi ladies sweeping Heathrow airport. I thought I'd arrived in Amritsar by mistake! It was during the 1970s, so I thought, "My God, I'm hallucinating. But no, no, I didn't take anything on the plane. This is amazing. I'll just keep calm, there'll be an explanation for it." Of course, when you live in India the only people you meet who go abroad are the elite who go to study or can afford to travel. It never occurs to you that there are Indians living all over the world, because you don't know about emigrants.'

Yet for Kusoom Vadgama, the working-class population of Britain offered a refreshing change in attitudes from the colonialists in her homeland Kenya. As with so many Asians from East Africa, who were used to being treated with contempt by the British there, the shock of being treated with civility in England is still fresh in Kusoom's mind. She vividly recalls seeing a white cleaner at London airport sweeping the floors, he was wearing a tie and called her 'madam'. 'I had never seen a white man pick up any piece of litter. If he dropped something, a servant would have to do it. So there's still a sense of disbelief that in Britain white people do menial jobs.' This realisation was also a pleasant surprise to Jinder Aujla, an executive life underwriter, who was 'somewhat expecting a change, but not to see a white man cleaning the stairs at the airport here. In East Africa the English were aloof. They would meet with you as managers, you could never really know them. Partly because they didn't want to let you, they wanted to keep the image that they were better than us, hide the fact that some of them were run of the mill. So it was a surprise to see that they did just the same jobs in their country as everyone else did all over the world. I wondered, "What's so different about them?"'

One difference which seems to have shocked many is the affection shown between men and women in public and the terms of endearment which are so freely used. When Yasmin Hosain arrived at Cambridge University, it took her some time to adjust to meeting boys and being able to talk to them. 'What shocked me at Cambridge was the totally relaxed atmosphere, though by modern standards it must seem like a nunnery. The women's colleges were at that time *women's* colleges; men were thrown out at 10 p.m. and women had to be back, like Cinderella, at midnight. Of course, this problem never arose for me because I continued to lead a fairly old-fashioned life.'

Impresario Daksha Kenney, a Gujarati Brahmin from Kenya and daughter of its largest publisher Mr T. A. Bhatt, came to do her A levels at Westminster College and was also 'shattered' when she first saw kissing in public. 'I thought, "Do Indians do this?" I thought kissing and cuddling was just Western!' Daksha had another shock when she got into one of the famous red London buses. 'I paid the conductor and he said, "Thank you, love." No one had called me "love" before, so I cringed and was very shy, blushing furiously. The next morning I had a good look to make sure it wasn't the same conductor before getting on.'

Many people were stunned when they heard people calling them 'madam', 'darling', or 'love'. We call people 'Auntie' and 'Uncle' when we want to be affectionate and so these terms, with their overtones of romance, would naturally have seemed peculiar. Perhaps it is a reflection of the different emphases of the two cultures that, in India, family is prized as the kindest source of language, whereas in England it is sexual relationships which provide the terms of endearment.

The difference in the respect and status given to language also made a powerful impression upon lawyer Naseem Khan who found accommodation in a working girls' hostel in Knightsbridge. 'I couldn't believe the words the girls used amongst and against each other, things like "bitch" and all that language I use now. I was "Thank you", "No, thank you", "Please". . .They used to abuse the warden, she used to abuse them back – incredible.'

Although the realities of living in Britain were a source of disappointment and distress to some, to others the promise of a new homeland was fulfilled at least to some extent. For law student Vina Shukla, Britain kept to its promise of politeness: 'I remember liking the way you *requested* buses to stop here. I always wanted to *request* a bus to stop, even if I didn't want to get on.'

Artist Sharon Lutchman found the general sensory inhibition of Britain quite alienating after having lived in Africa. 'What I notice in Britain is the repression of the senses, the greyness, the regimentation, even the rain doesn't smell sweet. People don't talk in the streets, don't interact with others, their body language is so inhibited. When I came here, I thought I would be isolated for life.'

At first Maria Couto, international author and lecturer, could not adjust to life in London. Alone in this vast and unfriendly city with her family thousands of miles away, the sense of isolation was doubled. 'I felt devastated. I missed my work and interaction with colleagues. I began to write a fortnightly "Letter From London" for the *Indian Express* newspaper, it forced me out of my house since I had to observe the life of the city.' Now Maria has begun to enjoy the benefits of London life, having the leisure to indulge in lifelong passions such as music and film, and the 'bliss' of Radio 3.

A similar joy is shared by Siromi Rodrigo, the deputy director of the world-wide Girl Guide movement, who loves the serious theatre in Britain. However, she also felt a stranger to the British way of life on her arrival. Siromi came to Britain as a child with her Sri Lankan diplomat family, she thought she 'was coming on a nice holiday. In our country things are so slow, all this rushing around really took time to get used to. Coming from Sri Lanka, we found keeping to time required discipline.' Once this change of pace had been made the family began to realise the new opportunities which Britain offered them in the early 1960s. 'We enjoyed being able to get around on our own. Even now, when I return to Sri Lanka, I wouldn't dream of walking along the road after sunset.'

It was this quality of relative freedom which nurse Saro Hutton also cherished. Saro found coming to England from Malaysia 'quite a novelty, quite scary. I didn't know anyone here and you heard about prejudice. But nurses have a sheltered life, living in a nursing home. I came with lots of Malaysian girls, so we had our own set of friends. We had a nice time without parental restrictions.'

Yet, while the escape from family constraints was seen as welcome freedom to some, for banker Farida Mazhar it meant loneliness and isolation. Farida came from the small Asian community in Aden to study in Britain and she was rather disappointed with the life she found here. 'Being an Asian, I was used to a lot of contact with my family, and I missed that here, although I was staying with friends. London is much less people-oriented than cities at home. Aden always felt a very secure place, particularly for the professionals, they felt they were somebody, it was a very small place, everyone knew everyone else. Coming to a city like London, it feels as if you sink into insignificance, you don't really have any social status, it's a very different kind of society.'

When antiquarian Yasmin Hosain travelled to Britain, she was shown kindness by a man who understood such feelings of insecurity. For Yasmin the journey from Pathan to study at Cambridge was her first time out of purdah since childhood. 'I was very excited as the plane took off from Karachi; it was my first flight. Having been used to a life where you were always surrounded by relatives, the fact that I didn't know anybody added to my exhilaration.'

Before direct flights from Pakistan were available, there was a transit break in Geneva. Yasmin went to the restaurant and stood around until an elderly gentleman came up to her and asked what was the matter. Assuming he was somebody to do with the restaurant, she said that she wanted a table and to eat. 'He found me a table and then, strangely, he sat down at the table with me! I was frightened, my heart was beating very, very fast, thinking that something awful was about to happen. It was a pleasant meal and the gentleman asked would I drink wine and I said "*No!*" – I was a good Muslim, frightened even to look at a glass of wine. The gentleman said to me, "You're going to London, would you like to come to a concert?" Of course I didn't really know what concerts were about, but he wrote his name down on a piece of paper for me. Later on he offered to take me to the plane. I was so scared, I ran off to the ladies' room and stayed there until the flight was announced and then rushed to the plane, imagining all kinds of horrendous things and thinking of something out of Jane Austen's *Northanger Abbey*, being pursued by someone you don't know.

'I stayed for a few days in London before term started and saw a familiar-looking name in the newspaper. I looked at the piece of paper from Geneva, and it was Andres Segovia, the Spanish guitarist. He was performing in London. I still keep that scrap of paper very carefully. I didn't go to the concert, not knowing much about Western music, so I didn't realise the importance of Andres Segovia until many, many years later.'

As Yasmin experienced, the arrival in a new land often leads to a mingling of emotions – excitement with anxiety, happiness with homesickness and opportunity with loss. For all the women in this book Britain has come to provide some sort of home and yet the common thread of Asia also runs through all of them. This other motherland is to some, like myself, the country of birth, and therefore holds a special emotional tie; to others it offers the promise of cultural and religious purity that England cannot provide. Indeed, while it is significant that all of these women have chosen to stay in Britain, it is also important that as Asians they have remained aware of their ancestral pasts and origins, drawn to them by a golden thread of genealogy and spirituality.

8

Coming Home

A vast and varied country, India holds many meanings and offers many promises to its peoples. Often to those not born in India the first journey there is as enlightening as that to Britain, yet unlike Britain, which is a land of new beginnings and material pull, the force that draws people to the Indian subcontinent is an ancestral and spiritual one. Like Mecca or Jerusalem, India is a land of pilgrimage, a country which reminds one that what may seem strange or self-conscious in their new homeland is natural in their old one. To many, India offers a sense of belonging and a spiritual and cultural renewal, but it also evokes feelings of frustration and longings for the comfort and convenience of the West.

To Janaki Menon, a law student at Cambridge, the journeying to India was a quest which led to a sense of complete experience and happiness. 'My first trip to India was in my year off before going to university. I went for three months. Although I felt it very important to meet my father's family to get my identity, and I grew to love my family very much, I don't know that I enjoyed it. They were very relieved that I wasn't too Western and I dressed in saris while I was there, even though they didn't ask me to. I think I was too big, too tall, too dark for them. My grandmother got very upset if I went out in the day, because I'd get darker. I was allowed to travel to India on my own, but there I couldn't even go to the end of the road alone.'

The multitudes of codes, the continual name dropping and the lack of privacy, which dictates Indian life, evokes a feeling of frustration in many. When Ella Vala's family were forced to leave Uganda, she wanted to settle in India rather than England, 'it sounded more interesting, but I'm glad now that I didn't. I'm more English than I'll ever be Indian. It's a beautiful country in every sense, but the pettiness, squabbles and non-working telephones.' The Deputy Director of the Guiding movement, Siromi Rodrigo also finds the same irritations in Sri Lanka. 'When I go home to Sri Lanka sometimes I feel really frustrated, especially with the people that I meet. They are all so busy doing nothing. Every friend of mine has at least two servants. To arrange a bowl of flowers they spend two hours. It is the heat also.'

Yet despite the difficulties in adjusting from the routine of Western societies, India still offers a unique charm. As an Asian, the subcontinent is a part of your history which cannot be denied, for me a journey back there is a remembrance and a renewal. For others too India has become a holiday homeland. Saadia Nasiri, radio presenter, feels this way about her native Pakistan. 'If someone asked me, "Where is your home?" I would say, "Pakistan is where I am from originally." But now, when we go back for holidays to Pakistan, it is just a place for a holiday.'

Although Amit Roy has chosen to stay in Britain where he is a feature writer with the *Sunday Times*, he also feels that, 'It is important to go back to India from time to time, it recharges my batteries. I find there is such a zest for life. I like the level of conversation. People are interested in you.' Sometimes though the feelings are not so clear, as Shruti Pankaj, a theatre administrator and poet, simply states, 'One may not like it, but one surely loves it.' This seems to be a sentiment echoed by others.

For lawyer Jyoti Munsiff, the feelings of dissatisfaction with India arise precisely because of her great affection for it. 'When I'm there, I get very frustrated with the place and the people. I love the beauty of their spiritual side, but, as a great generalisation, they are also apathetic and petty, our own worst enemies. So I also feel upset, and that's because I feel more Indian than English. It's like feeling more frustrated with your family than with strangers – your aspirations for family are higher.'

Belkis Bhegani found this mingling of emotions perfectly natural. 'Like any tourist, I was bowled over by India, I was frustrated by the country, I loved it, I hated it. I had no culture problems.' To her, India offered a land in which the Asian people could be treated according to their true worth – as the gold they really are, rather than the silver or bronze which is their Western value. 'There's a sense of absolute confidence about Indians in India which you don't find in them in Britain. They are totally confident about themselves, because they know where they are, they're in their country. Indians in Britain don't have that sense of complete confidence.'

Certainly, many found in India a sense of belonging and a cultural and racial identification that Britain cannot offer. To Belkis' Indian-born husband Samir Shah, BBC Deputy Editor of Television News and Current Affairs, India was a land in which the air-conditioning had been switched off in more ways than one. 'In Britain, racism to someone like me is a background noise, it's like air-conditioning, you only notice it when it switches off. It switches off in India and you never have the idea that the cab didn't stop because of the colour of your skin, the service in the shop was bad because of the colour of your skin.'

A similar contentment and ease was also felt by Kusoom Vadgama when she finally went to India for a holiday after its Independence in 1947. She recalls a magical trip to never-never land. She had thought of India, read about it, knew so much about it, and now she was actually there: 'I was amongst my own culture and there was no discrimination.'

Artist Sharon Lutchman also found India to be a place where the feelings of anxiety and self-consciousness could be left behind. 'When I went to India after college, I fell in love with the place. I felt comfortable about my body language, my hands, the way I move. Indian people are the most sensual people in the world, I know I am! It's how we speak, how we look with our eyes, how we react. It is a hot country, just luscious, that's how it is.'

Even to Asians born and brought up outside of the continent, India offers a homeland in terms of spiritual and emotional belong-ing. As Hena Mukherjee discovered when she travelled to India after taking her O levels, India is a land which offers a mirror to all Asians and one in which minor cultural differences become insignificant. 'I hadn't thought of myself as Bengali, I had always thought of myself as Singaporean. I felt at home in a very new and satisfying way, although the lifestyles were very different. They ate different things, they cooked with mustard oil and in Singapore you used ground-nut oil.'

Shakira Caine felt an equal sense of affinity and happiness in India, for her too it was a mirror of the qualities which she most cherished in the Asian people in her homeland of Guyana. 'When I went to India, I felt so at home there. When I arrived at the airport, it reminded me of the Indians from my country. Their faces say their souls are rich.'

For barrister Kim Hollis the emotions which a visit to India creates are so deep that they defy words. 'I am in that plane and just about to come in with the daybreak. . .My heart always misses a beat and I feel that I am coming home. It is really strange and I can't explain it. My husband has never been to India and I can't wait to take him.'

Yet to some, the very real tie to the spirituality and values of India is constantly being tugged at by the material luxury and comfort of the West. For Dr Natasha Bijlani, this is a division which causes much inconvenience: 'I want the best of both worlds, but that means commuting, and that's hell! I feel I belong in Bombay, it's part of me, I grew up there and return every year. London is such a big city, you could be anyone. In Bombay I feel part of society, in London I'm always going to be a second class citizen no matter how much I achieve. I can see myself living in Britain, it's cleaner, there are much better opportunities, but I'll never lose touch with Bombay, even with the corruption and petty rules.'

However, for some the lure of cleanliness and efficiency is strong enough for a decision to be made on a permanent homeland. Publisher Mishti Chatterji feels that it is important for her son, Arjun, to be aware of the source of his Asian culture, and each year they visit India to give Arjun a chance to experience both cultures and be with his other grandparents. 'When we first went back, he was 2 and we found him playing in the open sewers, "But it's puddles, mum." We wanted him to accept that people live in different ways, that's normal and you don't regard it with contempt. England is his real home, we know that and he knows that.'

The simple craving for cleanliness is a factor which dissuades many from India. As biochemist Kiran Kumar found, 'When I went to India I was so disappointed, my standards of cleanliness are Kenyan.' Indeed, for Koki Wasani, the first woman president of the UK Lohana community, the hygiene and other qualities of Britain compensate for both the weather and the work. 'It is hard in Britain, ladies have to work more, to go shopping, clean the house. I can also live with the weather, for the cleanliness of Britain.'

However, probably the most disturbing vision of India is the poverty and the comparatively low value of life. The feeling of impotence and the inevitability of acceptance which the poverty of others brings, has made successful equestrian Meera Mehta reluctant to return. 'We used to go to India every year, but I don't really want to go back again. On my last trip to India I was old enough to see the poverty and I couldn't understand it. There were people everywhere asking for money. I asked my parents how they could turn a blind eye to it. Within about two weeks I did turn a blind eye to it and that's what really disturbed me.'

Marc Zuber, an actor formerly with the Royal Shakespeare Company, experienced similar emotions when he travelled to India to pursue his international career in Indian films. 'For the first few months in Bombay I used to feel extremely guilty, I was in the Holiday Inn, drinking beer. On the other side of the wall, there were people who only make 18 rupees in a month. And there's me guzzling four, five beers if I'm bored. What really started to upset me was when I became immune to it.'

Whilst Marc did gradually harden himself to the poverty, he did not become immune to the sights of death, as others seemed to do. 'I was being driven back to my hotel after a long day filming. Suddenly the driver swerved and I looked back to see a figure lying in the road, really a nodding head, the rest was just squelched. I don't know how many cars had run over him. I'd had quite a few drinks and became hysterical, "Stop the damn car, call the police, call the ambulance." The driver advised me, "Please don't! Firstly, the cops will suggest we did it. Secondly, we'd be here for ever and we'd have to pay off the cops." To me the dead man was a valuable life. In Britain the *state* is far more caring, in India, 500 people die and nobody gives a damn. Maybe people feel overcrowded there, they see people dying in the street every day and it seems less urgent.'

Author Bapsi Sidhwa was equally distressed by the minimal worth credited to each Asian life. 'In Pakistan there was a front page story about seven Germans and Italians dying in a skiing accident in the Alps. Hidden away inside, twenty-seven Pakistanis dead in a bus crash. In our own estimation, we think we're not good enough, more coverage is given to Europeans.'

Although this seeming disregard of human life is difficult to cope with, maybe it communicates more than simple carelessness. For those living in a continent so over-populated and where reincarnation is a common belief, there is a spiritual solace which dilutes the absolute grief felt by the loss of a human life within Western Christian or secular beliefs.

For the Hare Krishna convert and devotee Akhandadhi das, England, and not India, appears as a place of real deprivation and suffering, as he judges according to spiritual and not material riches. After his first visit to India, he returned to the Hare Krishna centre from Heathrow airport and still vividly recalls how depressed people looked on the streets in Britain. 'My heart went out to them.

It just struck me that Britain is where the suffering is. I did not see suffering in India. I saw poverty, unimaginable poverty, but I did not see suffering. I saw that in the faces in England.'

Certainly, every vision depends upon the angle of sight and the eyes that inform it. Although Britain and India are undeniably different, even antithetical in some respects, there are many points of comparison and similarity. Just as the British left the time warp of their colonial values in India, the Indians have repeated this practice in Britain. As film maker Munni Kabir explains it, 'Most immigrant groups, wherever they have gone, and whenever they went, took the morality of their home country with them. So if you went from India in the fifties, the morality of India in the fifties is what you took with you. Because you haven't had the intervening years in India, your sense of morality, your attitudes, haven't evolved as they have there. You are stuck with your fifties attitude to women and religion and many other things. Religion is more complex, but certainly it is true for the attitude to women. So the result is that Asian men, here and now, are regarding their women like Indian men of the fifties, and whatever *his* attitude is to his wife, the British man is going to take on, because it's much easier.' Academic Sita Narasimhan discovered for herself that this applied to languages as well. When she spoke to the committee of a Tamil Saturday school, 'they all started laughing at me and said, "You lisp in Tamil!" The Tamil I speak is acceptable by modern-day standards, but they have frozen this language, in order to keep their identity.'

This was a realization which only struck radio presenter Saadia Nasiri when she returned to Pakistan. While she lived a fairly sheltered life in Britain, according to her parents' retention of their Pakistani Muslim values, she was surprised to find that in Pakistan itself women had more freedom. 'Our parents are more strict in terms of where, when and who we go out with. When we are in Pakistan my cousins come and say, "We are going to the disco tonight at the Holiday Inn." I think, "Oh my God! Discos in Karachi!" But it is quite common. There was nothing new about romances and things going on in Karachi. It was no big deal. Here you would probably think twice about starting a relationship with somebody, you would question, "Is he the same culture? Is he the right person for me? Will my parents accept him?" You know that you are away from your country, have a sort of obligation to really protect your culture, because you know that you shouldn't be influenced by Western ideas and morals, you should preserve your own.'

To academic Sita Narasimhan all that is truly being preserved is a time-warp. 'In some strange way, entirely out of goodwill, what we are doing here is to perpetuate outworn customs, habits, languages and attitudes from twice displaced communities.' Indeed, cultural identities are significant ties to one's homeland and heritage and reminders that each society has its own appeal and each its own flaws. Yet, the peoples of India and Britain are not only united by the common link of all humanity, but also by the golden threads of family and social structure and an interwoven history. While society emphasises the differences between us, if we look into the looking glass together we will see the similarities too.

9

Yours Was the Earth and Everything on It, and What's More. . .?

Rudyard Kipling's poem 'If' is, like Shakespeare and the Bible, one of the great texts of British conduct. Kipling's instructions for achievement and integrity may survive as the ideals of an Englishman and continue to offer an example to many, but the truths of history have now made his advice a parody of itself. The qualities that Kipling quotes are still widely considered to be the best of British, and are often used to judge the worth of character. Indeed, this mirror of British attitude was exported with colonialism as the ideal to be matched by other societies and in many ways it was. The mirror is now being turned around to examine to what extent the English can still fulfil their past reflection of perfection. The days of the British Empire are over, but it is interesting to see whether the many qualities which made them so powerful, and so politely so, remain. It is particularly apt that it is Rudyard Kipling, one of the very few authors to write of colonial India, who has left the Asian people a perfect set of criteria by which to judge their 'past masters'. Nevertheless, the views which emerge reveal how the natural affinities between the British and Asian cultures and the shadow of colonialism has produced a looking glass in which there are many features of comparison as well as of contrast.

> *If you can keep your head when all about you*
> *Are losing theirs and blaming it on you,*

The British reputation for staying calm during a crisis is one which many admire, it contrasts quite definitely with the Asian tendency to overdramatise a situation and to panic over the imminent disaster, rather than to appraise the solution calmly. Dr Navin Ramgoolam recalled that his father, the first Prime Minister and Governor General of Mauritius, felt that his ability to handle a crisis was developed during his time spent in England. When he returned to Mauritius he found that 'whenever something was happening, everyone else would be rushing around, reacting. I had learnt how to keep calm and would eventually be in a better position to act.'

Dr Roeinton Khambatta admires the British ability to cope in a crisis and sees it as a positive reflection of their 'impersonality'. 'The British are very undemonstrative in their ways. It's an attitude which quite frankly I prefer. I do not like emotionalism, I like the stiff upper lip. When there's a crisis, you need to think clearly and not just continue breast-beating. Perhaps it's my professional training which has taught me to look at things logically and coldly, analyse and resolve things.'

Barrister and journalist Devinia Sookia also feels that the positive quality of calm is related to the reserved nature of the British. 'English people do what they want without paying any attention to what others say. They are more diplomatic, know how to hide their real feelings and show a brave face in situations where many Asians would lose their cool.'

International journalist Amit Roy feels that Kipling's words proved themselves true during the Falklands crisis, which he covered from Argentina. 'The British truly rose to the occasion. They ought not to be underestimated, they appear to be easy going, but under pressure you see the British character at its best. For example, seeing the young men fighting in the Falklands, in the conditions they did, when it comes to the crunch I'd rather have Brits on my side than many other people.'

The sense of resilience and control which the British seem to muster despite adversity is a quality which some identify as typical of public school mentality fostered in the privileged classes. Business-woman Namita Panjabi sees British education as a right of passage into the kind of manhood Kipling advocated. 'The schooling means they rough it as kids and so aren't as soft when they grow up. Mark Tully, the BBC correspondent in India, will go places no Indian middle-class person would touch.'

Perhaps one of the most treasured qualities of the British is their sense of humour, uniquely dry and ironic. Rita Austin feels that it comes from a belief in oneself and a natural serenity. 'The

British sense of humour is wonderful; it shows their reserve and understatement, it was one of the things I first liked about my husband, it comes out as a sense of inner calm. A complete contrast to the Bengalis who are always jumping around about something.'

If you can trust yourself when all men doubt you,

The self-assurance and confidence that characterises the British was given supreme example by their colonial behaviour. Unlike other imperial powers who retained a fiercer hold but exchanged beliefs and customs, the British kept aloof and apart from the lives of the communities they ruled. Believing their ways to be naturally superior, they trusted in their own worth and did not examine the benefits or assets of others' cultures.

To law student Janaki Menon, this complacency is still strong today. Even direct questioning is not a display of genuine curiosity or interest to the British, as there is either no inclination actually to listen to the answers given, or else there is an alternate motive for the questioning. 'The British are xenophobic, they can't get used to anything strange or different. The question I hate most is, "Where are you from?" I always say "Harrow". "No, but where are you *really* from?" "Oh, I was born in Paddington. . ." Even in my French oral exam, the examiner asked me where I was from. When I said "Harrow" she looked really embarrassed, I'm sure it wasn't at my French.'

However, while the absence of interest and the segregation which this sometimes causes may be negative, the emphasis placed upon the authority of personal opinion and individual confidence is a quality which has often aided the Asian community in Britain. Syeda Jalali, the *Sunday Express*'s former Business Woman Of The Year and owner of Aquarius Designs, was happy to discover that her belief in her own abilities and her enthusiasm was rewarded when she was chosen for a course in business administration out of 2,000 applicants. 'The ten places on the course had been filled, but when I walked in there, two weeks before the course was starting, the interviewer was so impressed by my determination and confidence that he actually asked his governors to let one extra person onto this course.'

Educationist Piloo Nanavutty also remembers the stress that the British place upon the faith in one's own beliefs from her time at Cambridge, where she was encouraged to think independently.

'I was stunned when my tutor told me, "That's not correct!" I explained that I had found it in a book. "My dear child," he answered, "just because it's printed in a book doesn't make it true." I thought I was being good, I had consulted twenty-five books and included all the references in the essay. "Yes, I see you've read all these books. Now we will begin to discuss the subject." To Indians, the ability to understand and quote others is seen as a way to prove individual knowledge, whereas to the British it is seen as a poor excuse for the lack of original thought. Piloo took the British approach back with her to teach in India. She told her students not to just accept what others say, but to challenge, compare and think their own thoughts.

The indifference shown to the absolute authority of others may be a positive asset in education, but the British desire to promote their own beliefs rather than to explore those of others has also provided another aspect of the British character according to Dr David Dabydeen, author and lecturer at the University of Warwick. 'Tolerance is premised on a lack of curiosity. That is why the British can be tolerant, they are curiously incurious. The British people can't be bothered to be aggrieved or excited by something new.'

But make allowance for their doubting too;

However, tolerance of others was not seen as incidental by Kipling who advised his readers to make 'allowances' for others. Indeed, one quality which many admired in the British was their tolerance of others' cultures.

In the experience of some this was simply the British fondness for eccentrics. Such allowances were made for me at school at Roedean. Fortunately, some teachers expected a 'foreigner' to behave badly, and took it upon themselves to give me at least a veneer of 'well-bred ladylike' manners. TV presenter Shyama Perera was surprised by the broad-mindedness that reveals itself in all ranks of British society. 'I've had my hair pink and blue. The great thing is you expect to be stopped when you go to the House of Commons or the High Court but nobody ever stops me or comments on it. It is so British, they just let me through, "Oh hello, you're back again."'

Entrepreneur Namita Panjabi remembers the exception made for her when she received her degree from Cambridge, but also the cautionary tale which came with it. Namita was expected, like everyone else, to wear black for the graduation ceremony. Yet, after telling her tutor that she never wore black as it was an unlucky colour for Asians, the university's Senate gave Namita special permission to wear a white sari, which was more auspicious. On the morning of the ceremony, however, she was told that she had to wear white shoes as well. A rapid search of the university's halls of residence turned up only one pair in her size, a pair of slippers, complete with pom-poms. The ceremony at Cambridge involves climbing a few stairs to receive the degree and shaking hands with the Chancellor. Namita, already conspicuous as the only one in 3,000 people not wearing black, slipped in her borrowed slippers and fell, bringing the Chancellor down with her. As her tutor later remarked, 'See what comes of being different.'

Yet to the surprise and admiration of others, the British go beyond the acceptance of eccentrics, which presents no real threat, to tolerate cultural differences even when they are on a community scale. Journalist Amit Roy feels it is important to acknowledge that 'the British are tolerant, fair, reasonable people. That is not to say that there aren't problems or racism, but if we can show that far from their culture being threatened, we can extend it in some way, that we can make it more fun, by being here.' Amit also feels that there are few countries which would be so tolerant of cultures that seem to challenge their basic ideologies and social structures.

Radio presenter Saadia Nasiri admires and is amazed by the unquestioning acceptance which the British show to other ways of life amidst their own. 'Often I think, "Gosh, there are so many Asians here." I sometimes cringe at some of them because of the way they dress, the way they have not changed their life style at all from how they lived back home in the villages. And yet the tolerance which comes through from English people is amazing; like demanding Halal meat in schools, demanding that their daughters should wear trousers and cover their heads and demanding that they should have separate religious lessons, it is incredible that the British allow all this to go on.'

Yet, as Sarah Sheriff, a spokeswoman for the Islamic Organisation for Media Monitoring, sharply reminds us, the British are not the only people to have a history of tolerance. 'They are tolerant, but all the Indians, Pakistanis and Africans were tolerant when the British came out to their countries, so I don't see why they shouldn't be. They're the ones who wanted all these people to come here and work for them so they just have to put up with it.'

The British have shown tolerance to those immigrants who have settled here, but an unappealing attitude seems to be emerging in today's society, which my youngest son drew my attention to: 'The greatest British quality is tolerance, why waste it on foreigners?' This might be a humorous comment, but many a true word is said in jest.

To Mani Sidhwa, a market researcher, the restrained welcome and reserved tolerance of most British people is their endeavour to be as accommodating as their nature allows. 'On the whole British whites are very tolerant. They may not have welcomed us with open arms, but they have made concessions. At least they make an attempt to show that they are not racists.'

If you can wait and not be tired by waiting,

Perhaps one of the most famed virtues of the British, and another face of their tolerance, is queuing. To most who had come to settle in Britain, this quality was one which endeared them to the public. Kathak dancer Nahid Siddiqui remembers how this was the first quality of the British that appealed to her.

Queuing may be a minor face of British fair play, but it is a symbol of their attitude to life. As Dr Navin Ramgoolam comments, 'When you get to the end, you know you'll be served.' Also, its order is irresistible, and once Navin had become accustomed to queuing he found it difficult to break the rules. 'We were queuing outside a government building in Mauritius to get an identity card before the last election. Someone inside the building rushed out, as he'd recognised me. "What are you doing out here? You don't need to queue! Come in, come in!" He couldn't understand that I wanted to queue up like everybody else.'

The detailed decency and honesty of the British was also a quality which impressed Sister Jayanti: 'When I was young, with no concept of money, my mother would send me out to the shops, trusting that the shopkeeper would give me the right change. You couldn't do that in India; send a child out with a ten-rupee note and they'd come back with half the change.'

To child psychotherapist Asha Phillips the endless regulations which define British society make it fairly easy to fit in, if not to belong: 'The English are incredibly reserved, polite and civilised. It's a very easy place to live, they even drive according to the rules.' Indeed, the restraint and the ethic of 'playing things by the book' which the British display seems to be peculiar, even among other Europeans. As Asha noticed, 'At university, if there was something upsetting the students, they would *write* to the Vice-Chancellor. The slightest problem in France and you took to the streets.'

Certainly, within all walks of British life, calm and patience are prized virtues. Author Kusoom Vadgama has found that 'it takes time to build a relationship with the British, and you've got to accept that, and be very patient with them.' As Eartha Kitt sang, 'But an Englishman needs time!' For others, patience has been rewarded in professional as well as personal life.

Headmistress Shirley Daniel relied on the British admiration of perseverance when she was confronted by an anomaly in Britain's education system. Teachers qualified to teach in England are not accepted in Scotland and vice versa, but Shirley, who was recognised as a teacher only by the English Department of Education, needed a job in Scotland and so decided to be patient. She went to the Scottish Education Office in Edinburgh and asked to see the minister there. His secretary told her that it was impossible because he was 'too busy', so Shirley sat outside the office from morning to evening, until the secretary allowed her in. After he had looked at Shirley's certificates and references, he pronounced that she was qualified to teach in Scotland too. 'The Scots don't judge you until they see your work. I told the minister that I was educated at the Madras District College, founded by Scots, and my last Principal was living in Glasgow, so if he wanted to check on my abilities, he wouldn't have to go far!'

Dr Chandra Patel had a similar experience trying to gain admittance into medical school in Britain. Her age, marital and maternal status seemed to disqualify her before she was even given an interview. Chandra was determined to become a doctor and her persistence paid off. She visited King's College about twenty-five times. 'The Sub-Dean's secretary was really sympathetic to me. In the end, she talked to the Vice-Dean and he agreed to see me, about a week before the course started. He saw me, but said, "There is no guarantee that you will get into medical school." I said, "Don't worry about that. Just give me a place for the second MB, the anatomy and physiology part, and I will take my chances on that." I did so well I actually got the anatomy prize and I also stood first in biochemistry, which the Vice-Dean taught. In the end three hospitals were quite prepared to take me.' In Britain, the honest adherence to codes of practice means that the virtues of endurance and the evidence of ability are usually still justly rewarded.

Or being lied about, don't deal in lies,

Certainly, the willingness of the British to judge according to merit along with their high esteem of honesty were two of the most prominent characteristics to emerge. Many may feel that these are two qualities which Asian people do not share with the British, the constant queue-barging and privilege-bribing may confirm this. Nevertheless, Hare Krishna devotee Akhandadhi das explained to me that the tendency among Asians to flout their verbal promises, which annoys so many British business people, is not a deliberate breaking of one's word, rather a compulsive desire to defy an ordered code. 'The point of negotiating is to get the best deal you can. But they are just so oblivious to the etiquette that should be there, Indians just ignore all the rules.'

Although some of the minor traits of fair play, such as queuing itself, have become extinct along with imperial rule, the basic belief in honesty has retained its importance. This may be a quality to which the British would like to claim exclusive rights, but in fact it is also a virtue prized highly by Zoroastrians. Sehri Saklatvala's story about her famous MP father, Shapurji, illustrates this. 'When my eldest brother was 5, my father was undressing him for bed, when he found a cork in his pocket. "Where did this come from?" "From the lab at school." The next day was Saturday, the school was closed, but my father took him to the headmaster's house to give it back and explain why he had taken this bottle cork. I remember my father saying, "A child, like a plant, needs training."'

Perhaps the British quality most valued by others is their sense of justice, a female figure. The unique golden thread which runs through the British legal system means that each person is deemed to be innocent until proven guilty. Many people felt that however badly one was treated by the British there was ultimately a sense of justice. Shirley Daniel spoke for many when she said, 'In the end you can appeal to the law.' For advertising copy-writer Anjali Paul, it was the fairness and the sympathy of the British which endeared them to her. 'The one thing I do like about the British is that they are prepared to fight injustice for the underdog.'

When Mauritius gained independence some politicians wanted to form a Republic and abolish the right to make a final appeal to the British Privy Council. There was a popular ground swell in Mauritius which Dr Navin Ramgoolam's father, then Prime Minister, understood; the government would have collapsed if ordinary people had been denied the access to justice which they associated with the British, and Mauritians still have their final right of appeal to Britain.

Yet, despite the great tradition of their legal system, the British were quick to learn from their mistakes when they realised that their laws could be used against their own interests. Many Indians who came to Britain at the beginning of the century studied law in order to return to India to aid the struggle for their country's Independence. Consequently legal training ceased to be an option encouraged by the British to other peoples of their Empire. As Hena Mukherjee remembers, 'Malayans weren't invited to come and study law, as the British had learnt from the Indian experience. There was a new breed of Indians who went back to their country as freedom fighters, able to fight the English way, on their own battleground, with the same weapons.'

However, even the British justice system has its loopholes and Kiran Kumar's father, himself a lawyer, explored one of these. He proved that while the British might have had the law on their side, as an Asian he had the qualities of determination and resilience on his. 'In those days no Indian was allowed to buy land in the "white" areas of Kenya, it was like South Africa. My father wanted to buy a house in one such area, so he got an English client to buy the land first, then bought it off him.'

A more amusing display of her father's cunning was yet to come. Kiran's father was 'blessed with too many daughters', but he made them feel as though they were 'as good as sons'. Kiran recalls, 'My father also kept a cow, we had enough room in the garden. There were several theories about why he did this – one was that it was an Indian custom, if he didn't keep a cow, he wouldn't get a son. The city council complained about our cow, trying to find an excuse to politely move us from the area, but my father checked all the by-laws. He was taken to court and he defended himself. My father won the case because of his British legal training. He agreed with the judge that the by-laws stated that you couldn't keep a bull or cattle inside the city boundary, but there was no mention of the word "cow". The British had to amend the laws after they lost the case. The following day, all the headlines in Nairobi quoted my father as saying, "I may be bullied, but I refuse to be cowed". The cow was

kept on for milk, but everyone was relieved when a son was duly
born. I never found out whether there was any connection. . .'

Or being hated, don't give way to hating,

Author Farrukh Dhondy articulated the conflict between insulting
the British and trusting them to behave like gentlemen. 'We called
them bastards and swine, we wrote histories which said that they
looted our country dry, treated us badly, they were racists and
had two-tier legal systems. All these charges were true. But in
the explosion of nationalism we emphasised those charges against
the British without mentioning their qualities. Mahatma Gandhi
and Pandit Nehru tried to emphasise the decent qualities of the
British. They kept saying that whatever the British are, they are
gentlemen, they play the game, and we can rely on the British not
to beat us up if we offer them non-violence. In the end they will
have to go, they will do the decent thing.'

It is fortunate that it was the British, and not the Germans of
the time, that Gandhi had to deal with. Hitler would not have
been impressed with his campaign of non-violence. In contrast,
even though Churchill rudely called Gandhi a 'half-naked fakir',
the British respected him instead of shooting him. My favourite
scene in the film *Gandhi* is when Trevor Howard, playing the rôle of
a judge, stands up to honour Gandhi as he enters his court room. He
then sentences him to a period of imprisonment. This gesture shows
perfectly the British qualities of respect for an outstanding individual, personal dignity and unquestioning obedience to the law.

And yet don't look too good, nor talk too wise:

One aspect which has attracted public comment from the British
and Asians alike is the ostentation of certain Asians, who try to
'look too good'. Indeed, the recent trend towards the flashing of
newly-created wealth is far from the old British esteem of good
taste and modesty. Although Asian attitudes to money are naturally
flamboyant, the contempt for the *nouveaux riches* from both cultures
seems to confirm that the majority still believe in the understatement
that Kipling advises.

Money has great status within both cultures, but as Shruti Pankaj
points out this is for quite different reasons: 'In India there is
competition in spending rather than earning.' To the English, money

offers the chance to buy an island retreat, whereas to the Indians it provides the opportunity to erect a grand public stage on which to entertain and impress others with their wealth. The English with 'real money' are discreet about it, but to the Indians it is simply, 'If you've got it, flaunt it!' This Asian desire for conspicuous generosity also extends to social occasions and achieves its supreme expression in weddings. Unlike British marriages which are considered to be grand affairs if over 100 guests are invited, Asian weddings can entertain thousands and for days.

To some distinguished members of the community, the ostentation of a particular class of Asians seems both absurd and socially ungracious. Dr Roeinton Khambatta sees the exclusivity of certain wealthy Asians as self-seeking. 'They have divorced themselves from general society. Just as there are English sons of spivs there are Indian and Pakistani sons of spivs. They pride themselves on living in £2,000,000 homes in Hampstead, but all they do is to have parties to congratulate themselves. They might invite the odd English celebrity in the hope of being seen in the pages of *Tatler*.'

Kusoom Vadgama sees the conspicuous consumption of some Asian women as an expression of the futility of their lives. 'Some women feel there is nothing they can do about anything except spend their husband's money. They've been spoon-fed, provided with a house, servants, bank balance. So they go for coffee mornings, bridge parties and they end up with the same boring crowd competing with each other. Constantly buying saris, in case someone thinks that they haven't got enough.'

Many people commented that the need to be accepted and recognised had its roots in insecurity. One of many stories told was of an Asian with new money who had had gold taps installed, so when people visited her toilet they would know she was wealthy. Yet another remembered a telephone conversation with a friend's Filipino maid, who had been trained to discourage callers by informing them that 'Madam was jet-lagging'.

Certainly, if there is one quality which the British and the Asian old ruling classes have in common, it is a dislike of the *nouveaux* and their excessive flashing of money. One must never think that all the goings on in *Dallas* and *Dynasty* are exclusively for wealthy Westerners. Indians have their own equivalent: 'The New Delhisty Set'.

Princess Usha Devi Rathore shares the universal contempt for the *nouveaux*. 'The *nouveaux riches* are like children with bright coins, they want to play with their wealth, show it off. The new Indian moneyed is into copying the West, doing it better. They are not really my kind of people, but after all they are the sort of people who are able to give to my charities. I have two sets of calling cards, one normal set with my simple name and address, and the other for these people with our family's gold embossed royal crest and *Princess* Usha Devi!'

If you can dream – and not make dreams your master;
If you can think – and not make thoughts your aim;

The British, unlike the Asians, are not famed for their philosophy and tend to be more practically minded. In Britain learning is seen more as a means than an end in itself. Vocational courses are often given more respect and funding than arts or philosophy, as people cannot see what is to be 'done' with these. Thought has a more direct relation to action for the British and while this may seem to deaden the imagination, it promotes a single-minded commitment to causes for which they have always been admired. Many who had been educated in England spoke about the effects of the more ordered and disciplined system of analysis.

Shama Habibullah, film producer and director, remembers: 'At Cheltenham I had to accept the fact that there was a discipline. In fact I suppose I became part of it in order to beat it. It was something I reacted against very badly after I had left, I completely rejected anything that over-discipline had taught me. It was the kind of discipline through suffering that is supposed to build Empires, and Britain didn't have one by that time; anyway I was supposed to be one of those repressed by it.'

Yet producer and director Munni Kabir appreciated the education of Britain which was 'Anglo-Saxon structure and discipline. In Indian families there is a certain amount of chaos, a feeling that fate will come in and help you. So you just allow things to happen to you.' When Munni studied in France, she realised that the British way of learning is truly unique. 'The British system gives you the structure and allows you to think. The French tell you how to think, they give you a language to think in. The British allow you a space to grow for yourself. The French, they allow you that space, but intellectually they give you more definite tools.'

This difference in attitude and thought process was substantiated by so many that maybe the way in which we think is not merely defined by our social and educational background, but also by innate, ancestral, cultural ones. The rigid A–B–C process of Western analysis may be highly logical and suited to moving from idea to action, but its linear progression insists upon an exclusiveness of ideas.

In contrast, a thought pattern which can embrace A–Y–S, which many of those I spoke to identified as more their own, is a web of ideas, less ordered, but more able to hold complexities and contradictions and therefore less prone to generalisation and categorising. Whatever the reason, the East seems to place more worth upon the metaphysical aspects of thought than the British. The majority of British who judge according to deeds cannot understand the value of the labyrinth of philosophy or the wise passiveness of meditation.

> *If you can meet with Triumph and Disaster*
> *And treat those two impostors just the same.*

However, if there is one subject which the British have been able to treat philosophically, it is their own failure. Kipling's advice may seem noble, the epitome of the English amateur mentality, but to some his counsel seems a clever way to save face.

Princess Usha Devi Rathore felt that the British always knew that they were going to lose the Empire and therefore made a virtue out of losing. The great moments in English history have been moments of heroic failure: Dunkirk, the Charge of the Light Brigade, losing the Ashes to the Australians. Certainly there is something endearing about the way that the British do not take life all that seriously. They are not fanatics.

In one respect this has made the British willing to laugh at themselves, to make a comic success out of a dire failure. In recent years, ski-jumper 'Eddie the Eagle', the only British person competing, has amused people by consistently finishing last with a smile. The British have a sense of just being there and doing things. It charms people if athletes do not worry too much about whether they win or lose, just as long as they played the game and enjoyed it.

However, since the advent of Thatcherism, Kipling's words have waned, and the American philosophy of 'Winner Takes All' has usurped the great British 'Win or Lose' mentality. Even the English cricket team now blames their weaknesses on the Pakistani umpire, the West Indian fast-bowling or the 'damned weather'.

If you can make one heap of all your winnings
And risk it on one turn of pitch-and-toss,
And lose, and start again at your beginnings
And never breathe a word about your loss.

Courage, resourcefulness and acceptance were all important attributes of the Empire. The whole imperial success of the British was based on a gamble and, although they certainly came away from the table with substantial winnings, like all gamblers they ultimately lost. What is difficult for others to appreciate is that they have not accepted this loss, but have whinged about their misfortune and lost status. The British still have many qualities which could make them great and 'if' they could follow Kipling's advice they might find it easier to gain the world's respect once more.

If you can talk with crowds and keep your virtue,
Or walk with Kings – nor lose the common touch,

The dual obsession that the British have for the underdog and royalty has enabled them to retain some of the true liberalism for which they were so admired. Unlike the Indian caste system which mandates fierce segregation between its levels, with the higher not allowed to take water or be touched by the shadow of the lower, the cramping British class system developed from a relationship between the aristocracy and the working classes. To Asians there is considerably less value placed upon the society of those below one on the social ladder. For law student Sharmishta Chakrabarti this British attitude promotes a social conscience which she treasures in Britain: 'I like the idea of supporting the underdog.'

Dr David Dabydeen sees Kipling's advice as heeding a long tradition of British values: 'There is a liberal tradition in Britain that you can trace back to the Magna Carta, of common decencies operating between people. You see this at the height of the slave trade. There was also a very powerful anti-slavery movement. There have always been philanthropic movements in this country to save animals, to save human beings. There is also another tradition which is hostile to foreigners. The first tradition is polluted by the second, because the people who belong to the first, whilst they may sympathise with you broadly from a distance, would still be troubled if you came too close to their civilisation.

'You can see this in English literature. Coleridge, the great Romantic poet and critic, wrote a great poem against the slave trade when he was an undergraduate at Cambridge, 'Ode Against Slavery'. He won the university gold medal and it launched his poetic career. At the same time he was appalled by the fact that Othello should be hugging Desdemona in public on a stage. He argues that it is nauseating, and doubts that Othello is a veritable Negro. He cannot believe that Shakespeare would have such bad taste to have a black man having a relationship with a white woman.' Of course, what made it worse was that it was Desdemona, the fair maiden, who was more lustful than her husband!

> *If neither foes nor loving friends can hurt you,*
> *If all men count with you, but none too much;*

Coleridge's attitude may seem paradoxical, but in fact it is consistent with Kipling's advice and most English people's instinct to be kind in theory but not over-emotional in practice. Indeed, the slight distaste felt towards physical contact is an aspect of British life which has lived on since Coleridge. Writer Maria Couto felt along with many others that 'social conscience is apparent all the time, but it's depersonalised and the human touch seems to be dead.' In contrast to India, where there is a constant display of emotions and a sense of physical presence, in Britain, touching is taboo. I often feel that the British seem to be terrified of being physical or spiritual but do not mind being 'mental'! We now know that the expression of affection and grief is therapeutic and helps the body to rid itself of toxins and tensions; physical and emotional gestures should not be feared and on some occasions should be rightfully indulged.

In contrast to Britain, where even during rush hour people will withdraw from human contact on buses and trains, in India a journey on public transport means bumping and falling all over each other. The Englishman hopes to retreat to his castle and pull up the drawbridge, but for Asians the thought of such isolation is terrifying. The emphasis that Western culture as a whole places upon 'personal space' comes as a surprise to many Asians. Maria again expresses the sentiments of many when she says, 'I miss friends and the neighbourliness of the extended family. I enjoy company, the concept of privacy rather frightens me.' To child psychotherapist Asha Phillips, a 'room of one's own' at university was a new delight:

'I hadn't even heard the word "privacy". Being able to say "no" to people coming in. I loved it.'

I can still recall my husband Richard's first trip with me to India and the way his eyebrows kept moving up and down as people casually drifted in and out of our bedroom, even our bed! I do not think that for Asian people the word 'privacy' is in the dictionary. There would never be an Indian *Desert Island Discs*. Indeed, an English teacher I once knew set her class an essay about what they would take with them to a desert island; unlike the English children who wanted their TVs and hi-fis, the Asian children were taking their mummies, daddies, sisters, brothers, aunties, uncles, grandparents. . .

However, it is not only physical contact which is missed by many Asians in Britain, and indeed Kipling's words also counsel against excessively friendly gestures. To Devinia Sookia, a barrister and now women's editor for the *Asian Times*, the lack of warmth appeared to be both public and private: 'People are cold and selfish. In the street, bus and tube, people never seemed to smile. Even if you visit your close friends you have to give them a call. Back home you can visit people at any time and, rich or poor, they are always happy to share whatever they have. Here, even within your own community or circle of friends, there is competition.'

The insular and reserved social life of the British also came as a surprise to educationist Hena Mukherjee: 'I didn't think that people lived in as much isolation as I found they did. In Malaysia we were used to dropping in on people when we felt like it, but here people didn't invite you to their homes very easily. That was rather off-putting for me, having to make appointments to see people even if you were just going to have a cup of tea.'

What was even more surprising to people coming from an Asian culture was that these appointments were also kept too! All the same, a great number of Asians have found it hard to adjust from the spontaneous hospitality of their own countries, a quality which they have brought with them to Britain. Amit Roy recalls how his mother 'used to run almost a cafeteria, people would just drop in round the clock. I think that it was a good thing, as children we were aware of people and used to conversation.'

Amit's recollections brought my childhood back to me, as my parents owned a London hotel and so the Indian notion of 'open house' lived on. It seemed that our hotel was on the tourist map for every Indian coming to London. As a young girl I was brought up with an endless stream of visitors and the numerous arrivals and departures which made it feel as if I was living in Paddington Station. To me it seemed quite natural that my family home in Harrow should have an 'open door' policy, although it came as more of a surprise to my husband Richard, who has now accepted the inevitable with only an Englishman's ability to raise his eyebrows and make a wry joke or two. When totally exasperated by the arrival of so many unexpected guests, he quietly sighs and says, 'What can I expect from a hotelier's daughter?' and then teases, 'Maybe one day you'll be known as Lady Dharmsala!' This may sound grand, but the translation, 'Lady Doss House', somehow does not have the same ring to it.

To musicologist Nasreen Rehman, the restrained way of the British appeals as much as the Pakistani style of her family home. She amusingly recalls how she used her childish charm to avenge herself. 'Our house was like a circus with all the people visiting. I rather resented the way that every night there would be guests to dinner, I used to deliberately make trouble, "Oh, this is the person you said something very rude about", even though it wasn't true.'

Yet, despite their lack of emotional displays, the British are still valued as true and close friends, and to Nasreen the British way of forming friendships is the most genuine. 'It's like cooking on a slow heat, things that go slowly absorb more. Making friends with English people is like that, they don't bubble up and make friends with you like the Americans, but then they don't suddenly boil over either. When my marriage broke up, my English friends used to hide a key to their house for me, somewhere I could escape to at any time of the day. When they said it was as much my house as theirs, I knew they meant it, that was true friendship.'

Nasim Ahmed, Pakistan's Ambassador to the United Nations, only appreciated the depth of British friendship after he had lived in other countries. 'Before we lived in Scandinavia we used to consider the English insular and difficult to get to know. I realised that there are people even more insular. The British take their time to make friends, but when they do they are good friends. On the whole, with all their faults, the British are a tolerant and compassionate people.'

Indeed, while most confirmed that the British today live up to Kipling's criteria of self-control within relationships, it also became apparent that they continue to 'count each man', and the generosity of the British character was praised by many. Having worked for national charities myself as a fundraiser, I am continuously amazed by the big-heartedness of the British. Every religion prizes charity as one of the greatest virtues and while Asians and British people are both very generous in their own ways, their ways are certainly different.

Both peoples instinctively know that giving is an essential part of living. There is a parable about the nature of giving which my mother once told me. Every tree has to give in its own way. In the Spring it gives pleasure by showing off its beautiful blossom. In the Summer its abundant leaves offer shade from the sun. In the Autumn it has to give its fruit, either by allowing the fruit to be plucked or by dropping it to the ground when over-ripe. In the Winter when it appears to be dead, it can still give its wood for shelter and for fire. In the same way my mother instilled in me that I had to give whether it was with style or not.

Both the British and the Asians have got style when giving. Accountant Arunbhai Patel articulates the feelings of many Asians when he says, 'English people will always give money to disasters anywhere in the world. I have seen the same TV pictures, and I haven't been moved to send any money at all. Perhaps that is my Indian side telling me that my disaster may be round the corner, so I should conserve my money to ensure I don't need others' charity. But I want my children to have the English attitude.'

Saadia Nasiri agrees: 'The British are always there to help people out in a disaster. They respond when they see suffering on the TV, they obviously do genuinely care. We Asians just sit there. It doesn't affect us. We don't pick up the phone and say, "Here's my ten quid – this is my little for whatever."'

While the British Christian way of giving is typically understated, and follows the advice, 'let not thy left hand know what thy right hand doeth,' the Asian philanthropists have no inhibitions in letting people know what both hands are up to. The difference is like that between a man who lets his coin drop on a carpet so that no one hears the sound, and the other who drops his on a marble floor where the coin spins and jangles.

When English people attach their name to a gift it is usually in memory of someone whom they admire, for an Asian it is usually in memory of a relation. Indeed, I am conscious that in dedicating this book to my grandmother I too have followed this tradition. Indians like to give money to their temples and communities, they are generous and will always give one more for luck. This is the reason why, instead of receiving a cheque for the round figure of £100, there is a lovely surprise of £101. Yet, while Asians will happily act upon the saying 'Charity begins at home', the British are willing to give to complete strangers many miles away who will never be able to give a personal thank you.

Student Sheena Dewan heard comedian Lenny Henry say that it only took 5 pence to save a child dying from diarrhoea in Africa. So she 'ran around my school telling people this and in one hour collected over £20. That's 400 lives in an hour. There were about fifty other people at North London Collegiate School running around doing the same thing, and they did just as well.'

When counsellor Bidge Jugnauth was raising money for the Asian People With Disabilities Alliance, she found 'the English generous, but when I went to the Asian community, people didn't give me anything. These were the people and firms I had shopped with for years, the cash and carry, garage, sari shop. At our temple in South London, the altar is covered with coins. They give money to the gods, but not to people.'

Ameera Alli, well-known charity worker, prefers the discreet charm of the British public-spirited offerings to the hullabaloo that Indians make when giving. 'The English are now cashing in on the Indians' weakness to want to make a scene of giving. If an Indian can stand up at a function and say, "I will give thousands of pounds," they'll do it. But they won't do it quietly. Doesn't matter whether he's from Africa, the Americas or India, once he's *Indian*, he wants to show off.'

Ameera's own devotion to charity came from her childhood memories of life in Guyana when 'every Friday we had to feed 100 beggars from two big bags of rice. They each got a bowl of uncooked rice and a sixpence, I remember enjoying putting the sixpence in their bowl. This idea of charity definitely comes from Islam, my father felt he had to give to the poor.'

> *If you can fill the unforgiving minute*
> *With sixty seconds' worth of distance, run,*

While charity may be a quality which the British and the Asians have in common from their different heritages, so too is the emphasis on hard work. As poet Shruti Pankaj points out, in many ways commercial success is the best known hallmark on the golden thread of Asian global success. 'Alexander the Great went out to conquer the world. Columbus went to discover the world. But Asians went neither to discover nor conquer, they had only one capital, ENTERPRISE. And with their determination and faith, hard work and close family ties, they cast the ornament of success from the gold of opportunity. Britishers have often been obsessed by "race", and in that race one day they may lose.'

Others also saw hard work as a particular attribute of the British. Suman Bhargava, of the Suman Marriage Bureau, sees it as a quality which arises from the discipline endemic in British culture. 'I admire the English discipline – when they work, they work. In India, you can go to work for eight hours and only work for two hours. This means that the English enjoy their weekends more as they worked for them.'

In Britain, Asians have a reputation for being industrious and filling all the sixty seconds of their minutes in pursuit of business. The British admire this but personally prefer the 'well-rounded' balance of work and leisure. Hobbies are a particularly British phenomenon, a constructive waste of time designed not to allow idle hands to do the Devil's work. They range from the sublime, mountaineering in the quest to conquer Everest, to the ridiculous, the annual Convention of Tortoise Keepers! Yet while hobbies may appear to be a British quirk and not a quality, few can deny that the British take their time seriously.

For the British, time is a necessity and punctuality a virtue; unlike the Asians who identify more with the 'mañana' mentality of the Mediterranean, the British feel that life is a series of opportunities which need to be seized and acted upon promptly. Time is the tablet of history.

The passing of time has brought many changes, but it seems that to Asians the British have remained much the same. Now that the days of Kipling's colonial mirroring are over, Asians are bringing their qualities to bear on British society, and with common ideals and the new global emphasis of our time we can both fulfil his promise that

> *Yours is the Earth and everything that's in it,*
> *And – what is more – you'll be a Man, my son!*

With compliments to Rudyard Kipling.

10

Brownie Points

Politics, sex and religion are the three subjects considered most taboo in polite British society. They are also the three which make life worthwhile. In Britain at the moment there seems to be little political motivation amongst the people in general, with only 4 in 100 of the population involved at any level of political life. While democracy is one of the most treasured features that Britain and India share, there is still much to be achieved before the Asian community in Britain can fully identify with and be accepted by the mainstream British political parties. As Farrukh Dhondy, a commissioning editor for Channel Four Television, pointed out, 'The British believed that anybody coming to their shores lived under the protection of British democracy. A famous case proving this occurred in the eighteenth century, when an Englishman tried to claim that a black man who was living in Britain as a domestic servant was still his slave. The judge ruled: "Here in Britain no institution of slavery obtains and once you are on these shores, you are free, nobody's slave." The British respect for their own democracy has always been our protection.'

However, while justice does still triumph in British courts, the political system itself seems to operate according to codes and practices which subtly disadvantage certain groups. These vary from the unrepresentative voting system, which disenfranchises the real voting wishes of the majority, to the unsociable working hours of the House of Commons, which still accommodates the double lives of those male MPs who have dynamic daytime careers in the City or the Law, and moonlight in the House of Commons.

Although almost everyone acknowledges that the legislators of Britain are unrepresentative of the diversity of the nation, there is now a growing awareness within all political parties that women and the ethnic communities are hopelessly under-represented. This has led to a desire to find suitable faces in order to earn themselves 'Brownie Points'. Yet there are still many obstacles at every stage of the journey to Parliament as the stories of old, and those of more recent years, reveal.

It is a little-known fact that nearly 100 years ago in 1892, a Zoroastrian, Dadabhai Naoroji: was elected as the first Asian to the United Kingdom's House of Commons as the Liberal member for the London constituency of Finsbury Central. As those who have followed Dadabhai have to their cost discovered, the path to Westminster is not a smooth one. Sadly, much of the unpleasantness which Naoroji suffered still occurs a century later in Britain. In his day, Lord Salisbury, the Tory Prime Minister, tried to play on racial hatred by calling Naoroji 'a blackman'. Queen Victoria was not amused and Gladstone stated that, comparing Naoroji and Salisbury, the latter was the 'blacker'. Yet once again, a notable supporter was the indomitable Florence Nightingale who wrote Naoroji letters from her bed.

The Conservative Press also did their best to stir up racial prejudice against Naoroji: he was dubbed a 'fire-worshipping Asiatic'. One local paper, the *St Stephen's Review*, asserted, 'Central Finsbury ought to be ashamed of itself at having publicly confessed that there was not in the whole of the division an Englishman, a Scotsman, a Welshman or an Irishman as worthy of their votes as this fire-worshipper from Bombay.' Yet when Naoroji was elected to the House of Commons with three votes to spare, his delighted white constituents dubbed him 'Mr Narrow Majoritee'. Not only did the whole of India rejoice that at last they had a true representative to voice their needs where it mattered, the 'Mother of Parliaments', but William Gladstone, then leader of the Liberal Party, also publicly praised his victory.

General elections though, are decided on the record of the national parties and Naoroji, with his extremely narrow majority, could not survive any swing to the Tories. Such a swing duly arrived in 1895, bringing with it the second Indian Parsi MP, Mancherjee Bhownaggree as the Tory MP for Bethnal Green. He had earlier campaigned for Naoroji's election and was described by the Tories as a 'true British citizen', others quickly nicknamed him 'Mr Bow-and-agree' for his uncritical support of government policies. After two years in Parliament, Bhownaggree was knighted and increased his majority in 1900. Later, like Naoroji, he lost his seat due to a general swing away from his party.

The third Indian, and the third Parsi, to be elected was Shapurji Saklatvala who won Battersea North in 1922 for the Labour Party. Defeated a year later, he returned as a Communist with Labour Party support in 1924. He had left the Labour Party over the issue of Indian Independence, feeling Labour only wanted to be 'good rulers'. Then the only Communist MP, Saklatvala said that his was the only party which always spoke unanimously in the House of Commons!

His youngest daughter Sehri recalls his sense of humour. 'A Tory MP had said that there were a lot of sexual "goings on" in Hyde Park, you couldn't take your wife there for fear of what she might see. Another stood up and asked if it would not help to have more lights in the park? Father asked if the lady was offended by what she saw, would it not be better to put all the lights out?' Saklatvala was more famous for his fiery speeches and it was for one of these, made in Hyde Park during the 1926 General Strike, that he was charged with sedition and imprisoned for two months. Labour opposed him in the 1929 General Election, and once more the electorate voted along party lines with the result that Saklatvala lost his seat in Parliament.

With this background of political activity in all the major British parties, and the example of the significant rôle which women such as Prime Minister Indira Gandhi of India, Mrs Bandaranayake of Sri Lanka and Benazir Bhutto of Pakistan, have played in the history of Asian political life, it is perhaps surprising that no Asian women stood for the British Parliament until 1983. In that year, three women fought the election for three different parties, amongst whom I was proud to be one. We three pioneers all came from different backgrounds, with different political motivations. Nevertheless, we all had one thing in common, we had been selected to fight 'unwinnable' Parliamentary constituencies. Despite this fact we all learnt a great deal from our experiences; as Churchill said, 'No part of the education of a politician is more indispensable than the fighting of elections.'

I was selected as the Liberal candidate for Hertsmere, a constituency in Hertfordshire, just forty days before polling day. A year earlier I had been elected as a local government councillor in my home constituency of Harrow, a suburb of London. Thus proving I could win an election, I was asked by Liberals in the neighbouring constituency of Hertsmere to put my name forward for their Parliamentary seat. At the selection meeting I was competing with three men. I won, in my view, because I did not wear a pin-stripe suit, nor did I give the usual party answers, but more importantly a fair voting system of proportional representation was at work.

Shortly after that election, in which I doubled the Liberal/SDP Alliance vote and finished second, the Sarah Keays scandal broke around Mr Parkinson, the re-elected member, and at one stage it looked as if he would resign his seat and so cause a by-election. Several very prominent members of the Alliance, including the SDP's president, had lost their seats and were looking to get back into Parliament, but I was reconfirmed as the Liberal/SDP Alliance candidate. There was no question of an Asian candidate being regarded as a liability, even in a constituency like Hertsmere with an almost totally white electorate. As it turned out, Mr Parkinson resigned as Chairman of the Tory Party but not as an MP, and so I had to wait four years for another chance to get into Parliament.

Pramila Le Hunte, unlike me, waited until her children had grown up before beginning her political career. She chose to join the Conservative Party because of her belief in enterprise and sees herself as a pre-Thatcher Thatcherite. 'I thought that the England I knew was energetic and go-ahead, yet the talk was of child benefits, pensions not being high enough, the whole "give us more money" thing. I wondered why people didn't stand on their own two feet, they said that was what had made Britain great. I wanted the individual to be able to mould his own destiny. Injustices in Britain, such as bad living conditions or poverty didn't get me so het up. I'd seen the real thing in Calcutta, with bodies in the streets.'

Pramila applied to thirty constituencies and was finally selected to stand for Birmingham Ladywood. It was to be a very hard initiation, as Ladywood was a safe Labour seat. She felt that Clare Short, her Labour opponent, was 'very offish, she knew she would win, she had absolutely hundreds of canvassers. I had no help from the party at all, the Tories didn't have the local membership.'

The publicity given to Pramila was enormous, and interviews of her were seen as far away as New Zealand, where she was on the main TV news programme. Great emphasis was placed on her being bicultural by the Conservatives who thought that being 'able to change from a skirt to a sari' would be a vote winner in an area where 42% of voters came from the 'New Commonwealth'.

Nationally, Labour's vote collapsed and the Conservatives had a landslide victory. Yet in Ladywood, it was the Tory vote that fell badly and Pramila's result was the worst of any Asian candidate in that election. An able candidate, she feels that the Asian population in her area were so against her Conservative politics that they did not see her as their representative even though she was an Asian.

Rita Austin joined the Labour Party in 1963 and, like Pramila, waited until her children had grown up. Asked to stand in the 1983 General Election by her local party in St Albans, she agreed, knowing the experience would be useful.

Rita still vividly remembers one public meeting concerning private education. Both her opponents unfavourably contrasted her opposition to private schools with her attendance at Loreto, a Catholic private school in St Albans. Rita pointed out that they couldn't have it both ways. ' "If I had come to Britain and gone to a state-maintained school, you would accuse me of taking something to which I wasn't entitled. Quite right. I was not a British citizen then, so my father paid for my schooling." That shut them up.'

However, while this attempt at point scoring was dismissed by sharp thinking, the hatred and intimidation, which was the other common factor between we three, was not so quickly stamped out. It is interesting that, while all three of us experienced hostility to differing degrees, in each case it originated from a different source.

In 1983, as soon as my selection became known, my family became the target of extreme xenophobia. Death threats on the telephone were followed by an individual brandishing a knife at the window of my house and break-ins. On one occasion, my car was followed back from a meeting and after much flashing of lights, an attempt was made to force me off the road. My telephone calls were interrupted from time to time by someone cutting in on the line to abuse me personally, to the astonishment of the person I was talking to. My young sons had to be carefully watched at school in case of kidnap. Despite all this, my family insisted that I should not give in, but stay and fight.

While the campaign against my selection was obviously directed by ignorant racists, the hatred which hounded Pramila was more disturbing in that it originated from within the Asian community and was focused on her politics. Pramila feels that 'it was just hatred of Tories. We aren't very popular in areas of Birmingham.' After threats to herself and her children, one of whom was driven at by an Asian in a car, a police guard was provided. Rita was not the target of such a blatant campaign but rather one of racist whispers, with opponents saying that Indian people should 'go back to their own country and practise politics there.'

Only I stood again in the 1987 General Election. Pramila's marriage had broken up and she had left her job as Head of English at a private girls' school. Even finding her through her party proved very difficult as no one remembered her. Eventually, she was discovered to be living and teaching in Harrow, only ten minutes away from my home.

Shortly after the 1983 election, Rita and her family moved to Cardiff, 'leaving behind the complacency and smugness of the south-east of England for the sense of humour of the south-east of Wales.' She soon became a county councillor for the area in which she lived and became Chair of the council's Finance Committee, the most senior position that the Labour Party has there.

However, Rita encountered hostility when her local ward party tried to 'deselect' her. As she explains, 'I'm quite good at being a councillor, and they don't like it! Women and Indians are allowed onto the council only as long as they don't spread themselves too widely or do the job too well. It's a very subtle form of racism, but it is there.'

Recently, Rita let me know that she had finally been deselected by the Labour extremists in her ward. She did however fight the local elections in another area, but unfortunately lost by only 81 votes to a Liberal Democrat. In 1987, Rita had missed the nomination for a potentially winnable Parliamentary seat in Cardiff by just one vote. Ironically, it was possibly her opposition to the implementation of Black Sections in the Labour Party which deprived her party of an outstanding MP.

Local politics seems to be a more rewarding field for many women, as the hard work and personal commitment they put in is often acknowledged and valued at this level, in sharp contrast to national party politics. However, this does not mean to say that Asian women do not face problems at this level too. When I was the Liberal/SDP Alliance representative for the Harrow borough council, I quickly realised that Thrity Shroff would be an asset to any political party with her grass-roots knowledge of the ethnic communities and determined articulation of their needs. Like all successful politicians, she was a hard worker, unwavering in her opposition to what she felt was wrong and willing to stand her ground, even when times got tough.

When I suggested that she would be an ideal Liberal councillor, Thrity's first reaction was to wonder if anyone would vote for her, an unmarried Asian woman. Thrity, unlike Pramila, Rita and myself, would not have an English surname on the ballot papers, with which English people could identify.

I pointed to my success, achieving a 25% 'swing' to win my council seat in an area regarded as safe Tory territory which meant that the English must have voted for me. In the event Thrity rose to the challenge and after three recounts she won a safe Labour seat. Thrity's reception from the Labour group on the council was the cold shoulder. She puts this down not only to losing a seat Labour thought was 'theirs', 'but more importantly they couldn't accept, despite their claptrap about promoting the black cause and supporting the ethnic minorities, that the local community might want an Asian as their representative.'

I was disappointed, but not surprised by her experiences. When elected, I was then both the only woman with young children and the first and only non-white councillor. The response to my 'intrusion' was to try and test me. At my first council meeting, I was asked by one councillor why 'Miss India' was not wearing her sari that night. One Tory hesitantly approached me, fearful that I did not speak English. I wondered to myself how he could have thought I had won my seat without opening my mouth, then I realised that was how the majority of Tories managed to hold on to theirs. At least they had heeded the old saying, 'Keep your mouth shut and people will think you are a fool. Open it and they will know you are.'

Once my ability to talk was proven, the next tactic was to see if I could shout as well. My speeches were accompanied by catcalls and rowdiness, familiar to anyone listening to Prime Minister's question time in the House of Commons. When that failed to unsettle me, my presence would be ignored and the chairman would deliberately look surprised if I wished to make any contribution to the meeting.

When Thrity was elected in 1986, things had not improved and the insidious intimidation continued. They soon found out that she was also determined to speak her mind. 'I think that quite a lot of my colleagues have now begun to understand that I will not let matters pass by lightly, and that when I do feel strongly about issues, I will make sure that they have heard my viewpoint. I'm not going to fit into the pigeonhole of being meek and pussyfooting which they want me to fit into. I'm determined to ensure that what needs to be done, gets done.'

As an Asian woman, there is a constant double bind to be confronted. One does not want to be type-cast as the only speaker on race and gender issues, as this often means that one is only asked to comment on these issues. One consequence of this is that valuable insights which Asian women politicians have on a wider range of issues are simply lost. On the other hand, most of us became involved in politics because we felt that such a voice was lacking and that, if we do not articulate it, who will? Both paths have trapdoors. Thrity found the excuse of not stereotyping her as an Asian woman councillor was used in order to avoid consulting her on issues concerning both women and Asians.

Another Asian woman to enter politics at a local level is Gurbans Kaur Gill, who stood as a Labour candidate for the Aylesbury district council in 1979, feeling it to be the worst blunder of her life, as she had never believed in Labour's moral values and overall attitudes. Initially, she was not interested, putting her family commitments first, 'but the Labour Party said they had already nominated me, and I can't let people down.'

There were two seats in that ward and she came third, ahead of the other Labour candidate who had been the town's Mayor. 'She was in tears and wanted a recount. She couldn't believe that I had got more votes than her. I was very naïve, I said she could have my votes if she liked. I had lost, but I was laughing.' The next day, when people were congratulating Gurbans on her result, she could not understand it – after all, she had lost. Yet when her achievement in beating a former Mayor was pointed out to her, she realised how good a result it had been.

Gurbans never rejoined the Labour Party and when the Social Democratic Party came into existence in 1981, she jumped at the chance to join. 'At least it wasn't Labour and it wasn't Tory – I didn't like either of them.' Once more, Gurbans was told she was standing without first being asked. The SDP wanted her as a 'paper' candidate for the district council elections in May 1983, and told her that the party would put no effort into getting her elected, as they assumed that it would be wasted in an 'unwinnable' seat. Gurbans, like all the Asian women I have encountered, felt that if she were campaigning for a political seat, she would work to ensure that they won, which she duly did.

In October 1983, a county council by-election was called and Gurbans was approached to contest it. Like the other successful Asian women, she was elected by a predominantly white electorate but only won by a tiny majority. Gurbans is now the only SDP Asian councillor in Britain as well as the only Asian on both of her councils.

The stories of these women may offer some reasons as to why there are so few women MPs, let alone Asian women MPs, in Britain today. One of the main reasons is that there is a national trend away from political affiliations and for many people the 'certain sorrow, uncertain joy' of politics is not worth the heartaches.

Sehri Saklatvala remembers how different the situation was when her father, Shapurji, was in politics. 'There was no TV and even the newspapers dealt in facts, not escapism. Political meetings were packed. People don't want to interest themselves in politics now, it's a snore and a bore. They've got escapist entertainment freely available: pop music, TV, videos on tap, they don't even have to read any more. The British people have allowed themselves to be diverted by other things: "Oh I'm not political, I take no interest in politics". You've no right to call yourself a democracy and take no interest in politics.'

The fall in membership of the youth sections of all political parties has been the most dramatic of all. The desire to change society amongst the young is still there, but as copy-writer Anjali Paul says, joining the Young Conservatives, Socialists or Liberal Democrats is no longer seen as the way to achieve it. 'Everybody tells you that in order to change things, you've got to be part of the establishment. Fair enough, but you spend so much time and energy becoming part of the establishment that you lose the reasons why you joined in the first place. You end up being what you sought to replace. Now I'm wondering whether it's worth it, whether there isn't another way of changing things. There must be a way an individual can stand up for themselves and say that this is wrong, and I want to change it, *now*.'

One of the most energetic young women in SDP politics, but who now feels a similar disillusionment is Sharmishta Chakrabarti. Her family was always quite political, so from an early age she was involved in discussions on the subject. For her sixteenth birthday present to herself, Sharmishta got her own SDP membership card. The SDP was always a small party and she found it easy with her enthusiasm to rise quickly within it. 'At one General Election, I was sticking leaflets through people's doors. At the next one, I was responsible for quite large sums of money, producing important pieces of campaigning material.' Her most famous project was the youth recruitment video, which starred SDP leader David Owen doing a 'Max Headroom' impersonation, complete with artificial stutter and moving electronic background.

After the 1987 General Election was over, Sharmishta bowed out of active political life because of 'exhaustion and disillusionment'. She had been a rose bud that had been forced into bloom, not given a chance to develop naturally. Today, she is studying law at the London School of Economics. 'Even though I've become disillusioned with politics in general, it doesn't mean that there aren't injustices that I want to do something about, that have to be dealt with. Things won't change in terms of inequality for Asians or for blacks unless the whole attitude of the nation towards inequality changes. In a country where the vast majority seem to enjoy the existence of an unemployed underclass, you can't expect them not to enjoy the existence of racial underclasses as well. Clearly, inequality is in some people's best interests, and unfortunately the Tories seem to have succeeded in making it seem to be in a lot of people's best interests, that's how they stay in power.'

Sharmishta's youth and her decision to leave party politics may have made her more free to be honest, but the task of persuading most politicians to tell you their true feelings about their fellow politicians and their politics is usually almost impossible. They seem to be afraid of going 'on the record' about anything, fearing perhaps that years into the future they will be challenged with what they once thought. Yet all the women I interviewed for this chapter had no such inhibitions. Although many of us had opposing political beliefs, the golden threads of being a woman and an Asian meant that we had an understanding and could be truthful and respectful of each other.

The anxiety that politicians usually show when asked to give candid comments on each other or on controversial issues undoubtedly stems partly from the fear of how the mediawallas might misuse these comments. As an Asian woman in politics, I knew that my views were bound to be considered topical, but felt that they might also be vulnerable to manipulation. It is difficult to draw the fine line between exposing what is unjust and damaging, and simply conforming to the image of the cry-baby politician.

After 1983, the British media had become obsessed with the issue of black MPs. As the Liberal/SDP Alliance's sole non-white Parliamentary candidate, I was continually being invited onto television to discuss black participation in British life. At times the optimism about ethnic minorities entering Parliament bordered on euphoria. However, the grass roots reality for us campaigners in no way reflected the media hype.

When you stand for election you expect your record to be examined and, where justified, some criticism. But you don't expect smears and lies from parties who claim that they are not in any way racist. My community work in Harrow as a councillor working for the whole community, and not just for Asians, did not protect me from the irrelevant diatribes about the excesses of the Labour-controlled Greater London Council. It was all too evident that the Tories were trying to identify all ethnic minority candidates with the so-called 'Loony Left'. People seemed to believe that any black or Asian was bound to misuse power, as allegedly had been the case in the neighbouring Labour-dominated borough of Brent. Black and Asian candidates were often the subject of orchestrated whisper campaigns from all political directions, and insidious racial leaflets which attacked them were often circulated.

Five years earlier, during my first political campaign to become a councillor, the British Movement, an extreme racialist fringe group, put out 'whites unite' leaflets on the council estate in my ward. The local press respected my request not to make it an issue, as I felt that it would only give publicity to a group not worthy of any.

During the 1983 General Election, I was the target of explicit racism once more, but again chose not to make this public for two reasons. There was the desire not to give publicity to my attackers, but also I knew that some uninformed circles would see it as whinging about something I should have to live with. I can still remember one policeman saying, 'If you can't stand the heat, get out of the kitchen.' I had to ask him who would be left to do the cooking.

After four years, attitudes towards my candidature had changed very little. In the reputedly genteel Harrow, a London suburb where I was now standing as a Parliamentary candidate, I was being spat upon in the high street and called a 'nigger lover'. The general atmosphere of uninhibited racial hatred was epitomised when one of the local papers, with a change of editor since 1983, printed a letter suggesting that I get out of Britain. When the editor was challenged, he said that the people of Harrow felt that they were being swamped by Asians, and that it was his job to reflect local opinion.

When the threats restarted after my selection as a candidate in 1986, I finally 'went public' after much thought. It would place me in the hands of the national media, who could have slanted the story whichever way they liked, but I wanted people in Britain to know what it was like for a mother to have herself and her children subjected to terror, simply because she was Asian and had the audacity to want to stand for Parliament.

I need not have feared. Once the *Mail on Sunday* had written a sympathetic page-long article, several newspapers, radio and TV programmes contacted me to find out more. The story made BBC TV News, and their main 'heavyweight' news programme, *Newsnight*, made a serious examination of the epidemic of racial violence plaguing Britain.

In contrast, Independent Television broadcasted a special chat-show which managed to trivialise the issue. The most memorable outburst came from an MP who claimed that racial attacks only happened because black men wanted to rape white women. As I had feared, the serious issue of racial attacks had been hijacked by those prepared to outrage in order to get publicity for themselves.

There will always be those who promote sensationalism and thereby ridicule real suffering, but in general I felt that my political candidature was being taken seriously. The national Liberal Party responded to my wish to be involved in the mainstream of political life and gave me real political responsibility. I represented the party's leader, David Steel, at a major Anti-Apartheid rally in Trafalgar Square, and was invited to sit next to him at the conventionally 'masculine' party debate on defence. I was also actively involved in policy proposals.

During the party conference season, the TV cameras always try to find an Asian or black face to focus on from time to time. It is normally a hard task as so few are present at any party's week at the seaside. In 1986, the Liberals debated the report of their 'Commission on Ethnic Minority Involvement in British Life' which I had chaired. The report was a best-seller in the party, and attracted positive coverage from the media. It also attracted probably the highest ever attendance of Asian, black and Far Eastern people to the conference, which was not overlooked by the media.

Most of the newspapers and especially women's magazines took a serious interest in my life without patronising me. *The Sunday Times* colour supplement followed my 'Life in a Day', *Options* magazine portrayed my 'Lifestyle', *Sunday Today* highlighted my clothes' style, *Cosmopolitan* magazine chose me as their political judge for their annual awards and *The Times* invited me to write for them. These were just a few of the opportunities given to me by the British media.

However, the daily paper that most prides itself on being sympathetic to the ethnic minorities, the *Guardian*, did not match these examples. A sympathetic reporter of theirs spent most of a day with me and I told him about other Asians in Harrow who had suffered appalling racial attacks. One such man, a Sri Lankan law student, had had his legs smashed with iron bars when he had gone to the aid of a woman screaming for help. Another had had decapitated birds put through his letter box, while yet another had received obscene telephone calls and threats against his children.

The only things we all had in common were that we lived in Harrow, we were Asian and we were presumed to come from middle-class backgrounds. No article ever appeared. When I asked why, I was told that the issue was not news any more, although soon afterwards they printed a piece about working-class taxi drivers in Birmingham who had suffered racial abuse and attacks when picking up clients.

Perhaps the so-called 'left' press is more concerned with maintaining its own stereotypes about Asians and Afro-Caribbeans suffering racism than confronting the issue. I was interested to hear the complaints of the Labour Party's Black Sections, who feel that they get the roughest deal from the *Guardian*, and are no longer surprised at being misrepresented in its pages.

Some of the so-called right-wing press were consistently fairer and willing to condemn publicly the 'Merchants of Hate', to quote the *Daily Express*'s headline. I am willing to accept that they were more interested in my plight and the racism which I suffered because I had been educated at a top English private school, and was married to an Englishman. It was as if the British establishment regarded the matter as an affront to its own dignity and reputation for fair-mindedness, but at least my experiences were listened to and reported fairly.

Despite the even-handed coverage of my personal experiences, in general the national media still seems to be uncomfortable about including the views and experiences of Asians, consoling themselves with the fact that they have a specific slot of their own on radio and television. On the tenth anniversary of Mrs Thatcher coming to power, *Network East*, the BBC programme for Asians, chose author Amrit Wilson to put forward the 'radical' view of the decade. Amrit argued that the Asians who voted Tory were misguided and in turn were misguiding others. 'The ideology of Thatcherism consists of a very powerful nationalism which gives the impression to the English that, whatever class they are, there's something in it for them. It is very striking that it completely excludes black people, Thatcher's nationalism never includes us. We can never belong.'

A very different view is given by Sir 'Jay' Gohel, former chairman of the Anglo-Indian Conservative Association. 'I have always found members of the Tory party meeting we Asians more than half way, making us feel at home. I think the Asian community has a very bright future here. We have everything in common with the Conservative Party way of life. Private enterprise, freedom of religion, family feeling, love of God, we all want to be millionaires and pay as little tax as possible! I feel safer with the Tory way of life.'

As a Liberal Democrat, I strongly believe that Asians should be free to express all political views and should be encouraged to join the party of their choice. It is outrageous when Conservative Asians are howled at and called traitors as they have every right to hold their views. In the same way, the Conservative Party must be challenged for promoting itself as the party of 'God and the family'. Actions speak louder than words. It is the Tories who have consistently refused planning permission for the construction of temples and Mosques on the slightest pretext of traffic congestion without ever trying to find a solution, unless they are fearful of losing a political seat. They have callously divided many Asian families by 'firming up' Labour's immigration policies, seemingly fair in words, but racist in action. If political parties are truly so understanding and obliging to the Asian population, then why have they left many feeling overlooked, undervalued and marginalised?

Nasim Ahmed, who has recently left London to become Pakistan's representative to the United Nations, gives a balanced perspective on why Asians have rarely succeeded in any political party in Britain. 'The fault lies on both sides. There has been a reluctance on the part of the political parties and trade unions to accept Asians, except perhaps as ordinary members. Secondly, many Asians are much too busy making money and therefore are unwilling to invest time in politics.'

Frene Ginwala, an ANC representative, believes that commitment to the mainstream life of the country where people have chosen to settle is of absolute importance. 'People whose only interests are themselves, their family and making money have no loyalty to Britain or anywhere else. When things go wrong, you can either just walk out, or stay and fight. If you have made it clear that you'll "do a runner", the bulk of that society will treat you as a foreigner. You can't blame them when they do that, because you've conveyed, in one form or another, that you are a transient, a tourist, only there when times are good.

'If you're going to settle anywhere, you can't then say you're just going to have a little cultural island. You've got to accept that over time, cultures merge and at the end of it something different will come out of it. If you don't accept that, if you want total cultural isolation, then again you're in this limbo. You can't then complain you're not being accepted and feel excluded.'

Certainly one crucial reason why Asian politicians have not been elected in numbers is to be found within the workings of their own community. There is a popular joke about lobster fishermen not needing to cover the pots which catch Indian lobsters because any lobster trying to escape is pulled back down by the others. Asian communities all over the world do seem to show an incredible ability for in-fighting and pettiness.

This is partly a residual mentality left over from the time of Empire. Moved by the British around their empire to act as the 'second class', below them but above the 'natives', Asians were not allowed to mix with the British and preferred not to mix with the local population. When the British finally left, leaving the more numerous locals in power, the Asians had not built up the acceptance and goodwill necessary to be included in the plans of the new rulers. The importance of participating in the life of the country cannot be overestimated. It is one of the lessons that some Asians throughout the world have been slow to learn.

The most quoted example of this situation is East Africa. Although Asians ran the economy of Uganda until expelled by President Amin in the 1970s, they had little political muscle or affection from the majority of other Ugandans. There is the lesser known but equally sad story of Tamil rubber plantation workers in Malaysia. Living in abject conditions on the estates, the workers started their own

Tamil schools and brought their teachers and textbooks from South India, and so a mini Tamil Nadoo was created in the Malaysian peninsula.

After independence in 1957 nobody told the plantation Tamils that they were entitled to Malaysian citizenship. When rubber prices fell, the government tried to put them on boats back to South India, as they did not have Malaysian citizenship papers. For those left behind, there were other problems. Although the three main racial groups in Malaysia the Malays, the Indians and the Chinese, had their own political representation in parliament, the Malay language became compulsory and, without fluency in it, government jobs could not be secured. The tragedy of the situation was that some of the so-called Tamil leaders insisted that the plantation workers maintained their own Tamil language, culture and schools, in order to secure their own political positions and remain the spokespersons for their community. In effect they held their people back. After the children had been taught only Tamil in primary schools they had to attend secondary school in the Malay language and this placed them at a disadvantage. Put into remedial classes, they never seemed to catch up and so were doomed to repeat the lives of their parents on the plantations.

An example of political disunity, so characteristic of Asian communities, occurs during election time in the island of Mauritius. The caste system and religious differences are whipped up for electoral purposes. Such debilitating divisions affect the Asian community in Britain too, as BBC editor Narendhra Morar points out, 'There's no such thing as one Asian community. There are various groups based on things like caste, language, religion. Until you can get Asians who can cross those divides, you're not going to get any national Asian leaders.'

Although the system in which one person is relied upon to articulate and act for a whole community would delight the British, who have always preferred the 'take me to your leader approach', such a system could easily perpetuate the indifference shown towards the needs of the community as a whole. The Jewish community, one of the many minority groups in Britain, has adapted to this need by allowing the appointment of a Chief Rabbi. The appointment of the Chief Rabbi to the House of Lords has followed the success of Jewish MPs of all parties and has no doubt been an inspirational model within Jewish politics. It would be a welcome move if other heads of communities could also be granted a public voice, but it must not be forgotten that while a representative voice is important it is not always as truly representative as one might hope.

One of the reasons pointed out by many as to why the Asian community has never been a united force in Britain, was their petty rivalries. Journalist Naseem Khan suggested a valid reason for this in-fighting. 'Because we are a minority, we don't have such access to power and the suspicion, jealousy and paranoia does get very extreme at times. We've just got a little, little plot of land in Britain, while the British have a whole world out there, so there's not so much emotion invested in defending what there is.'

One of the best examples of the Asian ability to keep pulling others down in British politics is the parliamentary seat of Southall. A safe Labour seat with a very large proportion of Asian voters, it has attracted many attempts by Asians to try to win the Labour nomination, all unsuccessful. Now that the white male MP may decide not to stand again, the race is on once more in the 1990s.

Investigative journalist Sadhana Ghose reported on Southall politics for several years and believes that 'there is no unity in Southall, and never will be. Already, fifteen or so Asians are preparing to try for the Labour nomination. They should have said, "We want an Asian MP in Southall, let's settle our difficulties", but there are too many egos to deal with. The English are very amused at all this, obviously they take advantage of it. Southall is up for grabs for any candidate who can rise above the sibling jealousy that exists there. But I can't think of any Asian who can do that, so I expect they'll have another white male Labour MP.'

Although there is some relic of the British policy of 'divide and rule' within the tragi-comedy of Asian politics, it is also true that the Indians had the divisions of the caste system long before the Empire. The lack of unity among the different faces of the Asian community not only affects its chance of having an effective political voice, but it also affects British foreign policy.

Margaret Thatcher still refuses to support meaningful sanctions against South Africa's apartheid regime, saying that they are ineffectual. This has not stopped her imposing them against, for example, Argentina, Poland and Libya. Jeya Wilson, whose doctoral thesis was on the power of sanctions, thinks a major cause of this stand is the absence of an American-style 'black lobby' in Britain. 'The Asians and West Indians will never come together. In the States you're talking about a civil rights movement which did unite the blacks, but there's nothing similar in Britain, and so Mrs Thatcher is indifferent to what British blacks and Asians feel about racism in South Africa.'

One of the issues which minority communities in Britain must negotiate is their relationship with each other. While there are significant historical, traditional and cultural differences between, as well as within, the Afro-Caribbean and Asian communities, they are often perceived by the majority of the British public as a single group, defined under the umbrella title 'black'. For some this is an asset in terms of politics, a path to building a 'rainbow coalition', while to others it involves an unacceptable compromise of racial identity.

Frene Ginwala identifies politically with the term 'black' and finds it very strange when other Asians object to the word. I told her that many Asians felt it ignored their heritage, but she explained 'what we have to face up to is that racism is a black/white issue. Perhaps the old terms, which we resent, were more accurate. When the whites were deciding who would be allowed to do something, how did they define us? They said "whites" and "non-whites". We're all non-whites and the sooner we realise that, the sooner those in power will see it in those terms. The term 'black' emerged because we refused to be non-something. We are not a negative factor, we are a positive one. That's why we said we are blacks. Labels are, in very many ways, indications of one's attitude. If you want to distinguish yourself from others, then you are being racist as far as I am concerned. If in a racist society you are part of that group which is being discriminated against, you don't start making fine divisions, because where would we stop?'

Rita Austin can appreciate the solidarity conveyed by the term 'black', but feels that sometimes labels can be restrictive. 'I find it odd to refer to myself as an Asian, although I do so quite regularly these days. I was never comfortable with calling myself a black politician. I only adopt the term "black" in certain contexts in order to make a political point. I'm an Indian, as opposed to a Pakistani or a Bangladeshi, I'm a Bengali if it comes down to it, I was born in Bengal. But the white world, this world, seems to wish to call us all Asians, and we have fallen into that definition.'

However, Sehri Saklatvala sees the drawbacks of both the usage and the nature of the label 'black'. 'I think my father would have been very much against this blanket term, "black". Asia is one continent, Africa is another, Europe a third. Why do you lump everyone from India and Africa together? Being oppressed does not

Sister Jayanti (right) *with Archbishop Trevor Huddleston* (left) *and Dadi Janki* (centre)

Aruna Paul (front row, second from right) *with her family*

Siromi Rodrigo (far left) *with international Guiders*

Kim Hollis, Barrister-at-Law

Roshan Horabin, Prisoners of War Intelligence Department 1942-45

Bapsi Sidhwa, author

Meera Syal, author and actress

Koki Wasani presiding at a Lohana function

Asha Phillips with her daughter

Katy Mirza as a 'VIP Bunny'

Sudha Bhuchar in 'Jawaani'

Safira Afzal, international model

Kristine Landon-Smith (seated) *with Rita Wolf in 'Jawaani'*

*Frene Ginwala with the late President
Samora Machel of Mozambique*

*Jinder Aujla surrounded by the press and Mrs Thatcher during the 1987
General Election*

Councillor Gurbans Kaur Gill with 'SDP 1'

Pramila Le Hunte, teacher at North London Collegiate School

make us black! What should unite us is being ex-colonial people, not the colour of our skin, which is as varied as any human skin is varied. The word "black" is also associated with largely negative imagery – black arts, black magic, black market, black sheep. . .Besides, it's inaccurate to say anyone is black or white, no one is 100% either. These descriptions fit no one. I haven't seen a black person or a white person.'

In 1987, out of the 650 MPs elected, there were four black MPs, all Labour Party members. There was a mixed reaction to their success from the Asian community, even though one was an Asian from Aden. Even when Asians do attain some political success, this is not always seen as the solution to the problem of lack of real representation by many members of the community, nor are they given whole-hearted support.

Farrukh Dhondy feels that these black MPs have not yet done anything constructive for anyone. 'Blacks got into Parliament because of guilt in the parties, "we ought to have one of them." I don't know of any black politician in Britain who has made one jot of difference to public policy. Instead we got all sorts of cry-baby politicians, the people with a mission to complain.' Others who spoke with me felt that the MPs were jumping on the 'black wagon'.

Sharmishta Chakrabarti believed that they have 'used their race in a very cynical way, they haven't addressed the problems most of the people of our background have faced. Having five or six or even sixty "Professional black" MPs doesn't do anything unless they try to do something for the population at large. If they are only there for their own careers, it achieves nothing.'

Sharmishta herself played down her Asian background in politics, 'not in a sense of being ashamed, but I didn't want to use it as a stepping stone or a platform. I didn't want to be a professional Asian.' When others told her that being 'the token Asian' was the route to success, she looked at their motives. 'It was obvious that it was only their vested interests talking. If there was a certain number of places, they would suggest going only for the woman's position or use my "ethnic-ness", so they could stick another man in the position I wanted.'

Those Labour Party members not on the left felt that the four MPs elected had ruled themselves out of being taken seriously in politics by 'ranting and raving for publicity'. In contrast, some Labour supporters felt disappointed when the four suddenly stopped or toned down their statements on issues of race. It is interesting that the one black MP who has now rejected the 'Black Caucus' in Parliament is the one to be promoted politically by his party and is now one of their 'front bench' spokesmen.

The contempt shown for the 'Professional Black Politicians' was also shown for the Race Relations industry which many felt was simply a way to easy money. As Sadhana Ghose commented, 'It's just a massive ball game, the most successful industry in Britain, everyone's in for their own £25,000 local authority job. For all their money, they go to meetings, they take the radical line, they scream, they shout, they take part in demonstrations, but actual services? Never.'

The Asians I spoke with did not identify with the national Commission for Racial Equality or their local branches of Community Relations Councils because they felt that all the money and concessions went to Afro-Caribbeans as the terminology used was 'black' and, therefore, as Asians they were only an afterthought. Many remarked candidly about how the now defunct Greater London Council tried to impose equal opportunities but failed to take the majority of the British people with them, as it assumed an opposite but equally extreme position to the Tory party on race relations. The 'opportunities' offered only seemed to be available to those who supported their political beliefs. The Asian community may have taken the few grants offered but they were not taken in by them. The project failed because, instead of trying to identify and remove the hurdles which Asians and Afro-Caribbeans confront in British society and thereby enable them to run in an equal race, it looked as if certain politicians sought to give them a head start which was extravagantly emphasised by the media to the real disadvantage of the ethnic minorities struggling to make successes of their lives in Britain.

While popular opinion might wish to suggest that Asian women have never sought to enter the race of public or political life, this is another injustice. Asian women, like all women, do not see life as a spectator sport and have been forerunners in many aspects. While there has not yet been an Asian woman MP, this has more to do with the lack of support, encouragement and commitment shown by local members of political parties, than by the British electorate themselves, who have shown consistently that they will vote for Asian women in local elections if only because they get the job done.

Indeed, it must not be overlooked that many Asian women are very involved and hold positions of authority in the organisations within their own communities and many charities. Koki Wasani made history by becoming the first woman President of the British Lohanas (a section of the Gujarati community), Tara Kothari motivated other Asian women to come together across community lines as a founder of the UK Asian Women's Conference, and accomplished women such as Aruna Paul have worked tirelessly for the benefit of those less well off in Britain and abroad. It is time that Asian women, who have given their talents so generously for the whole community, should be acknowledged. It will only be a short time before Britain will have an Asian woman MP because, as everyone knows, a woman's place is in the House. . .of Commons!

11

Mirror, Mirror on the Wall. . .

The mirror has long been an important symbol of self for all women. So often judged by others according to their physical beauty, the mirror appears to enable women to see themselves as others see them. Yet, as Brutus reminds us in *Julius Caesar*, 'The eye sees not itself, but by a reflection by some other', and all too often women are admonished to match their reality to the images which others hold up for them. For many women this becomes an obsession with the mirror image and they either distort their bodies to gain its approval, or perceive themselves as an object of the male gaze and not a subject of their own. In both ways the reflection in the mirror encourages them to live only as shadows of their true selves.

Women are particularly vulnerable to the power of the mirror because, as Virginia Woolf points out, they have for so long acted as 'looking glasses possessing the magic and delicious power of reflecting the figure of man at twice his natural size.' Certainly, we should remember that the looking glass does hold the power to deceive; making us look thinner in fashion stores and fatter in fairground halls, it can flatter and entertain us by playing on the knowledge that few of us want to behold the reality of our appearances.

When Snow White's wicked stepmother questioned her looking glass she sought only to know the quality of her own beauty and was infuriated when it gave an honest reply. 'Mirror, mirror on the wall, who is the fairest of them all?' was answered even then by Snow *White*! Today when Asian women look into the mirror, they too judge their own beauty according to fairness, although to them this term has added significance. To be 'fair' is to be truly beautiful, as the shade of colour is a primary factor on the scale of Asian beauty and a pale skin is highly prized. Yet the beauty of Asian women, whether physical, spiritual or intellectual is consistently betrayed by the 'unfair' and ugly nature of stereotypes. These unjust and untrue images are perpetuated most powerfully by the mediawallas who project a static reflection of woman which simply repeats the evil queen's question without a care for its significance. The stories of Asian women's lives which receive attention are rarely 'fair' in any sense of the word. Instead of portraying the diversity of women's lives within the communities, the mediawallas have only chosen to give a one-sided story of victimisation.

For some Asian women the rituals of violence and oppression do characterise their lives and it is important not to forget this. One story which reveals the serious reality of violence was told by Rani Sharma, a radio presenter, who was asked to interpret in a hospital for a woman who spoke very little English. Her husband had brought an Englishwoman back to the house and asked his wife to cook for them. When she refused, he beat her up using a stiletto-heeled shoe and broke her wrist. The husband then only took her to the hospital on condition that she did not say who had done this.

However, the very real problem of violence against women in every sector of society means that it is an injustice to portray Asian women as exclusively brutalised. The abuse of women from all races and classes needs to be treated seriously and sensitively, and not hijacked by the mediawallas as a sensational 'story seller' or a riveting read. A little learning is a dangerous thing, and too often British society is only exposed to the truth of one face of Asian womanhood. The result is that others see Asian women's lives as an exclusive story of pain and repression. Not only does this make true suffering of all women seem mundane in comparison, but it also confirms divisions between different communities, congratulating one for its relative perfection and condemning the other for its total brutality.

A mock autobiography of Anjali Paul, a copy-writer, confirms the notion that all Asian women's lives are uniformly dismal. 'Sometimes, I get really fed up with what people want to hear, so I tell them I was forced into an arranged marriage, I've got seven children and I've been beaten up and never allowed out of my home. And they actually believe me, because they want to believe me, it's what their idea of us is.' Asian women's lives need to be treated sensitively and it is necessary to give those women in oppressive situations the confidence and support to break free, but this has to be done by judging the contexts of their own lives, and not merely imposing the standards of another, however well meaning they are.

Tara Kothari, founder of the UK Asian Women's Conference and voluntary social worker, encountered one such case from Cambridge. 'A woman had just got married and came over from India. The husband was beating her, the mother-in-law wasn't very nice to her either. She was very unhappy, and wrote to her uncle in India, telling him what was happening to her. Back in India, the uncle sent a telegram to the British police asking them to please do something. The police went to her home, and the woman was sitting with her husband and mother-in-law, how could she be expected to say what was happening? She had to stress how kind her husband and mother-in-law were. The police sent a cable back, saying she's happily settled here.

'The woman then wrote to her uncle asking why had he asked the police to intervene as she was now in even deeper trouble with her in-laws. So the uncle wrote me a letter and I got another Asian woman to visit. She started off by talking to the mother-in-law, befriended her first and then the daughter-in-law, so that everyone trusted her before she started to find out what was going on.' This story illustrates the necessity of cultural understanding and the importance of having members of all communities within the caring services. A knowledge of Asian family traditions enabled the female Asian adviser to identify the situation and respond to it in a way that the English police could never have done, even with the best of intentions.

There is a story in one of Zehra Nigar's poems which does relate the suffering of many women through all societies in a more honest way than the tales of the media-melodrama. Set in no particular place or time, it tells of a knife thrower whose talent is seen by every circus in the land. In each act his wife stands against a wooden board while he throws the knives at her, each time they come a little closer and she is in constant fear that one day the knife will be misthrown and wound her. Each performance she suffers the mental anguish of fear and expectation of ghastly pain. For many women the trick of the knife thrower is a familiar one. They are tortured in psychological ways which never leave a visible scar for others to see. While some women are the victims of physical violence, many others endure the invisible daggers of fear and oppression which seek to pin them against the walls of silence and isolation throughout their lives.

For women there are stereotypes which aim to confine from the moment of birth to that of death, images which deny individuality and dismiss genuine interest. They are a shorthand for the complexity of the truth, exploited by the mediawallas for maximum effect and maximum sales, they conceal and seal the threat of knowledge which might subvert the fragile belief in an exclusive version of the truth. As Ira Mathur, a BBC World Service presenter and journalist for the *Trinidad Guardian*, commented, 'When it's obvious there's another way of thinking, of living, they feel threatened. So it's easier for them to put us in a box and throw it away.' However, it is not only people who are subject to stereotyping and even though the experience of Empire should have given the British public some small knowledge about India, it remains a land of largely imaginary and extreme images.

As author Maria Couto has found, 'the stereotypes of India as maharajas, famine and poverty, snakes and elephants persist. It takes a lot of passionate commitment and heart-break to change these notions, certainly a beginning has been made. But one does get disillusioned because the shocking, glamorous, or the extreme is always given precedence over the true and the mundane. Not that the media in India are more innocent.' Sales executive Varsha Mulchandani remembers an English person asking her if she had ever been skiing: 'I said yes, the first time in India. "What? But we thought India was always hot." I had to remind them that it's cold, it snows, Kashmir's close to the Himalayas.'

Councillor Gurbans Gill was even more shocked by the innocent question that confronted her while working in the Civil Service. 'One morning, I said I was gasping for a cup of tea. An old lady, a filing assistant, came over and asked, "Excuse me, dear, do you mind if I ask you something? Do you have tea in India?" I didn't know whether to laugh or cry. I told her that if Indians didn't export it, she wouldn't have any to drink.' So often our images are dictated by the vision of the world that our experience, education and media presents us, and this is a vision angled for national contentment and pride, rather than for enlightenment.

Stereotyping is almost compulsive. Often flowing inconspicuously through our language, it keeps our thoughts and lives simple and ordered. Many of us are constantly judging people according to these expectations without realising it, as Anjali Paul points out, 'Just silly things, like "Oh, he's English, he must be like this," or "She's a Libra, she must be like that." Then you realise how stupid that all is.' However, these images have a malignancy which is also overlooked. For Asian women living in Britain there are many stereotypes to be faced and, although some are humorous and free from malice, they all betray the thought patterns of society which inform them. Naseem Khan, the arts critic, discovered this when she took her driving test in Greenford, near Southall. After she had completed the test, the examiner told her she had passed, then said, 'May I congratulate you, Ms Khan, on your excellent English.' He simply could not reconcile this articulate and accomplished woman with his stereotypical view.

Jeya Wilson, former President of the Oxford Union, confronted a similar attitude when travelling by train to a conference with Oxford friends. 'There was a problem with our tickets. So the guard explained it to my friends, then he came up to me and said, "This. . .ticket. . .no. . .good." While the others collapsed into laughter, I just had to look at him with a straight face, as he explained the problem in "Me Tarzan, you Jane" English. He was trying to be nice, but there was the whole assumption, "Asian face, therefore can't speak English."'

This sympathetically patronising manner also confronted business-woman Syeda Jalali. 'I went to see someone about a grant for machinery and the most annoying man I have ever met took me into the director's room, introduced me and said, "Do be nice to her because she is obviously feeling a little frightened." That was being patronising, as a man he would have done it to any woman, but more so because I was an Asian. I find that attitude infuriating because I can hold my own against any man.' While Syeda was right to feel irritated by the inflexibility of her colleagues, stereotyping is a process which we can all fall prey to, as Sadhana Ghose, journalist and agony aunt, is keen to point out when she tells the story of her first day working for the *Bucks Examiner*. She was sent to cover a court case and, as she was sitting down at the press desk, a policeman stopped her and asked what she was doing. When she replied she was from the press, there was a slightly surprised pause. His stereotypes did not include women in saris being from the press, 'but I'm not going to damn him for that. If it had been a policeman from a small town in India, he would have had exactly the same mentality.'

Indeed, some found that as Asian women they were more rigidly typecast by people of their own cultures than among the British. The internalisation of prejudice means that Asian people may value a white skin above a darker one, and a European above another Asian. When Siromi Rodrigo, Deputy Director of the Girl Guides, is working in her office alongside her European secretary, she finds that most people who come for an appointment will approach her secretary, assuming she holds the authoritative position, but Asian people will nearly always do so. Similarly, Hena Mukherjee finds that her position in the Commonwealth Secretariat often commands less respect from Indian people, who would be very impressed by any European who held an equal post.

The combination of being an Asian and a woman is a special cocktail for initial disrespect as Jyoti Munsiff discovered in her job with the international oil company, Shell. When the company were negotiating the nationalisation of Indian oil companies Jyoti was responsible for South Asia, but detected a reluctance in London to send her to India for the negotiations. 'So, in my usual way, I confronted it, and asked my head of department why another lawyer was going to be sent. He said that our Indian side didn't want me for three reasons: one, I was a woman; two, I was an Indian; and three, I was not sufficiently senior. I said I felt that the first was irrelevant, in India their Prime Minister was a woman and the Deputy Minister of Justice was a woman. I found the second, that I was Indian, interesting. In the end, I was sent and it was my presence and knowledge of the Indian situation that smoothed the negotiations.'

Although all of these stories of stereotyping are mainly harmless examples of unfamiliarity, in the hands of the mediawallas and politicians the refusal to break free of distorting and damaging images often reveals more than the desire to retain popularity. By continuing to pander to people's ignorance and to reflect rather than challenge their unfounded fears, the opinion formers of this country are wasting a valuable opportunity to use their power of influence in a progressive and not an oppressive way. Although America, Canada and Australia were all once less liberal than Britain in their attitudes to ethnic minorities, these countries have now started to tackle their racist policies and changes have been seen. The Americans had their legacy of slavery and racial bitterness in the South; the Australians for many years operated an openly racist 'white Australia' policy, and the Canadian record was mediocre. However, over the last twenty-five years all three have made progress, while progress in Britain has been minimal. It would now be unusual in the USA to find a major company without a black manager, but in Britain it would still be unusual to find a major company *with* a black manager. It would be equally unusual to find an American or Canadian politician making the sort of racist speeches often heard in Britain from right-wing politicians, who talk as if black people are somehow a liability. Even those who are concerned about race issues place virtually exclusive emphasis on safeguarding of legal rights, and none on the value and benefits of being a multi-ethnic society.

It is important to realise that negative labelling can be a calculated and vicious process which promotes prejudice and deliberately obscures the perception of unity and equality. For Asian women the stereotypes possess double power to inhibit their blossoming as active members of British society, as Councillor Thrity Shroff expresses, 'Asian women have to go through a twofold "unwelcoming" process, once from within their own community and the other from outside, from the host community.' However, while many of the women did perceive their womanhood as a major barrier to success in British society, the racial stereotypes and prejudice were also powerful obstacles in their way. Banker Farida Mazhar is never completely sure of the origins of prejudice against her. 'There are more younger Asian women in the City now, but there is still a lot of prejudice against women generally in British institutions. A lot of it is hidden, so it's very difficult to identify and fight it. I think my customers have been fine, my internal battles have been much tougher than my external ones. I have not been aware of overt prejudice because of my Asian origins. But when I first joined Lloyds Bank there were people who refused to meet me. I'm not sure whether that was because I was a woman or an Asian. There are a lot of times when I don't know that, perhaps it helps not to know.'

Yet for barrister Kim Hollis, the nature of the bigotry which faced her became quite plain when she applied for chambers. 'It was the first and only time I came across discrimination. Cheltenham Ladies College opens up doors for you. I was rung up by the head of a set of chambers, exceedingly unusual and was almost offered a tenancy over the telephone. I was waiting to see him when his clerk came out, looked at me and rushed back into his room. The head of chambers came out, looked at me and his face just dropped. When I was called into his room, before I even had a chance to sit down, he said, "I'm terribly sorry to call you here under false pretences, but unfortunately we had a meeting last night and we decided not to take on any new tenants." He was so patronising, just because I was not what he was expecting. It was because I was Indian.'

This kind of obsequiousness was a mask which others also found to be veiling racial prejudice, as publisher Arif Ali points out: 'Racism is subtle in Britain, Americans will take you and hang you from the nearest tree in the South. They will say that they don't want you there. The British will say, "Of course we welcome you", then put you in the worst chair, the worst council house, the worst job.'

In this sense prejudice creates stereotypes as it offers only limited choices and therefore aims to give people limited ways in which to express themselves. Like stereotyping, prejudice also relies on a conscious blindness towards the nature of individuals, as international film director Waris Hussein discovered to his amazement. 'I went to a smart party in Campden Hill Square, one of those dos where it's port after dinner and discussions about the world situation. A very pompous man sat next to me, ex-army all over. When I told him my current project was on the abdication of Edward VIII, he announced to the whole room, "Well, I suppose we're going to need foreigners to tell us our history next." I said, "I don't know what you mean by foreigner, I've been here since I was 8 years old." I am, and was then, a British subject, born into British India. I've never changed my passport, when the time came to choose, my mother chose to be British, not Indian or Pakistani. To be insulted then, at the age of thirty-something, is pretty galling, you suddenly come to a skidding halt. My entire life has been governed by the British system of education, I did the full British thing. Clifton College couldn't have been more horrendous, a post-war private school, suffering all down the line, spartan colonialism. To go through all that and suddenly be told you're a foreigner is infuriating.'

This attitude manifested itself much earlier to others and for biochemist Kiran Kumar it was a realisation which came to her husband only three months after they were married. 'My husband came home and told me he had resigned from his job as a commodity broker. He had trained a junior man, a white blue-eyed blond, who had then been promoted above him. When my husband complained, he was told, "You know how it is, Kumar, we can't have an Indian running the company, think of our image." He could have the money, but not the position.' Kiran's husband now runs his own business and is internationally respected. Like other Asians he refused to accept the glass ceilings which stereotyping tries to impose and proved that his potential could not be confined by prejudice.

Actress Sneh Gupta was forced to negotiate a more directly offensive form of racism when she arrived in St Ives to celebrate the Queen's Silver Jubilee, as 'Miss Anglia TV'. 'Like everywhere else, I checked into the hotel and met the organisers. I could hear my manageress and an organiser talking in very hushed voices. When they finished, I asked what's going on. They explained that the night before we arrived, the National Front had gone around putting leaflets through people's doors, "Why the hell should we in Britain have an Indian, a black, for a beauty queen?" The next day I had to stand up on stage and give speeches, looking down on a crowd of people, not knowing which ones really supported me and which ones were part of the National Front.'

I too experienced a leaflet campaign by the British Movement when I stood for local council elections in 1982. Obviously it hurts, but one has to be determined and keep dignity, otherwise those ignorant and vicious people get away with it. As Sneh says, 'It's really just seeing it through even though you want to scream and get out of it. It's just holding up one's face for the whole community. It's being professional.'

Any form of racism is distressing to witness, but actress and producer Sudha Bhuchar found it even more disturbing to encounter such beliefs amongst her own community. 'We went to a Greater London Council conference, "Black Artists, White Institutions", on what the Arts Council was doing for black artists. The people there were overwhelmingly black and Asian, but there were a few whites there. They were the ones who were actually doing something, who'd bothered to come, yet they were the ones who were made to cry, were humiliated. I felt ashamed to be black, I couldn't believe the mentality. The slogan of the time was "Racism is the White Man's Problem", the idea was that there's no such thing as black racism. I don't believe that. Anti-racism teaching starts from the standpoint of "you whites were there, and now we're here". To bash people on the head, "we're the downtrodden, now you're going to pay for it", is totally the wrong way forward.'

It is difficult to break free of a single view of history and to realise that society no longer has to be divided between masters and servants. Some of the anti-racist gurus have fallen into the same trap as some of the feminist sages. The faults of history are to be understood and not repeated, it benefits nobody to relieve one's own anguish by trying to dominate and degrade those groups who in the past have tyrannised and demeaned your race or sex.

The uncomfortable feelings which often occur when one ceases to identify solely with one's own group are seldom rewarded by society. Journalist Iqbal Wahhab learnt this lesson while at school in Battersea. 'It was a run-down area then and there would often be a couple of National Front thugs standing at the school gates who gave every Paki a kick as they came in. Coming from a liberal, free-thinking family, I quite naturally took exception to this and befriended these people. They were quite shocked to find that I didn't have a "Paki accent", didn't smell, didn't run a corner shop and didn't swot all the time. I kept an arms-distance friendliness with them, and I could never claim to have totally talked them out of their racism. My Asian school friends, though, were not impressed and thought that I would do anything to save a beating. Consequently I never became that close to them either.'

Iqbal now has respect from both communities in his career as a journalist, writing and editing for the Asian press and Fleet Street. He co-founded the Black Journalists Association in order to encourage the mainstream media to employ more black journalists, and the journalists themselves to feel a sense of solidarity and confidence in their own ability. Fleet Street knows that they benefit from the writing skills and access to the truth that these young journalists can bring. It serves no one's interests to use black journalists to continue producing blurred images of the minority communities, when they could use their intimate knowledge and experience to give a clearly focused picture.

Stereotyping is certainly a two-way evil when it breeds complacency in both its creators and its critics. Farrukh Dhondy points out that 'it has become an Orwellian word, the kind people use without knowing what it means. The word stops you looking at the actual criticism you have to make. As soon as you have used it you have stopped saying what exactly is wrong with what you are doing.' No doubt Farrukh will be disappointed that I have not banned it from my vocabulary, but I feel that it is important to examine how the process affects the lives of many, and how it has been used to incite certain beliefs and emotions by those with the power to control it.

It was interesting that many felt that racist feelings had somehow been made an issue, that difference has become associated with threat and hatred rather than with interest. Actor Marc Zuber encountered racism once, as a youngster in 1950s' London. 'We were knocking a football around in Cricklewood with a few of my closest mates and our ball hit an English woman's car. She poked her head out of the window, "Get away from my car, you black bastard." I can distinctly remember looking around to see who she meant. I was an Englishman as far as I was concerned, I grew up with them, I spoke "fick cockney". I thought "'oo the 'ell's she torkin to?" The mother of one of my closest friends, Colin, came across the road, "You old cow, darlin', who you talkin' to?" She slapped the woman in the face three or four times for calling me this, sent the woman howling away, acting as if it was her son who had been insulted. Meanwhile I'm still trying to figure out who she was talking to!'

Antiquarian Yasmin Hosain has also experienced the change in attitudes, but unhappy with the indifference shown to the problem by those in power in British society, she has tried to identify its roots. 'In the fifties and sixties there may have been the British reserve, but this was applicable to everybody, not just us. That also is changing. Asians were not seen then as a threat. Now there is the economic factor, areas where they have done very well. The resentment which emerged was fanned by prejudice and the media in such a way that it has created hostility between the two races.'

The rôle of the mediawallas should in no way be underestimated, they have the power to create and direct, as well as to reflect people's attitudes. Yet the media does not have to feel altruistic in order to print occasional stories about the minority communities. They should print those stories and more in the knowledge that there is an Asian market that will buy their papers and magazines if they can read positive stories about themselves with which they can identify. It is the realisation that there is a viable Asian market which has prompted many to start their own ethnic papers to give a more informed view.

It was disturbing that many concurred with journalist Sadhana Ghose that the primary problem with the media was that it was their 'own people already in there feeling threatened and looking out for their own jobs' which stopped more Asians joining, rather than any white racism.

This sense of being betrayed from within also arises with Asian writers who are prepared to recycle fallacies about their own community in order to achieve personal fame and professional security. Author Rukhsana Ahmad believes that such displays of contempt for one's own Asian culture is a short cut to social acceptability in Britain. 'It ranges from highlighting some individual injustice, "I've been forced into an arranged marriage", to a complete renunciation of Asian values.' However, short cuts usually have a drawback and the golden thread leading to individual fame and glory, when followed at the cost of honesty, can wind itself into a noose.

Ultimately, it is up to all in the media to use the power they have to affect the opinions of the masses in a responsible and progressive way. For those who do not have the knowledge this entails making an effort to find it and to communicate an honest and not sensational version; for those who do it means achieving status by telling the truth and consolidating one's position by allowing others in as well.

Munni Kabir, *auteur* of the television series *Movie Mahal* and Channel Four's Indian film consultant, tells how the images projected by the media need not reinforce passivity and difference, but can play a significant rôle in combating prejudice. By being shown Indian films on the television, British people are given an insight into Indian culture and the golden thread of human emotions which unites them. 'Although the first few films produced comments like, "You shouldn't encourage these people, they've already invaded our shores, why are you showing these films?", "Do Indians really sing like that? It's giving me a headache!", there were also people saying, "I've never liked foreign films before, reading subtitles, but I sat through *Mother India*, and cried at the end." Letters from Asian school children told how other children came up and said that they saw the films too, and it became something more familiar and popular. Your neighbour, whether he liked it or not, found that you were human too, you both had emotions and cried during *Mother India*.'

Even this simple gesture was able to give the Asian people a renewed confidence in their own culture and also reveal to the British public the vast wealth of Indian films and the great range of Asian peoples which some seek to hide. Indeed, it is interesting that Munni chooses *Mother India* for her example, as this film is of particular importance in the analysis of Asian women's lives. Far from endorsing the trembling woman under the strong hold of the mighty patriarch, *Mother India* discloses the supreme significance with which female honour is valued in Asian culture. The defilement of the woman induces the mother to break the sacred maternal bond and kill her son in order to preserve another woman's honour.

The testimonies of the women within this book also confirm that, whatever one's race, being a woman presents a precarious road down which one must weave in order to avoid being parcelled into the pigeonholes which pursue us through all walks of life. Perhaps the art of playing hopscotch, which many young girls perfect, offers a valuable education for mature life. Indeed, as women

we are still forbidden to tread on the lines between the 'boxes'
of definition, which would enable us to defy categorisation and
perceive its absurdity. Yet, as we grow up, we also come to realise
that the safe boxes have trapdoors which swallow us whole, giving
us either the universal female label of anonymity, or a token title
by which we can be defined. It is a symptom of modern-day Britain
that we must all wear our labels on the outside, in order to allow
people to recognise our designer and our rôle instantly. People are
baffled when I do not identify myself according to a single rôle
and feel frustrated that they cannot pin a designer label of MP,
author or 'housewife superstar' onto me. Even those women who
try to defy the confines of categorisation can also fall through the
trapdoors which, although they close the lid on certain areas of
one's personality, do offer a security and status of sorts. As an
Asian woman in politics you can be sure of being called for any
debates on race or women and will always be asked to sit on the
platform to advertise the representation of neglected parties. Often
it is difficult to break out of the expected mould and the safety that
some labelling can offer, in order to challenge the basis on which all
people are identified. Indeed, some of the women in this book have
experienced the negative effects which stereotyping can have upon
an individual's progress and yet still fall into the trap of judging
others by their popular images only.

I was surprised to find that, although most women judged womanhood to be the most prominent determinant of their experiences,
some continued to see women from other cultures through a dis-
torted mirror. In a sense this is inevitable, as the most powerful and
damning images projected onto each culture centre on women and
their sexuality. In most languages there are far more terms of abuse
and insult to level at women than at men. Women are always seen
as the retainers of cultural purity and the repositories of moral value
and consequently any transgression on their part is more threatening
to the tradition than the faults of their male counterparts who are
somehow "naturally" less pure. In the mirror of any religion or
culture it is the woman who must offer the flawless reflection: for
a Christian woman this means the personification of faith, hope
and charity; for an Islamic woman it is submission and modesty;
for a Zoroastrian woman it is good thoughts, words and deeds.
By always seeking to divide and conquer, male power has given
women from different backgrounds antagonistic stereotypes of each
other, thereby preventing them from perceiving the uniformity of

sexual prejudice which informs every tradition of female archetypes and therefore stereotypes. There is in each one the worship of the virgin and the contempt for the whore; a common thread which should link women together in an understanding of male anxiety about female purity and sexual power, and not encourage them to perceive each other as extreme versions of these myths.

While some British women are guilty of perceiving Asian women only as silent and submissive, some Asian women are guilty of seeing British women as sexually promiscuous and untrustworthy. Indeed, such categorising is rarely a one-way equation, and the laziness which prevents us from judging each person as unique occurs within all societies. Although the predominant image of Eastern women is one of subjugation and powerlessness, in fact the Eastern mythology which offers cultural archetypes is more potent in terms of female figures than its Western counterpart. Western archetypes of womanhood, like the popular images which follow them, polarise into exceptional evil and exceptional piety. The images alternate between figures of corruption, like Eve and Pandora, who must bear the guilt and function as the scapegoat which the West is constantly in search of, and figures of redemption like the Virgin Mary. Whether they are damners or saviours, inspirers – the Muses, or dementors – the Furies, women in Western culture are always defined in relation to men.

While Western women are presented with the choice between two extremes, which only hold the power to affect male destiny but not to create their own, Eastern women can behold the omnipotent figure of the goddess Kali, who is so powerful in her own right that she is able to create and destroy. Unrestricted by the Western compulsion for a struggle between two opposing forces, the Eastern archetype is all-embracing, recognising life and death, spirituality and earthiness, weakness and strength to be two faces of the same ever-changing body and therefore not demanding adherence to one and abhorrence of the other.

The archetypes from religious and cultural tales may be fascinatingly different but the rôles offered to women within family and marital life are often more similar than expected. Each culture offers the exclusive rôles of daughter, sister, wife and mother but women throughout the world have defied these in order to create their own Russian Babushka dolls which appear to the unknowing eye as a single wooden doll. It is only to the understanding eye that the doll can reveal her secrets.

12

Queens of the Castle

Asian women are the 'Queens of the Castle', holding power over the home and its affairs. The West has undervalued the significance of family life and therefore women's domestic and maternal rôle, judging the lack of worth or status as a convenient way to keep women subservient. Within the value system of the Asian community, the rôle played by women within family life is of great significance and moreover does not preclude the possibility of a career. Indeed, far from congratulating themselves for being 'superwomen' when they hold family and career responsibilities simultaneously, Asian women see the balanced involvement in private and public life as more natural.

The myths perpetrated about Asian women as domestic house servants are misleading on two counts; firstly because they do not account for the diversity of rôles dictated by economic and geographic factors, and secondly because in truth some women are treated this way within most societies. By deflecting the problem on to the Asian communities the mediawallas allow the rest of British society to appear flawless. In fact, the same basic attitudes towards daughters and mothers are shown by all patriarchal traditions and cultures and differ only by degree.

When Saadia Nasiri went back to Pakistan she took with her the British view of Asian womanhood, powerful even then at the tender age of 9. 'The impression I had was probably exactly what the media had portrayed. When I arrived, I couldn't believe the standard of living that they had. The women have it made there. They have no hassles in their lives. The majority of them have servants and so much time to themselves that it is a matter of just sitting there and sorting out their clothes, jewellery and make-up. The women in Britain have so many responsibilities.'

However, Daksha Kenney saw a quite different, but equally iconoclastic, side of Asian womanhood in India. 'Women are equal in India. Every time I go I see women working alongside the men in the fields and villages, digging, carrying wood, they're such hard workers. So we have the physical strength, mental strength, we have *shakti*, power, and without us there would be no world.'

As these two views illustrate, there is a natural diversity of rôles within Asian women's lives which does not detract from the universal importance placed upon family commitment. Certainly, for many women it is the support of the extended family which enables them to lead such varied lives and consequently they feel happy to fulfil their own rôles within it. As the Social Democratic Party Councillor Gurbans Gill pointed out, the Eastern sequence of family dependence is more coherent and natural than the Western system. 'On the Social Services Committee they talk about looking after old people. One day I said, "What's the idea? You are looking after my parents, I'm looking after your parents. Why don't you just look after your own parents? 'Adopt-a-Granny' doesn't make any sense to me, where are these grannies' grandchildren?" The other councillors are mostly Tories and they all agreed with me.'

As Sister Jayanti discovered, the natural network of the extended family also offers a global sense of belonging and support, 'My grandfather was one of seven brothers living together with their wives and families in their home in Hyderabad. So my father was one of forty cousins who grew up together and their relationships are more like those of brothers and sisters than the Western idea of cousins. My relationship with my second cousins is very close too and it means I have cousins in practically every country around the world. When I lectured in Puerto Rico, a small country in Central America, a woman came up afterwards and introduced herself as my mother's cousin.'

While the web of relations functions as a comforting and useful safety net during personal crisis, it can also become a butterfly net which stifles the expression and flight of the individual. Devinia Sookia found through her work in the media, as the women's editor of the *Asian Times*, that Asian women do tend to use this web as a means of keeping many problems private. 'Asian women are more modest and shy, yet they tend to have an inner force. The majority of Asian women will rarely seek divorce, no matter what their problems are, they will try to find a solution. They will suffer for years in silence rather than bring out their personal problems into the open.'

Actress and writer Attia Hosain was one of several women who felt that their individuality was being suffocated by the proximity of family, only to realise its true value once she had left it behind. 'When I was very young and rebelling against everything, I thought the extended family was something that was holding us back. I was young, very inexperienced. There was a feeling that you were being strangled, not allowed to do this or that, there were always people sitting in judgement. It started as a child, distant relations would feel they had the right to tell my widowed mother how to clothe me, they didn't like me wearing dresses and socks. Who were they to me? They weren't part of my immediate family.

'But when I came to Britain, removed from that extended family, then I realised one is absolutely left alone, as in a desert, there is no sense of security. There are friends, benevolent, kind people who help, but they can never be the same as those who are tied by blood to one, brought up to believe they have to help when there's trouble. They're a nuisance when there's no trouble, perhaps! When I first came to Britain, I used to cry for most of my waking day, that sense of emotional security was gone. No government service, no professional can replace the human security that is taken away when you take away the family background.'

The real sense of belonging and identity which the family provides within Eastern societies in general can often be misunderstood by those on the outside. The reluctance which many Asian women feel about leaving their husbands and families is partly due to the different expectations that they have about relationships, and the higher threshold at which the value of family life is outweighed by personal discontentment, in comparison to Western women. Also, any wave which is made by family break ups creates a much wider ripple throughout their Asian community and consequently there is more family pressure placed upon all members to retain a unified appearance. It is this system of family repercussion which also creates the added emphasis upon female modesty and chastity within Asian families.

In all societies women are more protected and sheltered than men, simply because they are the ones to bear the visible proof and lifelong consequences of pre-marital sex. As designer Lally Dutt and her fashion journalist brother, Robin, identify, this is more significant within Asian culture. 'If an Indian girl happened to be pregnant she would be bringing shame on every single person in her family from the year dot. If this happened to an English girl in the same circumstances, she would just be bringing shame to herself and her immediate family. It's the pride in the name of the family that's so important, that's why Indian families probably stick together. It's a source of power, a source of strength.' Robin also points out that maybe it is the British and not the Indian tradition which is more unusual in this respect. 'It's not only Indians though, look at the Italians and the Greeks, to them it's the same.'

It is also crucial to realise that the protection of women, which can become oppressive, is also a sign of their value, but as Lally commented, 'It's a sort of paradox because women are also the jewels of the family. But the whole idea of a jewel is to see it and let it shine, not to put it in a box and hide it. The Eastern world is criticised for keeping its women isolated, but they would say that they're preserving their jewels, what is precious to them.' Jewels are living creatures and, like women, cannot reveal their true beauty when they are kept from human contact. The treasuring of women should be a balanced belief which advocates protection alongside personal freedom.

In most cultures which operate patriarchal lineage, including Britain, a son and heir is considered to be the basic ingredient in the recipe for family success. For Hindu families a son is also important in order to fulfil the exclusively male task of lighting the funeral pyre and to ensure the mother's future status in the family as a mother-in-law. Dr Navin Ramgoolam made his first two journeys to India from Mauritius in order to carry his parents' ashes to the Ganges, and therefore fulfil the ultimate spiritual quest on their behalf.

Contrary to Western society, where it is generally the daughter who cares for the family in old age, according to Asian customs it is the son who retains the strongest links, as the inheritor. The birth of a daughter also signals a future cost to certain Asian families in the provision of a dowry. Consequently, to most Western and Eastern families alike the birth of a son is a cause for celebration as it offers long term security for the family name.

Indeed, there are many other similarities between the treatment of young women in the two cultures. The West criticises the way in which Muslim families prefer to segregate their daughters in Islamic single-sex schools and yet choose not to take similar educational risks with their sons, but in Britain many families continue to scrape together the money needed for their sons' private education but seldom make equal sacrifices for their daughters.

Many Asian women feel that Western society trivialises its 'better half' and is more prescriptive in its expectations than the East, but the misapprehensions occur both ways. The inheritance rights of certain Eastern societies reshape the myth of Asian female subservience and dependence. The Islamic holy book, The Koran, initiated a tradition of female economic independence as Yasmin Hosain points out, 'The Koran lays down as law that a woman inherits the property of her father, husband, brothers and that each man and each woman must lawfully own what they have earned.' Ironically, until the long overdue change in the tax laws, in Britain a wife's income was still treated as her husband's earnings!

Jeya Wilson explained that Sri Lankan Tamils also reject any material trading in women's lives. 'The dowry law of the Tamils in the Jaffna area of Sri Lanka says that the money given was the women's, theirs to do with as they liked, it didn't go to the husband. Similarly on death, my mother's property came to me, not to my father, therefore a woman was able to be independent.'

Publisher Mishti Chatterji told how in Burma, where she was born, the birth of a girl child is celebrated. 'Burmese women are highly prized, because they do most of the work, while the men sit around drinking and gossiping.' The basic equality and respect which all of these cultural codes advocate, outshines the reality of esteem given to women.

It is customary that within most Asian family structures a girl only fulfils the rôle of daughter within her own family, as once married she becomes part of her husband's family. Nevertheless, it is interesting to explore the variety of influences and directions which she encounters during this formative period of her life. One particularly intriguing discovery was that many of the women saw their *mothers* as the static influence upon their life, cultural preservers seeking to set their destinies in the aspic of historical tradition, and their fathers as the pioneers in their educational success. This situation could be traced to the fact that in nearly every culture it is the mother's responsibility to find a husband for her daughter and to encourage her to continue the line of tradition and create a family of her own.

Nevertheless, this was the situation which both Sita Narasimhan and Farida Mazhar encountered when they expressed the wish to study abroad. Sita found that it was the male members of her family who understood her ambitions. 'For a long time I didn't need to feel feminist quite simply because when I wanted to come to England to study, it was the women in the family who were against it. The men who supported me.' Farida also found, somewhat curiously, that the feminist in her family was her father. 'When I first asked my father if I could go to a UK university, my mother objected, wondering why I wanted to go to a university as all I was going to do afterwards was get married and settle down. My father was very liberal, even more so than my brothers, I think he was the first enlightened man I came across, he understood and encouraged me.'

Traditionally figured as the preserver of family values and the ruler of private life, perhaps it was bemusement and a lack of experience of public and professional spheres which kept these women from encouraging their daughters beyond the world of fulfilment in marriage. In contrast, access to the opportunities beyond the family and the close paternal bonds established meant that to many their fathers are figures of both affection and inspiration. Businesswoman Syeda Jalali recalls the experience of being reunited with her father who had left Pakistan ahead of the rest of the family to establish a new life in Britain. 'I had longed for my father. It was lovely getting to know him, he wanted to make up for all the love that I hadn't had from him for those years. He used to buy me a present every day. At first they were very nice presents and gradually as the novelty wore off they became less grand. To this day he still brings me a present when he comes to see me, even if it is just a pound of apples!'

Newscaster Lisa Aziz remembers how being the first child meant that she was given the conventional male education and attention, despite being a girl. 'My father probably wanted a son first. Before I ever played with dolls, I knew how to fix a plug. I don't know how to cook and I have no wish to learn. I was never pressured to do typically female things.'

To barrister Kim Hollis, her father was a figure of love and security, the parent committed to his children's welfare and happiness. 'Although divorced, my father didn't remarry until I was grown up, for very sensible and lovely reasons which I didn't appreciate at that time. He used to say to myself and my brother, "Your mother has remarried and has another family. If I remarry and I have another family, where are you two left?" We were the most important things in his life, which gave us security.'

However, these stories of progressive and pioneering fathers cannot be told by all Asian daughters, as the experience of Safira Afzal, actress and model, reveals. 'My father was expecting us back early to watch the Wimbledon finals on TV together. When my sister and I got back late from shopping in the West End, he got very angry and just threw us out of the house. Finally we were able to get back in, take our handbags and some clothes, and then found somewhere else to live. I was 18, my sister, 16. It was very difficult and now that I think about it, I think we probably did the right thing. Many Asian women lack confidence and if they can only say, "Look, I'm not happy here, I don't want to be here, where I've got to do the housework. I want to be dating boys, go out to the club. I don't particularly want to be promiscuous, but I want to have the opportunity."' Today Safira and her sister have healed the family rift and visit their family every weekend.

While Safira's father provides an example of the strict paternal attitude, there remains a fairly strong tradition of discipline, guardianship and respect which operates according to age and gender in most Asian families. Janaki Menon objected to the gender ruling which meant that her brother had more freedom than her, a common complaint among girls in all families. 'My father wanted me to apply for London University, so I could live at home, like all Asian fathers. My first boyfriend, at 18, couldn't understand why I had to be in at 10.30, then it got earlier and earlier, down to 8.30. I'm not meant to go into pubs, "ladies don't do that". My mother can't either, or wear trousers or much make-up. She's adapted to that, but me. . .Certainly at home, there's no such thing as the feminist movement. My father once said, "In every army there has to be a General, in every household there has to be a head." Slightly humorous, but I think he believes that he'll take any important decisions. I had to get very bolshie before my brother was asked to do some housework as well. My brother had a completely different life, simply because he was a boy. He was allowed out, whereas I had to even say what film I was going to see. I was forbidden to see *The French Lieutenant's Woman*, so I bought the book and saw *Jaws* instead, violence instead of sex.'

For some Asian families settled in Britain, the Western ethic of more individual freedom and trust has led them to modify the traditional codes in relation to their daughters. Radio presenter Saadia Nasiri comes from one such family. 'My parents have never been strict. They have never said, "You are not going to do this." They left it up to me. It is a matter of trust. At college there were girls who came to school each day, covered from top to toe, yet when they arrived a sudden metamorphosis took place. They'd change into a pencil skirt and high heels, put on make-up. Those same girls went to university and have gone berserk there, going out with every Tom,

Dick or Harry, hitting the bottle, everything you could possibly do. I've been given that freedom, if I had wanted to I could have got away with a lot without anyone knowing about it, but I have never honestly wanted to do so.'

Indeed some Asian families feel that the scales of progress and care are inverted by the mediawallas, and that it is Western families which undervalue and discourage their children. Najma Akhtar's mother expresses this view: 'The English give the child very good attention for a little while, but then it stops, and they don't ask questions. If an English child says he wants to stop education at 16, they just let them, so they can earn some money. We'd make them study.' Najma herself also agrees and feels that family responsibility generates genuine loyalty when it is accompanied by progressive attitudes: 'I think the majority of kids want to leave home around a certain age, even I probably had moments of "Oh God, mother's nagging, daddy's nagging, I wish I could get out of here." But because of our society, the culture, I can't just run away. I have to think of the family name, what people are going to say. I don't want to go because my parents have given me the freedom, they've accepted me and changed with the times. They've seen so many broken marriages, Asians taking drugs, leaving home, because parents have been too strict and unable to understand their kids. Now, I'm free to go out when I like, they've really become extremely flexible about a lot of things. We can talk about sex, marriage, politics, anything.'

A humorous example of parents always considering their offspring to still be children is told by publisher Arif Ali. 'When I go to visit my parents in Canada it is not unusual for my mother to take all my money from me and keep it until I leave. I am 53!' Although this does seem comic, the power and influence which the mother has over the family is perfectly serious. The cross-section of women who speak here illustrates a natural range of ambitions and desires. Some certainly feel more fulfilled by the maternal rôle than others, but they all perceive it as an important rôle which should not be undervalued by society or women themselves, and as choice which requires commitment, but does not exclude the possibility of a career too. Contrary to popular opinion, most Asian women grow up knowing that they will be educated and will contribute to the work-force, and even when they marry, they continue to have interests outside of the home. The strongest belief to emerge from the women was that a balance between personal and family fulfilment was both possible and necessary.

Biochemist Kiran Kumar explains how this twin rôle operates: 'Asian women are not totally career-minded, we look after our family's interests first. Our next generation is getting all the love and attention, but it doesn't end there, the woman still participates in her husband's work, his business. The dual life Asian women lead is important to us. It's about time we taught non-Asian women about it; how to act as a sort of shock-absorber while also remaining your own woman. There's got to be equality and harmony.'

Kiran's theory, that it is the Western attitude to women which needs liberating, is also voiced by publisher Mishti Chatterji who, like myself, was shocked at the poor child-care facilities which are available to British women. 'Western feminism has affected me in the sense that I feel very strongly that the ability of a woman in this country to work, to further her career, is very difficult given you have so little support, no nurseries or day care. America was a revelation to me, schools were providing support to working mothers, not just supervising them after school hours, but actually carrying on with relevant education. It was similar during the holidays there.'

For Mishti, like many other Asian women, it was the support offered by the Eastern family system which enabled her to continue work. 'I couldn't have survived without an extended family, having my mother here to look after our son Arjun. My husband and I always came home late and this made him a "night bird", he slept during the day and stayed awake until midnight. His life-style adapted to suit ours, he learnt to crawl late at night! But I still felt I was missing out on his growing up, so when my mother went to India for a few months, I thought right, it is time to take a break and really enjoy Arjun. I stayed with him from just before his third birthday until past his fifth.'

Dr Natasha Bijlani also expects to rely on her mother, Pushpa, when she marries in order to balance her career and family commitments. 'I'm not going to give up my career, after all the exams, long nights on call. I'm going to have to rely on my mum, on having quality time, not quantity time with my child. I was lucky as a child, I had both.'

Community Relations officer Rita Austin's mother was also instrumental in enabling her to perceive the importance of valuing family relationships as well as personal success. Although for Rita it was her mother's example of extreme professional devotion which made this balance evident. 'My mother was somewhat of an academic and won an All-India scholarship to study at Columbia University in the US. She went there, leaving us, absolutely remarkable for that society. I was only 7 at the time, so she wasn't a woman I got on with at all well, she didn't come back until I was 15 and I had spent my childhood in boarding schools. My mother was expected to return from America with her Ph.D. and lead the teacher-training in India, but by that time my father had divorced her, and my brother and I had left India for Britain. She did not do anything else with her life, she didn't have a job, didn't have a home, and she was no longer my father's wife. A really sad, feminist, example. I've always kept it in mind, moderating my speed, not going too far, too fast for the interests of other people, my husband, my children.'

Mani Sidhwa, market researcher, sees family devotion as the most important aspect of an Asian woman's life: 'My first duty is towards my family. My son's future is more important than serving the community. Selfish it may sound, but I think most women think this way. Today's child is the parent of tomorrow.'

Mohini Samtani, charity executive and business woman, offers a similar view of the significance of the maternal rôle within today's materialistic society: 'People have become very selfish, and it's affecting the children. If you want to give your children anything, give them your time. You don't have to spend hours explaining your values, they'll see you live it, a living example. A nanny can't give the same depth.'

While Asha Phillips, child psychotherapist, advocates the need for each woman to make the choice best suited to her own life, she too feels that the mother has a unique rôle to play. 'If you are unhappy at home with young children, then go out. But if you are happy, then don't miss it for the world. They're only that age for a short time and there's nobody better to deal with them. It's very hard work, much harder than going out "nine to five". My work is quite similar to having children, you have to be patient, listen, understand. You also have to be available for the babyish emotions.' Asha, like many others, is keen to point out the benefits which the family network can provide: 'Having an extended family around defuses some of the emotions, it's not always the mother's fault, and there will be someone the child can turn to when everyone else is "horrible".'

Author Bapsi Sidhwa echoes this feeling, stating that in the East women have more support and also show a more caring approach to their children. 'The house is given over to women, the extended family. You feel sometimes that men are barely tolerated, it's the women's domain. Children in the East aren't the sole burden or responsibility of the parents, everyone is there bolstering the parents, it's one of the advantages of a society where people are so dependent on each other. Children are loved to bits and pieces.'

Without exception the quality of family life within Asian culture was highly prized and treasured by these women. However, when the mirror was turned around in order to view the British, the generalisations which emerged about British family values seemed to lack the understanding which my own experience has given me. The criticism that the English do not truly care about their children was often voiced. Certainly from the Asian perspective it could look that way, but in fact the difference is only one of emphasis. My own family offers an excellent example. When my sons were babies I insisted that they slept with us so that if they ever cried I was immediately at hand to feed them and change their nappies. Richard felt that they should sleep in a separate room and be encouraged to learn a measure of self-control and independence. Later there were similar differences over feeding. I would spoon-feed them whereas Richard felt that they should learn to feed themselves, no matter how messy it was. Both Richard and I agreed that they needed physical warmth and we used to carry them in the Red Indian style on our backs. As they became toddlers, Richard encouraged them to explore their environment, whereas I preferred to have them sitting on my lap, reading or playing. Now as they grow older, I look forward to the day when they will bring their wives to live with us and the house will be full with our grandchildren. Richard, in true English style, looks forward to the day when his sons will leave us in peace together and we will have the luxury of being pampered guests in their homes.

Maybe the lesson to be learnt is that it is a balance of both independence and security which is needed. The Asian cycle of family dependence would be enhanced by the introduction of more self-reliance and the English insistence upon self-sufficiency would be improved by an acknowledgement of natural interdependence. One of the women who are trying to balance the two demands is student Sheena Dewan. She is grateful that her parents have never pressurised her into going into the family business, even though she is interested in publishing. 'I want to achieve something on my own, I don't want to take what my father's built up. I think this is a combination of the Western and Asian approaches, the Asians as a race are very geared to performing and support, while the Western culture is geared towards doing your own thing and making your own living.'

Having established the general beliefs on their rôle and status within the family from the Asian women themselves, I decided to ask accountant Arunbhai Patel for a male version. It was equally positive and praiseworthy, 'My wife Mina has contributed a lot more to my success than would be apparent on the face of it. She is the mother of my children, and she looks after them very well. If it comes to a choice between looking after them or me, they get her time. I like that because I spend too much time working and it is important that at least one parent gives 100% to the children. I'm building up the company for my children, but the person who is building up my children is my wife. The real wealth in life, she believes, is children, not money. She's very strong willed, I like to believe I will get my way, but it doesn't always happen! But it's always done in a spirit of friendship and love. She gives me the strength to concentrate on work, without worrying about the home.'

The personal histories of the majority of these women banish the image of the Asian woman as dominated and confined to an insular and oppressive family life that makes no attempt to understand or accommodate her needs. Whilst the life stories of some illustrate that such situations do still exist and this is a problem which needs to be tackled. The high value placed on the education of all children and the support offered by the extended family show the Asian community to be more progressive than the British in some respects, a virtue often overlooked. Even in the area of Asian marriages, a major panic button for British society, the stories of these women displace the uniform image of the Asian community as somehow intrinsically regressive and repressive in its treatment of women.

13

From Here to Eternity

Marriage is the single most important decision in most people's lives; it is a bond intended until death and a vow which will determine the rest of one's life. In Hinduism the marriage ceremony is a literal binding of the golden thread around the couple's hands to unite them in happiness for eternity. In other ceremonies where the thread is not visible, the same emotional bond ties the lives of husband and wife. In all religions and cultures, marriage is perceived as a sacred state, for it is the relationships between men and women which secure the destiny of humanity as well as the future of individuals. Yet while there is little conflict between cultures over the significance of marriage itself, there has always been controversy over the various philosophies and rituals which bring about its fulfilment. The fundamental beliefs of Western and Eastern societies have been misapprehended by each other to create mutually mythic versions of the marriage saga. Indeed, the negative image of Western marriage as based solely on physical attraction and the positive one of its disregard for social or class considerations are as false and misleading as the Western view of arranged marriage.

Amongst many Asian women the sentiment of legal secretary Rose Barreto still rings true: 'In our communities, marriage is the pivot around which the whole communal universe revolves', but there is now a definite flux of opinion as to the meaning and significance of 'marriage'. To the lawyer Naseem Khan, the Asian tradition of marriage is surely preferable to the 'mistress mania' of Western men. 'The West complains about Muslim men having many wives, but in their culture they have affairs, mistresses. When I was at the Bar, all the male barristers I knew were having affairs, it was the accepted thing to do, but no one talked about it. They're just being hypocritical. I'd rather be a second wife than a mistress.' Certainly, for many Asian women of the older generation the more recent rejection of female marital destiny and arranged marriages is difficult to accept.

Community worker Koki Wasani sees the new trend towards female independence as the major reason for the high percentage of failed marriages. 'The main problem in this country is the young generation. There are lots of cases of divorces, even within the Asian community. It is very difficult to find the right person and even then women won't just put up with everything now. In the olden days the girls were married young, their ideas were still developing, they would adjust to the new life. Now they are becoming graduates and by the time they have finished their studies, they've got their own set ideas.'

For the young women growing up in a society which fosters career ambitions, independence of mind and contact between the sexes, the idea of being married to someone whom they do not know well is naturally bewildering. Meera Mehta articulates the anxiety and confusion which is felt by many young Asian women in Britain, caught between Eastern and Western ways. 'I remember watching a programme about five years ago, with an Indian girl being locked in a room, and told, "This is your husband." I was thinking, do my parents plan this for me too? Among my generation no one quite knows what is expected of them. I just confronted my mother with it, "Do you expect me to have an arranged marriage?" She said no, and I wondered why I hadn't asked her earlier, instead of worrying about it for months.'

In her work as an agony aunt, Sadhana Ghose found that this uncertainty and confusion about arranged marriages was common among those living in British society. 'I had letters from girls who didn't see why they should have to marry someone they've never seen, imported from an Indian village. I told them arranged marriages work very well in India, because there we don't really get the opportunity to meet men. As you start growing up, you're even segregated from your brothers and male cousins. You don't build up the reflexes you do in the West, where you meet men from a very young age.

'Arranged marriages are like computer dating, you take all your good points and bad points and compare them with someone else's. In India you'd compare horoscopes to see if the marriage would be compatible or not. Then the parents decide, "OK, you come from the same background, you've the same status, you speak the same language." If you marry someone completely out of your status, then you have to adjust to that person's food habits, social structure, family, when you should be building a relationship. It's not just the night you spend with them, you're with them during the day, your whole life. That needs a pragmatic analysis of two people and arranged marriages existed to do that. In Western society, you go to school together, you're being exposed to another culture, suddenly you're told you're marrying some man from some village. Even I wouldn't marry someone like that, there would be nothing in common. But the parents in Britain have the concept of arranged marriage as part of their culture, as part of the importance of the family. They have to explain that to their children, not just impose it.'

There is a growing acceptance among Asian mothers that their daughters may not wish to follow in their own footsteps, but there is also a sense of nostalgia and disappointment that valued rituals are being left behind. Geeta Dave expressed these feelings to me: 'If I could, I'd arrange my children's marriages, the right caste if I can, the same marriage ceremony as in India. That's my dream, but they'll probably marry someone they meet. I hope it's a Hindu though.' Ameera Alli also felt a similar mixture of regret and happiness at her daughter's marriage: 'I would have liked to arrange a Muslim marriage for my daughter, she's married to an Englishman, they've two children. But it was not to be, we have come to this country. She fell in love at 17, and whatever makes her happy, I agreed to. She has a wonderful marriage.'

However, it is important to remember that young Asian men are also put under family pressure to select a suitable partner and it is usually the man's responsibility to make the woman conform to his family's ideals. For Kim Hollis, a barrister, this pressure destroyed a relationship. 'I went out for two years with an Indian solicitor from Malawi. In the end we broke up because he was always trying to suppress me and turn me into something that was acceptable to his family.'

It is ironic that these requirements are often contradictory, specifying both family devotion and independent thinking, as radio presenter Saadia Nasiri pointed out, 'When young Asian men decide to get themselves a wife, they adopt the things that their parents want in a wife. The young men want a wife who is going to be nice and quiet, not too career-minded, perhaps who is just going to work until the children arrive, who is not really going to say much. But now parents are saying their son should want a girl who is a graduate. A degree is now a status symbol.'

While the Western emphasis placed upon individual choice may seem to suggest that only marriages chosen by the couples themselves can bring happiness, the Eastern belief in family wisdom creates a confidence and trust in arranged marriages. Accountant Arunbhai Patel remembers his own experience: 'My wife and I both came from Uganda originally, but when Amin threw us out, we came to Britain, my wife's family went to New York. Everyone in my family knew Mina, except me. I had never seen her in real life, until the day before our engagement, a week before the wedding. My sister-in-law arranged it, and I trusted her judgement.'

Suman Bhargava, who has now devoted her time to arranging marriages for others, also had an arranged marriage herself. Her sister met her husband, Ramesh, and then photos were exchanged. Ramesh's family met Suman but the couple only met each other after Ramesh had travelled back to India, just three days before their wedding. In the couple's professional experience, young Asian people living in Britain still value the priorities of social and genetic compatibility which the arranged system offers. 'Young Asians come to us. Physical attraction doesn't last long, a successful marriage is more to do with family background. We went to India to find a wife for our son, someone of the right family background, who would know what was expected of her. We could easily have married him in this country, but there's a lot of Western influences here.'

The careful matching of backgrounds and associated customs and values is a key quality of arranged marriages which remains relevant even as relations between the sexes change. Author Bapsi Sidhwa recalled her emotions about marriage: 'I married at 19. By that time your hormones are built up, you look at a photograph and you fall in love, you don't have to know him to do that.' Although things have changed somewhat, Bapsi still believes in the fundamental advantages of the system. 'Usually arranged marriages match the couple rather well, a good looking man with a good looking woman, around the same age, wealth, family. Perhaps arranged marriages stand a better chance of lasting, the parents have at least checked him out. His family have not just given him a set of genes, but a whole background of how to look at life, values.'

Perhaps the most contentious factor of Asian marriage is the custom of giving a dowry, goods given by the bride's family in order to secure the woman's future happiness, which can include property, cars, jewellery. To some people this custom is no different from

Western girls collecting for their 'bottom drawer', but I personally feel that dowries are pernicious and that there is no comparison. The Asian community has the power to wipe out this custom by simply refusing to accept and offer dowries. For Asians in Britain the custom retains prominence and is subject to additional pressure as the substantial wealth being created by the Asian community has ironically pushed up the demands. The practice of giving a dowry works against all members of the Asian community, and could potentially discredit all Asians if the British media is given the opportunity to report a 'dowry death'. The custom places financial burdens on those families who must give, anxiety onto the women who even after marriage fear that their in-laws will still pressurise their parents into giving more by making their lives miserable, and a low esteem onto the men who put a price on their own heads.

Suman Bhargava is a founder member of the Anti-Dowry Society and sees the acceptance of the dowry system as an example of the power of socialisation. 'Most women are taught from birth that their families come first, they come second. So they feel that anything to avoid shame on the family is all right. What society says doesn't come into it.' Rose Barreto also perceives it as complying with social pressures: 'If you have an arranged marriage system then dowry is bound to be there in some form or another. If the boy's family demand XYZ, then the family are going to give XYZ for the simple reason that if a girl is not married by a certain age, she is looked upon as a lost cause. She is "on the shelf", a terrible shame and disgrace on the family. The social and peer group pressures for Asian girls to be married at an early age are tremendous.'

The contempt that actor Marc Zuber shows for this romantic bargaining is representative of the feelings of many others. 'In India the whole family is on the look-out to promote the girl. India is more money-oriented than Britain. Marry your daughter into some rich family, but even then the father has to give a dowry, so parents are literally selling off their daughters into an easy life.'

Even when the dowry issue is not at stake, arranged marriages can prove unsettling for the women involved. Writer Rukhsana Ahmad agreed to an arranged marriage as a way to gain independence from her family and does not wish her own daughter to continue the tradition. 'I lost a stone in weight in the period between getting engaged and the marriage. I accepted the system because I needed to get out of being a single person in my parents' home. I was a lecturer at Karachi University and earning my own money but I

wasn't allowed to live independently, I was treated very much like
a 12 year old. I wasn't happy, but I accepted it. I don't believe in
arranged marriages, though the problem is not the arranging, but
that they are marriages. I think that marriage as an institution is
detrimental to the cause of women.'

Rukhsana feels that women need to develop and grow within an
arranged marriage, which I believe applies to any relationship, and to
both sides. There is a key difference in the expectations of marriage
in different cultures. In the East, marriages are often seen as links
between two families, with the woman's needs being subservient
to the group interest; in the West, the individual's desires are
paramount. Both these extremes can lead to unhappiness.

Lecturer Maria Couto married within her own Goan community,
but it was not a conventional marriage according to Eastern or
Western expectations. 'The BA degree was fine, the MA worried
my mother, although it was through my quest for education that
I met my husband. I was on the way back from Delhi, trying for
a scholarship to go to Paris. I went to a party in Bombay, and
met him. We found ourselves at the same place only because of
our traditional religious and cultural connections. We decided to
marry, it wasn't arranged, it wasn't a great love match either, we
just got on.' Maria's approach to marriage may seem very realistic
in comparison to the passionate stories of romance which many
young girls relish, but as Maria points out these are often no
more than fiction anyway: 'In England marriages from royalty
downwards are structured within complexities of religion, class,
family, compatibilities and affinities.'

For the young women who have grown up with both Eastern and Western models of society, the issue of marriage can
be problematical, as their wishes do not conform entirely to the
expectations of either. Banker Farida Mazhar has encountered these
difficulties: 'Once I was successful, it became very difficult to
meet and relate to Muslim men of my background, they were
much more conservative and felt terribly threatened by a career
woman. That's been one of the problems I've had to face because
of my background, I'm not typically anything. Even Pakistani men
who've been educated here haven't internalised any of the more
liberal Western culture, still preferring shy and retiring women,
not someone who feels she's their equal. I've become a different
breed of person, too Western for men of my background, but unable
to consider, because of it, the idea of marrying a non-Muslim.'

Jeya Wilson, a former president of the Oxford Union, also feels that her independent and ambitious nature made her unsuitable for an arranged marriage. 'As far as arranged marriages went, I was far too Westernised for any mother to inflict on her son, I just wasn't the sort of bride they would have been looking for. My father was an unusual Asian man in that he didn't mind whom I married, so long as I could stand on my own two feet and wasn't dependent on my husband.' Consequently, Jeya married a New Zealander and did not feel that she was 'marrying out' when she married Peter.

While several of the women felt that it was perfectly natural to marry someone from a different community, race or religion, this is often not a view shared by their parents. Princess Usha Devi Rathore came to England and fell in love with a rock musician, the first man she had ever been involved with, because of her sheltered upbringing in India. 'He was my mother, my brother, my sister, everything, because my whole family was far away from me in India. He was my family and my friend because he loved me.'

After her art and television course in London, Usha returned to India alone and when her future husband announced that he was to join Usha on her birthday, 'I was absolutely horrified. You can imagine my family's shock, a rock musician! Not the Lord Mountbatten type of Englishman they were used to. My poor father was faced with this Scots rock musician asking for his daughter's hand. I must have been naïve to think we would get my parents' blessing then. The two men used to retire after dinner with brandies to discuss the situation. It reached a crisis point when I heard my father saying, "Yes, I understand that you cannot keep my daughter in the manner to which she is accustomed, but can you keep her at all?" My poor innocent husband, who came from a working-class background in Scotland, had not thought of any of these practicalities. He tried to reassure my father, but said all the wrong things, "I wouldn't worry about it. You've educated your daughter, she can work!" My father went berserk, this was the last straw that broke the camel's back. He ordered him out of the house. I had to make my choice, "If you are going to marry this man, you leave with him now and you never come back to my house again!" It was all very dramatic, like Indian movies are. We got married in Bombay and eventually received my parents' blessings.'

Although lawyer Naseem Khan's parents had always told her that differences in religion were not important, when she returned to Pakistan with the news of her engagement to a Sri Lankan fellow lawyer, half Buddhist, half Christian, she found that they had changed their minds. 'My father said he'd disown me if I married him, my mother said she'd always thought I was a bad lot! I reminded them that they'd always said that religion didn't matter, it should be a good human being that you married. My father changed his mind, it now had to be a Muslim, I had to convert him. I said that if it was the other way around, he wouldn't want me to convert, so I wasn't even going to ask such a thing. In the end, they agreed, but I wasn't to bring my husband to Pakistan, and they wouldn't attend the wedding, even if they were in Britain at the time. That was OK with me. When I got back to Britain, this young man had found himself a Sri Lankan bride.'

When Madhur Jaffrey and her ex-husband Sayeed announced that they wished to marry, her father's beliefs in religious tolerance were also pushed to their limits. 'My father would never say, "Don't marry a Muslim," and all his best friends were Muslims, but, with Sayeed, my father said, "I don't like him, because he looks ill." He had to find another reason. Sayeed's family was the same, "Why doesn't she convert?" I said, "I can't, I am what I am, I can't change."'

To Sarah Sheriff, it is only religious affinity which bears any significance in the choice of marriage partner. 'There is no harm in Muslim girls marrying Englishmen as long as the Englishmen embrace Islam. They can marry anybody they like, as long as they're Muslim. Practically every week at the Mosque somebody comes up with an Englishman or an American who embraces Islam in order to marry his wife.'

For Asha Phillips, a child psychotherapist married to Trevor Phillips, the black television journalist and presenter, cross-cultural marriages are no surprise, as breaking the codes of arranged marriage was the tradition in her family. 'I don't think anyone expected me to marry within the community. My grandfather was one of the first Parsis to marry out, he married a French woman, they went and settled in Bombay. When my father had his *Navjote*, the Zoroastrian religious confirmation, Parsis didn't accept him. My cousin eloped on her eighteenth birthday to marry a Muslim, she had to bribe a servant as she was locked in her room. My parents took a little time to accept my marriage. Perhaps it was easier marrying Trevor than marrying an Englishman, although my parents would have been delighted if I had married Prince

Charles! Culturally the ideas about family life are more similar between Afro-Caribbean and Asian cultures, for both of us the family is the most important thing.'

When penal reformer Roshan Horabin married her husband Ivan, an English naval officer, the usual probing about family status led to some confusion. As her father had died, she had to ask her uncle for permission. 'He wanted to know if Ivan had any money, I didn't know. "What did his father do?" I told him he was an MP, to which my uncle replied, "Trust you to marry a Military Policeman's son!" Unfamiliar with the British political system, my uncle thought that MP stood for Military Police as it does in India, a job not very highly regarded.' In fact Ivan's father was the Liberal Chief Whip in the British House of Commons, but Roshan's uncle still was not impressed; after all: '"These days railway men and miners could be MPs in Britain."' In the end the couple married anyway.

Indeed, it appears that however compatible two people are, there will always be some objection to their marriage, no matter how absurd. Educationist Hena Mukherjee discovered this when she married a Bengali doctor before she finished her degree, as he had to leave for postgraduate study in England. Both families objected: 'From my mother-in-law it was because we were slightly different kinds of Brahmins. I came from the educationists, my husband from the priest class, and both sides considered themselves superior to the other. My parents did not bother about that, because one of my sisters had had a love marriage to a non-Brahmin, what they were more concerned about was that I had an elder sister still unmarried. I remember my father getting cables from my grandmother in Calcutta saying she would never be able to hold her head up in society again. We have a Bengali saying, *Chodho purush*, "fourteen generations". In other words, you are sending fourteen generations down the drain by marrying into this family just because they were not the same kind of Brahmin.'

One trend which did seem to emerge from the women I talked to was that those who had married English men had found it easier to gain access to and integrate into British society. From my own experience, I feel that this is a twin process, initiated by the spirited personalities which usually characterise women who accept the challenge of 'marrying out', but also facilitated by the contacts within British society made through one's husband and children. Nurse Saro Hutton also noticed this, and described it as 'partly the self-selecting process, these women have shown a sort of dedication to becoming part of that country. Their links give them accessibility, acceptability.'

Like many others, Saro experienced a change in attitudes among her family when her husband, Ron, followed tradition in requesting the marriage. 'They were saddened at first. Ron wrote to them and went through all the proper Indian ways of asking for marriage, and I think that calmed their fears. We had a registry wedding in London, and then flew to Malaysia for our honeymoon and had a blessing there from mum and dad, that was the main thing.'

Even though Saro's experience as one of many Asian women who have married Englishmen is proof that cross-cultural marriages can work happily, she still realises that feeling against such matches is strong. 'One of the mums at our children's school, a lecturer, came to me for advice, "I've two students, the boy is English, the girl of Sikh origin, and they have fallen in love. The girl's father has stopped her seeing the boy. She has said if she can't marry him, she will commit suicide." I explained that my situation was entirely different from the girl's because I didn't have my family in Britain, and my family were good enough to accept the situation. I rang a close family friend to ask his advice, but he acted just like the girl's parents, and was determined to keep them apart. He said that if any Indian girl marries an English boy, it is only because she can't find one of her own kind. I was stunned.'

Nevertheless, many couples who initially face hostility from their families receive their blessing as time passes and they see that their children are happily married despite their fears. When impresario Daksha Kenney first married her English husband, her family were 'shattered, very upset. They'd seen the British attitude in East Africa and could never imagine an Englishman changing himself to belong to an Asian family. But as the years went by, my ex-husband was welcomed and my father struck up a lovely friendship with him.'

For Lata McWatt, a corporate planner for race relations in Croydon, parental fears were allayed by the first meeting with her husband. 'Marrying outside my religion and culture came as quite a shock to my family. It's still unthinkable for many, and you have to be very brave to take such a step, but my family accepted my husband after meeting him. Compared to Indian parents living in Britain, I think my family is very open-minded and prepared to change and understand.' Amrit Wilson, a journalist and author, found that her family were equally understanding when she decided to 'marry out'. 'I just married someone I cared about, it wasn't a conscious decision.'

Her parents did not want her to have an arranged marriage, and even if they were not keen on her marrying a non-Indian, they respected her decision.

However, objections to 'marrying out' are not solely part of the older generation's thinking. In fact, when banker Farida Mazhar's brother married an English woman, it was Farida's generation who felt most upset. 'It's surprising how liberal my mother is considering the vast change in her life, first a small village in Pakistan, then Aden, now England. She had no objections to their marriage, but we did! You'd expect us to be more liberal, but Asian culture is so strong that it can be very difficult for a non-Asian to enter into the extended family. We thought we would lose our close ties with our brother. I think that an Asian woman and a British man works better than the other way around. Firstly, Asian women tend to be more solicitous, Western men are used to their women being more independent, wanting equality and everything. Asian men resent Western women wanting these things and being less solicitous. Secondly, Western men do treat their wives more as equals, and this is so refreshing to Asian women.'

In British society today there is a great demand for Asian wives among British men, who are attracted to the passive, devoted and faithful image which they have. The Suman Marriage Bureau has responded to this demand and from their experience feel that 'an English man and an Asian woman is much more successful than the other way around. English men like the way they are in control, an Asian wife won't go off with someone else. English women who see someone better will drop their husband and children. Asian women want English husbands because they are more broad-minded, there's no dowry problem, no in-laws problem, they are able to get a job. Even a divorced or widowed Asian girl with children can get an English husband, but never an Asian husband. Asian men are after younger virgins, even if they have been married and divorced themselves. If they can't find one here, they'll go to India or Pakistan.

'Some of the English girls who come to us are looking for a rich Asian man, because they can't find someone in their own community. I'm not sure how these marriages will last, most of those sort of marriages in the sixties have ended in divorce, and when the men come here for a second time, they want an Asian wife. Asian men demand a lot more of their wives, they expect them to bring in money and do all the housework and the cooking without any help. English men help their wives.'

While Princess Usha Devi recognised that this was indeed the image of the Asian wife, she felt that it was perhaps not the reality. 'There is a myth, because we look so feminine and retiring, that we make perfect wives.' The reality behind this myth was boldly and humorously expressed by the artist Sharon Lutchman. 'It is the desire for the exotic which historically is a fascination with the English. I think it is a combination of our sensuality, the different way of being and the imagined servility. But little do they know that it is not a terrible thing to be a strong woman in Indian culture, in fact it has been expected of you through history. This goes right back to Durga, and the other Indian goddesses, they are powerful and able to kill men, they *devoured* them.' I feel sorry for the unsuspecting Englishman, expecting a pussy cat, but finding a tigress.

Certainly Asian women are changing their attitudes and claiming a voice and a place in society in their own right. For some this means redefining the expectations and realities of marriage, while for others it means rejecting them altogether. Creating their own brand of feminism which allows a plurality of positive images and a diversity of desires, Asian women are now realising the possibilities open to them, and revealing the flair they have to fulfil them. As Kusoom Vadgama has seen, 'There is a very forceful, intelligent, determined group of women coming up, not getting married and establishing homes on their own. That was something unheard of, but it is happening, a generation of Asian women are deciding to be independent.'

14

Equal in Ourselves

Even more than in Jane Austen's England, every Indian girl is supposed to be in search of a husband. Although for many Asian women marriage has brought stability and happiness, for some it is a destiny which they have chosen to reject. As one young woman, law student Vina Shukla states, 'I'm not in search of a husband! My life isn't aimed at finding someone I can look after, it's about doing what I want to do.'

The rapid growth of the international women's movement in recent decades has given us a new perspective to the 'spinster stigma' of patriarchal societies, and feminists have redefined the rôle of women within them. Central to much vigorous debate has been the subject of marriage. Marriage is seen as the epitome of feminine fulfilment by many societies, but many feminists have argued, and still argue, that to be a wife involves unacceptable dependency for a woman and that the status of wifehood needs reconsideration by both men and women. Feminist exploration of marriage has discovered the ways in which it can stunt the growth of individual women and has therefore concentrated on building a network of resources to support women whose marriages break down.

For some Asian women, the examples of Western feminism have given inspiration and a new reflection of their own beliefs in female equality, but by appearing to overlook the lives of happily married women, Western feminism as a movement has not related to their lives. This neglect seems particularly disquieting to Asian women who place a high esteem upon family loyalty and often do not see this as something which conflicts with their individual ambitions. Indeed, the notable absence of Asian women's views within the libraries of feminist thought is not due to any lack of achievement, but to the fact that few have so far closely identified with Western feminist goals or felt that their views would be fairly represented and understood. Many of the women I spoke to felt that they had a natural affinity with feminists from all parts of the world because of their common aim of equality of opportunity, but that, equally naturally, they did not share the exact ideals of some feminists from the West. Western feminism has been misrepresented by the mediawallas who have obscured the fact that there is much common ground between all women. Misleading images have led to mutual misunderstandings, with Asian women believing that Western feminists are man-haters and Western feminists believing that Asian women are man-servants. Despite the fact that womanhood was seen by the women I spoke with as the strongest common bond, in the discussion of Western feminism, tensions were apparent.

The term 'feminism' obviously has different meanings to different people, but many of the women I spoke with found Western feminism 'soul destroying' and did not identify with its tendency to place priority upon acquiring political and economic equality. Their own goals were changes in the nature of relationships and not in the nature of power structures.

In terms of marriage, it was the West that they felt actually needed liberating. In many respects Asian women see themselves as equal to their men and as natural feminists within married life. As a movement, Western feminism has concentrated upon promoting the profile of women in public life and the importance of being economically independent and offering the confidence and support to reject unsatisfying relationships with men. In the struggle to achieve self-determination and equality in previously male dominated areas, Western feminism has perhaps undermined the fulfilment open to women through family life. To most Asian women, the thought of life outside the structure of marriage and family is not a desirable one. Artist Sharon Lutchman points out that this is one reason why Asian women do not identify with Western feminists. 'I would say feminism is a Western concept. I look at the Indian version which is completely different.' Many people expressed a reluctance to identify with this term as they could only see one version of the movement and did not appreciate the diversity of goals and forms which feminism has pursued. One key difference of Asian feminism is that Asian women have not had to make such a deliberate choice between family and career, as Sharon states: 'An orthodox traditional marriage in the West is at the kitchen sink. It needn't be like that for us. Our psyche and needs are different. We perhaps do want to get in the kitchen and cook curry, we perhaps do want to wear the *salwar kamiz*, we perhaps do want to go to the Indian movies and watch something romantic, we do want to be with babies because we were brought up with them, I don't know any Indian who wasn't and that is part of our "Indianness".'

Indeed, Sharon and many others felt strongly that the narrow version of Western feminism portrayed in the media was more restrictive than Eastern feminism in its approach to women's lives. 'In Britain if you are feminist, you are pigeonholed, wearing dungarees with Campaign for Nuclear Disarmament peace badges. Intelligent young Asian women who could be part of this change become confused because they want to relate to other independent, creative women, but when they come across a certain kind of Western feminism they find it fails to consider their differences and leaves them feeling outsiders.'

For some Asian women it was the experience of coming to the West which made them aware of the reality behind the images of liberation and equality for women, fictions by which they had been led to judge their own cultures. When writer Maria Couto came to Britain she realised that, 'Some of my assumptions about the much vaunted freedom enjoyed by women in the West have been quickly belied. Apart from sexual freedom and state benefits, I often feel we are better off in India, with the high place accorded to motherhood.'

When Hena Mukherjee took a Fulbright scholarship at Harvard and temporarily settled in America without her husband and children, she too discovered that attitudes towards women in the West were more restrictive than in her homeland. 'At home I never felt discriminated against as a woman. As a Bengali I always grew up with the idea that women are very important people. To come to what one thought was a more developed society and to find that women were not having too good a time, was very strange.

'An American man on the university selection committee asked, "Isn't it going to be difficult for you as a woman to leave your husband and family?" I was so angry. "Surely I'm a mature person and if I came to present myself at this interview I must have thought it through, I must have discussed it with people who are important in my life."' When Hena was finally awarded the scholarship and had moved to America she found that the women there were 'obsessed by the fact that I was married and had two children who were at home with my husband. They were positive that I was on the brink of divorce, otherwise I wouldn't have left my husband. I found this very hard to figure out initially. Why was everyone talking about divorce and separation? To me there was nothing unusual about this situation. We were quite used to living apart from time to time depending on where my husband's career took him. My husband went off to Sweden two days before my son was born. He came back nine months later. Nobody turned round to me and said, "How difficult it must be for you to have your husband away," during those nine months.

'I wasn't used to wearing a wedding ring, it wasn't very important to me. The Bengalis wear an iron wedding bangle, the equivalent of the Western ring. In America another woman student came up to me and said, "You know you are misleading people into thinking you are not married because you don't have a ring." She was quite annoyed about this. It's like there was a competition and I should indicate that I am out of it, you're meant to make it very clear. I was irritated by this, but I went out and bought a cheap $1 ring from the local Woolworth's, put it on and that made everybody happy around me. I did it to make life easier for me. After some time I was confident enough not to bother about it.'

For the land which claims to be the flagship of freedom and feminism, America showed itself to be suspicious of a married woman who followed a career independently. I found a similar attitude when travelling around the newly liberated China shortly after my marriage in 1974. Everyone kept asking me where my husband was; I simply replied that he was at home in England paying the mortgage on our new home. I was surprised to find that so soon after the Cultural Revolution married women who showed independence were still seen as somewhat strange. True liberation and feminism is giving women the chance to express themselves as they wish and it means accepting that a contented marriage is an important aspect of many women's lives, but not the only one.

As feminists we should be seeking ways in which women can achieve maximum fulfilment, trying to accept the 'Compleat Woman', whose life embraces all aspects without the need for total sacrifice. The different elements of one's psyche or personality can all be realised, being 'compleat' leads to a more balanced view of oneself and life. The most consistent objection to be voiced against Western feminism is the suspicion and criticism shown to men. Not only is this ideologically wrong as it devalues their central premise of equality, but it is also flawed in practice, as it ignores the lives of many women that are linked happily with men.

The insistence upon segregation is seen as anti-progressive by Hena Mukherjee: 'The tendency of women's groups to isolate themselves by not including men is absolutely wrong. Our goals are the same as men's goals.' To Rita Austin, who echoes this common criticism, feminism and female fulfilment is not about exclusion or selfish satisfaction: 'The extreme forms of feminism don't do human beings any good, let alone women any good. They have no room for men and little room for children, they don't actually accept that in order to provide young, growing people with a secure future, women have to tone their aspirations down.'

Devinia Sookia sees her marital and family life as a source of her strength and independence and not an obstacle to it. 'Asian women realise they are equal, but also respect their husband and are proud and happy to look after their house and take care of their family. I can only function properly if my mood is good, so I need a stable and happy home life. The force behind me is my husband, I share everything with him: work, ideas, housework and even my moods.' The stability that a happy marriage can offer is an important quality which I also value. Knowing that I have a strong base to grow from and to return to, gives me the confidence to be adventurous and independent.

Indeed, many felt that the movement towards true equality could be jeopardised by the alienation of the younger generation of men. Maria Couto believes that men have opposed feminism because they feel threatened and not included. 'Young men are less open-minded and definitely keen to see their future wives in traditional rôles, but this is a characteristic within white communities as well. I have a tolerant husband who shares the challenges of my work and who is ambitious for me rather than competitive.' Many women I spoke with thought that feminism has simply regarded men as the enemy and stressed the changes which women need to effect within society, ignoring the potential to change men's attitudes and therefore effect a more united and fulfilling sense of equality throughout society.

It is not only the more flexible definition of marriage and relationships between men and women within Asian culture that has allowed Asian women to feel equal without naming themselves 'feminists'. Their ancestral and mythological heritage also offers positive images of independent women. The balance between the public and the private and the masculine and feminine is a natural belief which originates in the religion and philosophy of the East. The genesis in which man and woman grow together, the Yin and Yang and the animus and anima all tell of how we are each composed of both qualities which cannot be denied within our personalities or within our societies. Women from all cultures now have the chance to create their own destinies and disprove the false images of myth, as poet Shruti Pankaj so concisely says, 'Eve may well have been created from the spare rib of Adam, but today's Asian women have their own backbone.'

Indeed, powerful and resourceful women are an important part of Asian culture. For Jeya Wilson, the commitment to female equality comes partly from the feminist fables of her Tamil background. 'In classical Indian literature and epics, Nalan and Damayanthi, Rama and Sita were couples where the female characters were strong. My mother used to teach me a lot about them, they were chaste women and, sure, there's also this "their husband was a god" bit, but there was nothing about being a servant, they were women in their own right.' The myriad of Hindu goddesses offers women a whole range of positive and powerful images. Durga and Kali are the protectors and destroyers; Laxshmi is the guardian of wealth, and Saraswati is the goddess of knowledge. These are not icons of virginity or pure divinity, mocking the lives of real women, but figures who have been realised through the family power, economic independence and educational advancement of many Asian women's lives.

The strong bonds between mother and daughter, and all female relations, are another natural source of strength in the East, one which Western feminism has also emphasised. This stress upon bonds between women is Western feminism's version of sisterhood. In the East, there is a natural sisterhooding which has arisen from imposed social structures and which means that the value of other women is never underestimated. We do not need to be told that sisterhood is strength, as we naturally experience it. Family heritage has affected many of the women; the paternal encouragement to enter public life enhanced by the authority of the mother within the family. Far from admonishing their daughters to be passive and meek, many of the female figures in these women's pasts have inspired strength and involvement.

Producer and director Munni Kabir is one woman who feels an instinctive solidarity with the feminist movement, but realised that her own mother had already dispelled any notion of female oppression by the time she became aware of it. 'When the women's movement came about, with the whole question of identity, I didn't know what it was all about. I had always identified with my mother, a strong woman. My mother was the boss and I didn't know that men had anything to say about anything. There were all girls in my family and there was no question that a man had anything to say. Not just my father, we respected him all right, but we would go to my mother when we needed to come to a decision.'

The mother often plays an important rôle in forming her daughter's approach to life, but it was quite surprising to discover that the female figures to whom many Asian women looked as rôle-models of powerful and contented women in their own right were the nuns who educated them. The history of Christian educational influence within Asian society meant that many women were taught by the Loreto nuns and naturally grew up to see them as examples of womanhood. Although married to God, these nuns lived their earthly lives without the restrictions and responsibilities which come with marital and family life and consequently offered their pupils a positive image of self-determination without communicating any bitterness about men. Film executive Devika Bannerjee decided that in order to achieve self-fulfilment she should remain single. The support of her family and the example of the nuns gave her the confidence to do so. 'I do not want to rely on a rich husband, lover or father. I don't discredit men in my life, but I want to establish myself, without compromise. My parents gave me a taste for liberty and freedom of expression. Also, the nuns who taught me reinforced that.'

Another religious example of female autonomy is to be found in the Koran, the Islamic holy book, which follower Sarah Sheriff explained to me, presents the basic ethos of feminism. 'There is one fundamental difference: Western society as a whole is becoming a unisex society, the female rôle has been downgraded altogether in the drive for equality and identity. In the Koran, women and men are equal in the sight of God.'

In the ideal, this belief is truly liberating as it enables women to choose their destiny, as either marital and maternal or professional, and to feel equally valued and fulfilled. Indeed, to some women, Asian societies do offer this 'feminist' possibility, as Sharon Lutchman found, 'Men respect women in India, whether she is working or not. People tend to lose this respect in Britain because the rôle of the wife and mother is undervalued.'

Rukhsana Ahmad feels that equality of the sexes is a worthwhile ideal, but that the emphasis placed upon being different usually becomes an excuse for inequality. 'I don't disagree with a lot of feminist philosophy, it's based on good sense, I think that women are equal. I don't think there's much to be had from the "women are equal but different" stance of religions, particularly Islam. It always claims to have given great rights to women, but "because women are different, those rights must be different" is usually a premise for inequality. They believe they have a status, but they don't recognise that when difference gets codified, the inequality gets codified.'

Inequalities still characterise women's lives in all corners of the globe, but the common assumption that it was the West alone which pioneered the concept of feminism and is more liberated in every respect than the East is a misapprehension. Equality in terms of the work ethic is an important feminist goal which women in the East have experienced alongside those in the West. Like women from all societies, Asian women found opportunities to flourish in their own right when men relinquished their control over the family land or businesses. Pireeni Sundaralingam, a research psychologist, recalls how the women of her family naturally assumed this responsibility. 'My mother used to drive tractors in Ceylon. I don't come from a repressed female background, my grandmothers are both widows, both running their estates.'

The great emphasis which the West now places upon economic feminism is also a phenomenon natural to other models of society. In many non-Western societies women have a long history of contributing to the work force, moreover of being the sole supporter of their families. To some such women, working from nine to five each day might not appear to be desperately liberating. Jeya Wilson also found that the professional world of British society, although often thought of as more progressive than that of Eastern societies, had sexism rooted in the very titles of its many powerful institutions. 'I could not believe Britain has government bodies with names like the *Man*power Services Commission. They still haven't learnt the importance of language. It's the whole mental attitude, language does influence a person's thinking, it's not just a matter of semantics; people say, "Oh, so what" if they're talking about a chair*man* instead of a *chair* or a chair*person*.'

The privilege given to men in the English language also appears in more subtle ways. Consider the difference in status conveyed by the terms bachelor and spinster, stag party and hen party, even man and wife. Certainly, the English language does seem to convey a bias towards male power and authority. The 'objective' terminology used often confirms this point of view to be male. Journalist Ira Mathur felt that women are only ever given titles according to traditional female rôles. 'I don't like the idea of "our women" or "my daughter", it's very cramping. You're expected to go straight from daughter to wife to mother and I want to be an individual.' Feminists have made attempts to correct this imbalance and the invention of 'Ms' means that women need no longer make their marital status part of their title if they do not wish to.

However, while women must fight sexism together and assert their rights to be treated equally across all cultures, they must develop individual strategies which best serve their own situations and needs. These are two lessons which Gita Saghal, journalist and TV presenter, has come to appreciate through her involvement in feminism in India. Gita knew that Indian women had long since fought oppression but felt that the global movement instigated in the West had given women throughout the world a new fervour and determination. 'There have been women's movements in India since the nineteenth century, but it was in the late seventies that a new kind of movement evolved, taking inspiration from Western feminism and campaigns for social justice.' Several strands developed to deal with the differing problems, so 'village' feminism could be different to the 'urban' feminism which Gita was actively involved with. This flexibility and the treatment of specifically Indian problems meant that the movement moved in different directions to the women's movement in the West.

'The agendas were set by Indian women, largely middle-class, but women who were wondering about Indian problems like dowry. Rape is also a different issue in India, there it is not only an individual matter, which is horrific enough, but also very clearly a weapon used by the state, where women are raped in police custody, the army have been involved in mass rapes. So this was an issue connected to a whole series of women's issues. It was about women's position, but it was also a critique of South Asian society.'

Although they cater for different communities, the dominance of middle-class women is a problem which nearly all women's movements have encountered. Gita knew that this caused certain difficulties, but also recognised that it had some benefits. These women had access to the mediawallas and therefore their protests were well reported. When a campaign against dowry murders was started there were street plays outside the homes of murdered wives to bring attention to their plight and they received good coverage.

When Gita returned to England she found that feminism had quite different connotations to Asians living in Britain. 'There was a lot of rhetoric about the community and about defending it against racism, with a lot of hostility towards white feminism. Something called black feminism had developed. The idea was that racism destroys all our families and white women are against the family, because only we, as black women or Asian women, are for family and that our families have been torn apart by the immigration laws. This seemed to be a very simplistic view. Yes, of course the immigration laws are pernicious, they do divide families and one has to fight for that unity, but I don't think that fighting against the immigration laws means that once you are here, you should shut up about the fact that Asian men beat up their women. Or that large numbers of women are being beaten in all communities. It's not just an Asian thing, you can be quite clear about that. It happens right across the board, but people want to pretend that it doesn't happen to us Asians.'

I am a feminist and believe that the stand taken by feminists in the West has been a crucial step in writing women's issues onto the agenda and instrumental in changing attitudes towards us in all areas of life. However, as is the case with all radical movements, the need to be outrageous in order to attract the attention of the mediawallas creates the danger that the extreme image portrayed will jeopardise the popularity and success of the movement. Western feminism in the past has often given an uncompromising image of itself, the strict choice between being feminist and feminine. This has meant that, although many organisations believe in and promote future opportunities for women, they cannot identify themselves with the term 'feminism'.

Siromi Rodrigo, speaking on the modern Guiding movement, said their aim was to help young girls to take the future leadership rôle in their country and society. 'We want the advancement of young women and help them stand up shoulder to shoulder with the men, not to push and demand things or try to be better than them. We prefer to be feminine, not feminist.'

Many Asian women have their own brand of feminism which can unite the feminist and the feminine. There is a natural affinity between the female members of the community, a support structure based on genuine appreciation of and interest in each other. It is not a deliberate attempt to 'network'. For myself, my grandmother, mother, sister, aunts and female cousins are the golden thread that tie me to my heritage and give me the confidence to be myself.

Author Bapsi Sidhwa found that in the West women are conditioned to look to the man as the source of interest and authority, a habit which opposes their feminist awareness. 'When women talk to me in Pakistan, they make eye contact, but this is not so in the West. The Western woman will always look at the man. If I'm at a cocktail party and a man comes over to me, I find he embarks on a little monologue, leaving me to provide the "yeses", "oh reallies" and "how wonderfuls". They'll button-hole you, bore you to tears about their job, then move away as soon as you start talking. In Pakistan, some men are so monosyllabic, they're happy for women to do all the talking.'

Feminism may have liberated the feminists, but it is still to change the lives of the majority of women. Although feminism has enabled many women to achieve positions and goals which would formerly have been denied to them, it has remained a 'movement' and has not been a set of ideas fully integrated into society. The laws may have been decreed, but women still do not have equal pay, equal job security or equal opportunities in many fields. Certainly many men are to blame for this, but so are some women. There is a breed of woman who, once she has succeeded, forgets other women; she flourishes by being 'the single red rose'. A single rose may be exquisite but it is a vase abundant with roses which arrests the senses with its unsparing fragrance and incomparable beauty.

Many Asian women do feel themselves to be feminist, part of the same rose garden, but in a different sense. Their quiet evolution and their refusal to conform to the imaginary choice between 'feminine' and 'feminist' has meant that their beauty has been unseen by most in the West.

But Shyama Perera, a television presenter, feels that because Asian women have not been so extreme or conspicuous in their assertion of feminist goals, they are more likely to be able to challenge the system in a permanent way. 'I think because we are possibly more thoughtful, less abrasive and aggressive, we will actually get there in a far more subtle and possibly satisfactory way.' Mohini Samtani also sees the virtue in Asian women's quiet power: 'Asian women do things very subtly. People feel they are very meek, that they don't say anything. But it's like the wind and the air, you can't see it, but it is very strong.'

However, whatever type of social freedom feminism has granted women, it is the sexual revolution that would be expected to clash most with Eastern beliefs. Yet the sexuality of Asian women is also a mythic concept which has been misapprehended by many. This story told to me by agony aunt Sadhana Ghose, may shatter many people's illusions of the rôle of the 'Asian agony aunt'. 'I had an ambassador's wife of 56 whose husband was fooling around. She fell in love with somebody else, then her husband started taking an interest in her again. Suddenly she wanted to give it all up, go hang-gliding with a tall, dark, handsome man. So she asked me what she should do.

'I told her to keep the husband, keep the lover and also look for a third man. With the husband she had the power and status. With the lover she'd have a good time and feel great. Now she should look out for a nice "toy boy" to go hang-gliding with. Why give up all these good things? Men do it, they have their wives and their mistresses, what's wrong with women doing it too? So that's what she's doing now.

'Men have one standard for their sisters and their daughters, but another for the woman they want to go out with. That's something I don't like. If you want to have fun with me, say so. If I feel like having fun with you, I'll say so too. But don't clothe it with "I am in love with you and I can't sleep at night and I look at your picture constantly. . ." For heaven's sake!'

While some young Asian women welcome sexual freedom, viewing it as an opportunity to express their sexuality openly, many see it as a symbol of Western society that only values women as sexual objects. The scandal generated by Pamella Bordes, a pale imitation of the Profumo Affair, created a new stereotype of the Asian woman as sexually manipulative and it is one which all the women in this book found offensive. Within Asian culture, sex is seen as a blessing rather than a sin.

Katy Mirza, actress and former VIP Bunny Girl, emphasised the Eastern view that sex is an important part of human life and has both a physical and a spiritual dimension. 'Human reproduction is not a man-made thing, it's a divine system for creating more human beings. Because of this, sex is not just for pleasure, it's a divine duty. That's what Indian philosophy, the *Kama Sutra*, is all about. It teaches the art of love-making. Sexiness is next to godliness!'

15

Karma, Kismet,
I Did It My Way

Religion is like a travel agency: there are many different ways to reach your destination, and many routes which take you there. Similarly, there are different religions and various roads within them that lead to enlightenment. As on any journey, the spiritual quest offers a choice of tour operators, each with their own special features and appeal. The decision on which way to travel is often made for us as a provisional booking by our ancestors. For most this booking is confirmed as we reach adulthood, but sometimes we realise that a different way of travel is more suited to our individual needs. Some people wish to arrive as quickly and easily as possible, others enjoy the lingering pleasure of the journey, a few wish to travel solo, while others simply prefer to stay at home and never experience the joys and hardship of travelling.

While the choices available add interest and variety to life, it is important to remember that ultimately all religions travel to the same destination: total self-knowledge. The lives of the prophets and the teachings they have left act as maps and landmarks to guide us through this life. Yet a few reject the well-worn paths which these maps offer, preferring to explore unknown routes for themselves, also leading to the same divinity.

As global journeying between East and West has become easier, and migration has become more popular, the religious identity of nations has naturally become plural. The organised worship of many different religions is a fairly recent phenomenon in British society, which has a predominantly secular profile. In contrast, for centuries India has been host to all the world's great religions and a mutual acceptance has naturally evolved. When I am in India it is not unusual for me to worship at a Hindu temple, light candles in a Catholic church, give offerings at a Sikh Gurdwara and say my Zoroastrian prayers at the fire-temple. I have never felt unwelcome. Outside India, I often visit religious centres, but somehow feel a tourist.

An understanding and experience of different religions was a subject about which many others also spoke. The father of educationist Piloo Nanavutty insisted that as a young girl she learnt about other religions as well as her own Zoroastrian faith. 'One day you will have the fragrance of all religions in your heart. Never forget, in a garden you want a variety of flowers.' Asha Phillips, also a Zoroastrian, was brought up to respect all religions. 'I grew up praying to them all. If you felt religious at all, you should be thanking all the prophets.'

We are now beginning to live in an inter-faith world which can no longer promote religious superiority and complacency. The face of British religious life is changing dramatically. People may be surprised to hear that there are more Christians in India than in Britain and more practising Muslims in Britain than Christians. For British society the emphasis upon spirituality which is characteristic of the East, should be a welcome gift which immigration has brought. The rituals and significance of the act of worship may differ between religions, but a higher priority on spiritual matters may be a corrective perspective to the fanatical materialism which is sweeping the world. The acceptance and tolerance of other ways need not jeopardise the beliefs of each religion, or the trust which God has put in them, to worship according to His many ways.

Recently when I was in India, I had a meeting with a Kashmiri cabinet minister and half way through our meeting he disappeared. Later I learnt that he had gone to pray. God is a full-time affair in the East. Western society is more familiar with the New Testament concept of 'Render unto Caesar that which is Caesar's' and so find it more difficult to come to terms with the Eastern way of giving everything unto God.

It is only as we gain a fuller understanding of each others' lives that we can appreciate how the fundamental beliefs of all religions are basically the same. Actress Sehri Saklatvala's parents came from different religious backgrounds, but found that they had much in common. 'Both religions were very noble and what was deemed good in my father's Zoroastrian religion was deemed good in my mother's Christian one. The things that divide religions are usually the rites, the rituals, the extras. Most religions teach you to be truthful, self-disciplined, kind to others. Goodness and love are the basis of them all.' Certainly, there is a golden thread which runs through the fabric of all religions and which advises all humanity to 'know thyself', 'love thy neighbour' and 'seek life everlasting in God'.

The Christian philosophy that the way to God and salvation is through Jesus Christ, has made the religious identity of the British seem more exclusive than others and possibly less receptive to the value of other spiritual ways. However, Christianity has affected many people of other religions. Jesus and the Virgin Mary have had great impact upon the lives and psyches of many Asian people who were educated by Jesuits and nuns and who consequently have a greater understanding of Christianity and the Bible. This influence extended beyond spiritual lessons. Educationist Hena Mukherjee feels that her familiarity with the texture of Christian language gave her an advantage in understanding the subtleties of English literature. Naseem Khan, the barrister, remembers the powerful images presented by her Catholic schooling.

My own father's life is also an example of the influence of religious education and a natural generosity of spirit. He was taught by the Jesuit priests in Poona and so had a respect for them and their religious doctrines. When my father's education finished, he began his engineering career by building ice factories but found it hard financially as at that time there was no regulation over the cost of ice. Consequently, there was a price war and some large ice manufacturers even gave ice away free in order to create business. About this time the local Catholic priest in Bandra, a suburb of Bombay, approached my father for the loan of one of his lorries in order to transport a statue of the Virgin Mary of Fatima from the airport in a cavalcade around Bombay. Even though my father was a practising Zoroastrian, he willingly offered to help the priest. However, when the day came it was the monsoon season and all his lorries were stranded outside the city. My father approached the local butcher who also had a lorry and asked him if he would lend it for the occasion. He refused, but told my father that he could hire it. After my father had paid for the lorry and the fuel, he delivered it to the priest in time for all the school children to decorate it with flowers before it was driven to the airport to welcome the statue of the Virgin Mary. When the statue was finally in place the priest thanked my father for his kindness and told him that the Virgin Mary would bless him. That very night a cartel was established which fixed a minimum price for ice and my father's cash shortage was solved overnight. To this day, my father visits Lourdes in France, Fatima in Portugal and Mount Mary in Bombay to show his gratitude to the Virgin for her blessings.

Many Asian people respect and have faith in the figures of other religions as in India the pantheon of gods and goddesses which Hinduism offers creates an easier acceptance of religious figures. It is not unusual to see pictures of prophets and gurus whose devotees live in India. The visibility of gods within Hindu culture may seem strange, even disrespectful, but the displays of gurus and gods in shops, taxis, homes and even on the roadside function as a constant reminder of the spiritual side of life and the possibility of happiness which they hold for the believers.

In my own house I have statues of the Virgin Mary, Laxshmi, Ganesh and Hannuman. I have a cross blessed in Bethlehem, copies of the Koran, *Bhagavadgita* and the Bible, a set of Buddhist prayer beads, a drawing of Guru Nanak, as well as a portrait of Zoroaster painted by my mother. For me, each adds blessing and spiritual influence to my home. All of these symbols can exist side by side as they provide a vision of religious harmony. There is no sense of demeaning any faith, just a belief that they are all there for us to gain from spiritually and there is no conflict. Headmistress Shirley Daniel, although a Christian, has a statue of Ganesh, the Hindu elephant god, in her house. 'I was brought up as a Christian, but the temple round the corner in Madras was a Shri Ganesha temple. I've always kept a statue of Ganesh; superstitiously, I believe that he'll bring me luck.'

For Asian people it is common to be exposed to several religious traditions and the density of people within the countries has created a mentality which is naturally accommodating. There is not the space to be exclusive nor is there the will, all religions have merged so that rituals, symbols and philosophies are now more complementary and not conflicting. Sarah Sheriff, a worker at the Islamia Schools Trust, sees this as rather awkward. 'If you go to India you wouldn't be able to see any difference at all between a Hindu marriage and a Muslim marriage, in ritual or whatever, there's been so much borrowing. What happens in a Pakistani marriage nowadays is so un-Islamic, it's embarrassing.'

A more positive side of this inter-religious mixing is a natural contact and understanding which combats religious prejudice. Mahatma Gandhi was brought up in a village in Gujarat where they studied the Koran in their temple. The lessons in other people's religions offered an insight into their cultural lives which was transformed into social tolerance. In today's society this balance between spiritual fulfilment and social responsibility has often not been achieved. In one extreme this has led to the neglect of spiritual life, as businesswoman Mohini Samtani believes, 'We have been so busy with our lives, we have forgotten to look after our souls. Our soul is the sum total of us, it never dies, but you can't see it, so you don't bother with it. If only we had someone to explain how to look after it, teaching "Soul Care".'

The other extreme of imbalance has led some to religious fundamentalism, which often means the sacrifice of national harmony and individual development. Fundamentalism is the triumph of the letter over the spirit and while 'the spirit giveth life', 'the letter killeth'. The main problem with fundamentalism is that it is always looking to the past for answers and security. The past is not really a suitable model for the future as it shows injustice, persecution and the broken myth of the golden age. Religion is not about looking backwards, it is about using this life to equip oneself for the next. A story which Renoo Zaiwalla told me explains this need for growth and makes clear the modern enigma of spirituality: 'A baby in the womb grows arms and legs which it does not need while it is inside its mother. The life inside the womb is a time of preparation for life outside of it. In this life we might feel that we do not need a spiritual side, but our earthly lives are a time of preparation for after death.'

For Eastern and Western religions the means of preparation and the expectations of life after death differ. The Eastern philosophy of trusting in God to guide one to one's destiny and the belief that nothing is possible without God, subtly contrasts to the Western emphasis on self-determination and the Catholic need to worship in order to triumph over original sin. There is a general truth that in the West, problems are there to be solved, whereas in the East, something will be done if God is willing. However, this is a deep philosophical premise which does not exclude the need to confront evil during the earthly life. Yasmin Hosain explained that the understanding of destiny in Islam does not preclude human action, as a religion it is not fatalistic. 'Destiny is there, but *you* have to tie the foot of the camel. Fate won't stop him wandering for you, you are responsible for your destiny, your actions are important. Although it may be that God knows everything that will happen to you, humans are responsible not only to God but to themselves'.

To many, a belief in destiny, one's kismet, gives a sense of peace and security, without leading to complacency. A trust that things will happen when the time is right tempers the stress and ruthlessness of competitive feelings. For singer Najma Akhtar, this philosophy has enabled her to accept limitations. 'I believe that what God has written is written, I don't want to force it. With my singing, my ambition is not to get a number one. I'd like to, but it's not an ambition; if it's written, it will come naturally.'

This sense of purposeful inevitability offered real solace to community worker Vasuben Shah when her husband died shortly after they had settled in Britain. 'I used to ask myself that having started life together how could he just leave me. But Jainism teaches us that he would live only the time that was given to him by God. I could not extend his life, even he could not extend his life, not even for a second. And I have accepted that.'

Hotelier Gulshan Jaffer had always derived great strength from her religion, 'You never feel you don't have friends, you can always go to the Mosque, see someone you know and feel you belong.' Although, as she went on to say, 'whether they'll help is a different story. When my husband died, nobody wanted to know us: not the community, family, or the banks.' Islam has no intermediaries between the individual and God, so Gulshan was able to turn to God for strength and help. She sat down with her sons and told God that they were going to fight and that He was going to help them! After that, the doors did start opening, the bank lent her money to start again.

Not only does the belief in God's will help one to cope with the feelings of grief when a loved one dies, but it also offers a philosophical view of one's own destiny. It is a view which Shakespeare coined beautifully in Western terms with the words, 'There's a divinity that shapes our ends, rough hew them as we will.' Indeed, despite the common assumption that the notion of kismet is somehow intrinsically Eastern, it also emerges at a very simple level within Western philosophy. When life does not turn out as well as expected it is not unusual to hear an English person exclaim, 'Well, maybe it wasn't meant to be.' In other words it was not in your destiny.

Syeda Jalali feels that her belief in kismet has been formed by her experiences: 'I have been in too many places at the right time and too many things have coincidentally happened to me. That has really made a difference. I am a firm believer. I don't fear death, I've been on a train when somebody said that there was a bomb on board. To me it was of no significance because I think what will be, will be.' Like Syeda, I believe that when my time is up, it is up. I was recently involved in a car accident and, much to the amazement of those who rescued me, I simply climbed out of the crunched car untouched. As my car was hit, my life passed before my eyes, but I knew that I had not finished here yet; indeed, in many ways I felt I had not started! For others too, it is remarkable incidents which have happened in their lives which have confirmed their beliefs.

Shakira Caine has good reason to trust in destiny: 'I believe very much in fate, our life is mapped out for us somehow, there's a power up there, guiding us. I had my fortune told before I left Guyana and it was predicted that I'd be all right, I'd travel and meet lots of people. My mother had four kids to bring up, struggling to pay the school fees, so I didn't believe it at the time, I thought I'd be married off, have ten kids and suffer just like her. It was fate I came to live in London and met my husband.'

Certainly, astrology has a long tradition in the East and Bapsi Sidhwa sees it as having roots in earthly suffering. 'We believe in destiny, it's part of our tradition. The moment a child is born, its horoscope is cast. There's not much you can do by your own willpower. Fate is a very strong belief brought about by poverty, helplessness. In the West, people feel more in control of their own lives.'

For those who travel to India, this faith which becomes a state of resignation is difficult to comprehend. Veena Ramgoolam, from Mauritius, spoke for many when she commented that, 'In India they seemed to be content with the situation they were in, I couldn't understand that. Their philosophy was that God put us here and that's where we're going to live.' It is important to acknowledge that while Hinduism may appear to be the most encompassing and tolerant of all religions on a spiritual level, on a social level it advocates acceptance of life and seems to teach people not to rock the boat and so, unwittingly, it protects the status quo.

Whether socially or spiritually inspired, the trust in one's destiny is certainly a significant part of most Eastern psyches, but journalist Sadhana Ghose feels more of an affinity to the philosophy of *My Way*. 'The way my life has gone has always been because I've directed it, not because it was just fate. I have a philosophy: when I die they should play *My Way*, except I want a woman to sing it and not Frank Sinatra!'

Although some may reject the notion of a divine blueprint for human life, to a varying degree we all share a fascination and belief in phenomena beyond our understanding. To some they offer comfort, to others bemusement, but there is little question that, 'There are more things in heaven and earth than are dreamt of in your philosophy.' For Asians the spiritual dimension of the personality is not so mysterious and bears a direct relation to one's actions. There is a spiritual mirror of one's deeds which reflects into the future, one's karma.

Mathematical genius Shakuntala Devi does not believe that the past dictates the future even though her other business is astrology. 'I live for the moment, day by day, not for the past. Maybe that's because I don't have such a glorious past. I don't believe in past lives, or future ones, just my present life. Karma has no meaning for me. I don't believe in a Day of Judgement either. If I smile at you, you become a friend. If I frown, you become an enemy. The behaviour has already been judged and you can't be tried twice for the same crime.' In a sense Shakuntala does believe in karma, just a more instantaneous version which judges each action as it happens.

Nevertheless, sometimes you help people and show kindness and it comes back in indirect ways or after a long period of time. Karma is an ultimate balance and not necessarily an immediate reaction, just a belief that somehow the deeds of your life will return. In fact the belief in karma is also mirrored by Christian teachings and by British common sense. The Christian parable about sowing seeds in fertile ground, for 'as you sow, so do you reap', is the Western understanding of karma. Yet, the religious counsel is more commonly heard as a foreboding. It is common to hear people say, 'Don't worry, he'll get his come-uppance,' it's a very typical British reaction. So, although English people think they have very little in common with Eastern spirituality, they unwittingly believe in both kismet and karma although they seldom recognise it.

Although one's karma is altered by one's actions, karma can also be a collective force generated by the actions of families and nations. This is one reason why there is more emphasis placed upon family reputation in the East, as there is a deep belief that one's behaviour will affect the quality of life for the next generation. I believe that the spontaneous philanthropy which has characterised my ancestry has affected my outlook and possibilities in life and I know that on many occasions I have benefited from my family's goodness.

This is a belief I share with accountant Arunbhai Patel. 'God must have made it possible for me to get my education, to be in England at the right time because of the goodness of my family.'

Publisher Arif Ali hopes that his deeds will continue his family's reputation for kindness. 'Many things happened to my family in Guyana because my parents and grandparents were good people. I'd like to leave that legacy for my children, so that people will say to them, "Oh, you are Arif's son, that's nice," rather than, "Oh you are Arif's son, that bastard!"'

Equestrian Meera Mehta feels that it is her karma and events in past lives which have dictated her love for animals and she practises Jainism to show respect for all forms of life. 'I have become a stricter vegetarian, I won't even step on a spider knowingly. You can sustain your own life without killing something else, so why do it? If we've come on since the cavemen, why do we still kill animals?' Meera explained why she felt so attached to her horse, George. 'When I bought him, he had just been condemned as insane, he'd been kicked as a foal and some bone went into his brain. Every so often, he'd do something mad and dangerous. My mother was worried, every week I'd come back with some new war wound. Then someone who goes into past lives explained that George had been my horse before and had saved my life in an eleventh-century battle. I believe in karma, I was put on this earth to look after animals. Eventually, I'd like to start an animal refuge.'

It is ironic that the British assume that they are a nation of animal lovers because of the fuss and attention which they show to domestic animals. While their example has been effective in highlighting sickening cruelty in the form of bull-baiting, cock fights and the trafficking of exotic birds, they have been slow in being outraged at the cruelties of factory farming and animal experimentation. In contrast Eastern societies, although less protective to domestic animals, have acknowledged the inter-relationships within the animal kingdom and have even incorporated them into their spiritual pantheons. In Hinduism there are many animal gods, vegetarianism is a natural part of their philosophy and the cow is accorded a sacred status. The Greeks too had animal gods, Pan the part-goat, part-man god is often pictured playing his reed pipe, but few know that this musical instrument was created by the rape of the nymph Syrinx who changed herself into a reed to escape his lecherous advances. This aspect of Greek civilisation has been underplayed by Western society since the rise of Christianity and Islam.

One religion which provides a bridge between Eastern and Western philosophies is Zoroastrianism. Although no animal is personified as God, the religion advocates care for God's Good Creation which not only includes fellow men, but also plants and animals. Throughout life one is not allowed to pollute the elements and on death, as in birth, one is placed naked and equal in the Towers of Silence; a final resting place, where the body is offered up to the vultures. It is a reminder that if one does not perform acts of charity in life, on death it is inevitable.

The Zoroastrian beliefs about one's rôle within the natural world encompass philosophies from the East and West, as does its balance between spiritual and physical life which has enabled the religion to offer an action plan for this life. Although Zoroastrianism is the first monotheistic religion and the first to create the concepts of good and evil and heaven and hell, even today, it appears modern in its attitudes. Most other monotheistic religions which came after Zoroastrianism told of the same concepts: of an archetypal struggle between good and evil; a judgement day, when the scales of justice will weigh the worth of one's soul, and the final arrival of a saviour.

It is interesting that in the Old Testament there are few words of praise for anyone not of 'God's chosen people'. The exception was made for the Zoroastrian Cyrus, the founder of the Persian Empire, who was called the 'King of Kings' and 'God's anointed'. It was Cyrus who operated a policy of resettling uprooted peoples, communities who had been exiled by the previous Babylonian conquerors. Not only did he allow the Jews to return home from captivity in Babylon, but he also had the foresight to provide funds for the rebuilding of their temple in Jerusalem. Yet, as Farrukh Dhondy pointed out, the faith which inspired such great acts is now forgotten by most, 'What did the Zoroastrians do? We invented God and I have often regretted that we did not patent Him.'

One quality of Zoroastrianism which is seldom associated with religion is the enjoyment of life; it is a positive faith which advocates the expression of all forms of goodness. As Dr Roeinton Khambatta explains, 'Zoroastrianism is a religion of joy where the whole world exalts in the presence of the almighty God. Where everything is done for good. Evil does exist in this world but good will eventually triumph. We do not have to sit down and beat our breast about original sin or anything like that. Nor do we have to constantly be told about the wrath of God. God to us is a fun person, good, kind, tolerant. He understands that man will have foibles and err. He is merciful. He is not going to be angry with us for ever. Our religion teaches us to spread happiness not gloom. There is no place for misery in our religion and way of life.'

Dr Hoshang Jungalwalla also sees Zoroastrianism as a religion which offers happiness, but demands action. 'We are taught to enjoy life to the full, to *do* good, not just think good. We are invited to be co-workers with God and given the hard option of responsibility to sustain order and overcome the evils of disorder. Not the soft option of fear of God and helplessness.'

This contest with evil has become a life principle for Aban Bana who feels that the religious goals of Zoroastrianism relate closely to her professional vocation. 'My life ethic has been based upon my religion and I have discovered that Steiner's educational philosophy is very close to Zoroastrianism. He acknowledged that it was the Persians who first recognised the Prince of Darkness, whom they called "Ahriman". This was the being that we had to overcome in our lives. You don't slink away from evil when it approaches you, but you have a head-on confrontation.' For Zoroastrians it is a duty to transform chaos into order, unravelling the golden thread and freeing it from all the knots is a divine purpose.

The popular understanding of Hinduism may lead people to believe that as a religion it does not demand this same kind of strategy for positive action, but rather consoles with the faith that there will always be another life in which to get it right. Certainly the trust that one's position in life is inevitably decreed by past lives may take the urgency from personal ambition, but this does not mean that complacency or indifference to evil are acceptable.

Hinduism also has a strong code of communal action which encourages people to use their minds and bodies not only to benefit themselves, but to service others. This is the aspect of Hinduism which Aruna Paul most values, as it relates to her strong sense of duty to her family and community. 'Hinduism is a series of duties, towards your family, country, humanity. You don't look on someone as a European or an African, but as a neighbour, a person. There is no sense of superiority in Hinduism at all.'

However, while all religions are united by the common threads of fighting evil and helping others, Hinduism is in many ways fundamentally different to Christianity. The Christian ideal is one of control, it is like a square, it has very clear sides to it, it has an inside and an outside, there are straight lines, edges. It follows a certain path and people have to live within those parameters, live by the book. In contrast, Hinduism is more a system of concentric

Dr Chandra Patel, founder member of the British Holistic Medical Association

Meera Mehta, equestrian

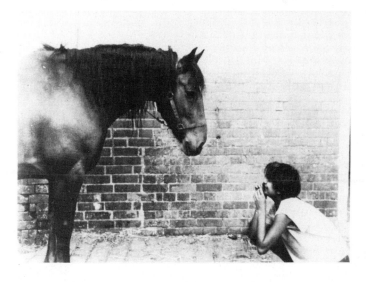

Bidge Jugnauth, presenter for Channel Four's 'Same Difference', one of the rare series by and for people with disability

Syeda Jalali (left), *dress designer*

Nahid Siddiqui, 'Kathak' dancer

Naseem Khan, author and arts critic

Najma Akhtar, Gazal singer

Sharon Lutchman, artist

Rani Sharma, radio and film producer

Lisa Aziz, TV AM newscaster

Shakuntala Devi, 'Human Computer'

Saadia Nasiri, radio journalist

Shakira Caine, former beauty queen, international business-woman

Ameera Ali, charity worker, with HRH Prince Michael of Kent

Zerbanoo Gifford in India with her mother, Kitty Irani, before leaving for England. The daughter of Khan Bahadur Mazda, Kitty was one of the last pupils of Mme Montessori, the world-famous educationist.

Zerbanoo Gifford as a young girl with her father, Bailey Irani, the founder President of the World Zoroastrian Organisation, outside the family's London hotel.

circles. You start at the centre and go on and on. The philosophy does have grey areas, there are not always clear differences between right and wrong, but there is a pattern to it, there is an on-going process which I think sheds light and dark over our lives.

The sense of overlap and of slight chaos which Hinduism evokes relates to the nature of life in India and also the natural admixture of peoples living there. For many the Hindu philosophy and the Indian mentality are mutually responsive and tolerant, they create a belief in general rules which do not need to heed particulars. This causes problems in an appreciation of Christianity, as business-woman Namita Panjabi found when she was at a missionary school with its hard-working, disciplined approach. 'As a Hindu, I couldn't accept the idea of being told what's right and what's wrong, ten commandments et al. One's soul tells you how to get your own salvation. There is much to learn and mistakes will be made, so you get more than one life, but you'll get there.'

Hinduism, although essentially one mode of spiritual journeying, has many routes to offer. Sister Jayanti was always interested in religion, but couldn't believe in the images of orthodox Hinduism or see Christ as God rather than a very beautiful human. However, she was immediately drawn to the spirituality of the Brahma Kumaris when she visited their Mount Abu centre in her teens. 'Brahma Baba's personality was very charismatic, he was a tremendously beautiful person and showed a lot of love. I had fallen in love with God through Brahma Baba and when he died in January 1969, all the devotees went to our centre, Mount Abu, there was no split or power struggle. Two women devotees naturally took over the administration.'

It was the harmony, peace and spiritual fulfilment in life which attracted Akhandadhi das to Hare Krishna. Many people feel confused by the Hare Krishna devotees' chanting and believe that they are doing little practical good for the world. It was explained to me that the Hare Krishna philosophy is not just about individual enlightenment but about helping others reach spiritual fulfilment. 'We want to help people, not just materially. You may feed them today, but tomorrow the same hunger arises. If you really want to help them, help them spiritually. That will not only help them in this lifetime but help them in future lifetimes, to go back home to God.' This reminded me of the Oxfam slogan, 'Give a man a fish and you feed him for a day. Teach him how to fish and you feed him for life.'

For Muslims, religion is also a way of life. Coming to Britain gave Yasmin Hosain a new perspective on Islam and actually strengthened her faith. 'One of the main appeals of Islam is that it is totally egalitarian. Everyone is equal from the Caliph to the beggar. We are not born with the burden of original sin from which we have to be released by religious ceremony. We are born responsible for our own actions and will be rewarded or punished on what we have done.'

There is an Islamic story which emphasises the responsibility of each individual to fight evil. God was going to destroy a village because it was so sinful, but Angel Gabriel, who was ordered to carry out this destruction, said, 'Oh Allah, there's a man in the village who prays five times a day. If we destroy the village, we'll destroy him.' And Allah said, 'You begin with his house, because what good has his worship done? He has not gone out to enjoin good or forbid evil in this society.' Just praying in your corner is not enough, if you've got some talent or ability you must give it to society.

In Islam, the worship of God is manifested by all forms of positive action. It is a Muslim's duty not only to worship God, but also to establish justice, enjoin the good, forbid the wrong and to establish peace and harmony. Worship encapsulates not just prayer, but doing good. Every aspect of doing good is worship.

Certainly the emphasis upon positive action and the ethic of anti-violence is another golden thread which runs through all religions and offers believers a way in which to view life as worship. Jyoti Munsiff is a Baha'i and to her faith is ever present. 'When people think about religion, they think about concepts apart from themselves. To me, being a Baha'i carries the same feelings as other people have when they talk about being English or Indian, what constitutes their very being. It is not a creed or dogma, but my way of life, if you were to remove my Baha'i beliefs and values, I would be an empty shell. The Baha'i faith touches on all aspects of life and so provides a reference point for me. I can see in the Baha'i faith a way for human beings to live collectively in a manner that fully endorses and fulfils that potential. It is the objective of Baha'is *everywhere* in the world to participate in the life of the country they're in. There's no segregation.'

For others, though, it has been their Christian faith which has enabled them to integrate more fully within British society. Siromi Rodrigo felt that it was easier for her to take up her job in the Guiding movement's headquarters in Britain because she was

Christian and could accept the beliefs and ways of the society. However, she was a little surprised to find that, 'at home in Sri Lanka, Christians are in the minority, but our churches are always full, but in Britain you don't see full churches except at Christmas.'

Maybe the fall in numbers of church members is not due to disbelief, but rather to a realisation that we no longer need communal worship in order to feel secure. Many people in Britain feel that they can worship God through individual prayer and action. Sister Joseann, of the Order of Missionaries of Charity founded by Mother Teresa, explained to me that she has devoted her own life to Christ and that Christianity is about offering the love of Jesus Christ to others in the form of spiritual and practical aid. 'We know Jesus suffered and the Cross is a reminder that loving people isn't always easy. Helping people in trouble is hard, but if I feel sorry for them, avoid seeing them, it's no good to them at all in their suffering. When we make efforts to pray, we meet Jesus and He gives us His love, His peace. This we can share with others. That is the greatest gift we can give to each other. We meet a lot of people who are hurt, unwanted, unloved, spiritually as well as physically sick. We cannot do anything by ourselves, unless it comes from Jesus. Jesus gives the Word of God to us to give away, give until it hurts.'

Common religious bonding often creates an understanding and acceptance of other cultures. Mother Teresa, although from Yugoslavia, is never challenged for wearing a sari because her calling from God and the beautiful life she has led makes any cultural differences insignificant. For headmistress Shirley Daniel, being an Asian Christian means that she has an affinity to both communities which helps her as a headmistress. 'It leads to the rôle of mediator, quite often people imagine I can see things from both sides and sometimes I do. I don't flaunt my Christianity in school though, it's a very private thing but I believe in fate too and that's a very Indian thing.'

When research psychologist Pireeni Sundaralingam came to Britain she missed the social contacts which Hinduism offered in Sri Lanka, but continued to worship. 'I was always quite spiritual and prayed every night. I thought all English people did that for an hour before they went to bed!' However, Pireeni began to feel that her prayers were not being answered. 'When I was 6, I got very fed up when I found out that you had to be a man to be a priest. Being told that if I was very good, in my next life I could be a man, just sowed the first seeds of disgruntlement with my religion. I stopped praying overtly at 14. At 15, I started asking questions at temple, like why couldn't I go when I was menstruating. That caused problems, my father was incredibly embarrassed and took me out. He said he accepted that it was silly, but it was tradition and I should go along with it. He believed in religion because of the tradition and culture, whereas I believe in the spiritual side. I didn't believe you had to go to temple to be religious.'

Like Pireeni, many women find the codes dictated by religions concerning menstruation difficult to accept, but they have a long tradition in other faiths. Zoroastrianism treated women fairly in all respects, as Piloo Nanavutty states, 'Apart from menstrual segregation, she was an equal partner in every way, there were women priests. It's the prejudice of men that there are no women priests now.' Piloo also explains the segregation: 'All old religions and primitive societies segregated menstruating women for those few days to protect the rest, as in that condition she attracts evil spirits and has to have a purifying bath afterwards. It was not that she was so impure, but it was felt that there was a temptation for evil spirits to come near her. We think menstruation is perfectly natural now. If women did not menstruate, they could not bear children.'

As science has progressed, we have discovered many facts to substantiate the cultural codes which religions have long since assumed. As actress Katy Mirza points out, menstrual segregation may be one such practice. 'A Parsi woman's separation from her spouse during menstruation is a custom now being validated by science. Statistics now show that Parsi women have a very low incidence of cervical cancer; one reason may be because they don't have intercourse during their period.'

'When you have your menstruation you should not touch plants or flowers. You shouldn't make pickles, neither should you touch them as your vibrations are all topsy-turvy during that time. I remember an incident where a group of school children were taken on a tour to visit the sacred caves outside Bombay. Someone disturbed the hornets' nest there and the tour guide immediately shouted that all the girls who were having their periods should run out, quickly. We were stunned because it was embarrassing, but a couple of girls ran out immediately. Those who stayed behind were stung badly, all over their bodies. Hornets and bees can sense the enigmatic vibration around the body generated by menstruation. This magnetic field surrounds the body and is the reason you shouldn't utter holy words because the current defiles all pure things.'

Cultural laws which have dictated eating habits are also now being recognised as practical measures enforced for the survival of the population. Publisher Mishti Chatterji has a range of books on 'ethnic' food and explained why the meat eaten by both Muslims and Jews is prepared in a similar way. 'Halal is very much like kosher meat, which is why it comes out looking a bit whitish, all the blood has gone. Blood is a favourable medium for bacteria to grow in, so these meats are less likely to give you food poisoning.'

Many religions see food as a symbol of earthly life and satisfaction and so set aside a time for fasting, when the spiritual side can be nurtured. Nahid Siddiqui was fasting for Ramadan when I stayed with her. 'It is a fifteen hour fast. Not even water should pass your lips. When you wash yourself before praying, you rinse your mouth, but you must be careful not to swallow. Food is available to you, but not eating it reminds you of the people who have none. You thank God for giving you the food, which is something you otherwise forget.'

Within Hindu culture, food is a means to enhance the spirit and not to detract from it, cooking expert Madhur Jaffrey told me. 'The whole of Indian vegetarian food has very little to do with taste, it is to uplift the soul. The philosophy behind it is that man goes through four stages. The first when he's studying. The second as a householder, with all the responsibilities of a house and family. Then he begins, slowly, to give it all up and distance himself. And then, if he's capable, he becomes an Ascetic and finds his soul and therefore God.

'The foods that you eat during all these stages are different; as you achieve a higher and higher stage you eat only those foods which are meant to be uplifting. It's very interesting how they are divided: red chillies are downers, green chillies are all right; ginger is marvellous, garlic and onions are not. You start early by giving them up on fast days and then you keep working your way up. So there is very definitely a whole philosophy of eating. Ultimately, the idea is to calm the passions; your insides are like a basin of water and if water is always shaking and trembling, you don't see the light – which is the soul – that is shining inside. When you let the water get calm, then you see the light clearly. The whole aim in everything you eat is to calm the body so that you can see the soul. Yoga is practised for the same reason.'

Princess Usha Devi Rathore, a professional yoga teacher, explained the significance of yoga. 'It is not what they think in the West, just

a series of physical exercises for your health. You do need a healthy
body, because that houses the soul. Yoga is a spiritual science. The
postures serve to rid physical tensions, to vitalise all the different
centres of your nervous system and your brain. The whole body
and mind has to be purified so that the spiritual energy can rise
and awaken the dormant nine-tenths of the brain which is the
super-conscious. When you awaken that, you are awakening your
own divinity within you. It's a way of recharging your batteries.
Yoga is especially relevant in this modern age because of all the
stresses and strains and the pace of modern life. Now is a critical
time in the earth's evolution. Either we all grow *en masse* spiritually
and survive, or we blow ourselves up in a holocaust and start all
over again.' The belief that humanity has reached crisis point and
must commit itself to a new age of unity and shared faith and ideals
in order to survive seems to have emerged in all parts of the world.
Even for those who do not participate in religious life, there is an
appreciation of the need for global understanding.

Indeed, to writer Rukhsana Ahmad, it is the frequent disunity
caused by organised religions which has caused her to reject it. 'I
like to think of myself as a humanitarian, who believes that human
beings have a lot in common, but most of that commonality is lost
because of various practices in society. State, religion, nationality,
provinces, everything about us tends to divide us, culture, languages, *everything*.' Jeya Wilson also echoes this same emphasis: 'If
I have a philosophy, it's a oneness with everything; I'm interested in
what makes me part of the whole oneness of humanity. That is why
I have strong feelings against racism and sexism, they're barriers to
that oneness. It immediately says, I'm brown or black and you're
not, or I'm female and you're male.'

Whatever our beliefs, it is the golden thread of humanity which
leads each of us to the 'X' which is marked in the same spot on the
treasure maps of all religions. It is a sign which promises not the gold
of this world, but the riches of the next and which prefigures the
ultimate union of all peoples in God. 'The golden age only comes
to humanity when it has, if only for a moment, forgotten gold.' In
our earthly lives we must use our ability to make the world more
beautiful, but we must also prepare ourselves for the glory of what
is to follow.

One of my favourite stories recalls how there was once a kingdom
in a far off land where every five years the people would elect a
leader. For many generations the corruption of the land meant

that despots were elected, who continued the greed, brutality and injustice among the people. At the end of their five years of rule, horror and fear came to the rulers too, as each was put onto a boat and made to cross the river to a wild jungle on the opposite shore, where a dreadful fate awaited them. Eventually a wise young woman was elected, who, unlike her predecessors, used her power to improve the conditions of her people, by educating them, providing free medical services and good housing. She even reduced the taxes! More importantly she inspired her people to cross the river with her and clear the jungle on the opposite side. When her five years were over she stepped into the boat with a smile on her face.

16

Quo Vadis?

For many Asians whose families journeyed to Britain in search of happiness and success, Britain is now their terminus and not their waiting room. The decades of Asian immigration are over and the time has come for us to work together towards the future with a positive vision. The presence of Asian women in British society has enhanced it in many ways. They have succeeded in commerce, public life and culture; indeed every walk of British life has the imprint of Asian influence. They have offered their hard work, skills and intelligence and, not least of all, their children.

As Kusoom Vadgama believes, the time has come to recognise the history of injustice and to place it in our memories and to use our minds for a creative future. 'We should find areas where we can function efficiently, impressively and show people the positive side of our lives. Much of the hope lies in our children, they are growing up alongside other cultures and the relationship that they will develop is something we have to look forward to. It will be of a much more harmonious variety. They will have a much better understanding of each other. There is already an interaction between the two communities. Our achievements and their understanding will make the British regret the pockets of discrimination that they have held against us.'

Our children are the golden thread which ties us to the future; through their lives we are kept alive and can continue to grow. As parents we have a responsibility to give our children a sense of belonging, but we must also give them a sense of possibility and of adventure. For many Asian families their children are their link with British life and while the parents can teach the children about their ancestry and traditions, they can also learn from them about another's. An honest and unbiased knowledge of each others' histories and cultures can only aid mutual understanding and respect.

Education, which brought so many Asians to this country, can now help to make them feel more at home here. Publisher Mishti Chatterji sees children as catalysts for adult learning. 'The educational emphasis now is on having books in two languages, side by side. Children find that they can learn by reading from one to the other and parents who are also learning English can feel involved in their children's education.'

The thread between two cultures which is being woven by the new generation should not be broken by the fear of cultural contamination. Certainly change is inevitable within any society, but we can feel sure that Indian culture which has developed over thousands of years will not disappear overnight. Jyoti Munsiff feels that true integration is a two-way process, 'It's like being a stranger in someone else's house, you have to see what it is you can do for the people already there. As Asians, we have a lot that is beautiful in our culture, from the mundane, like our food, to the philosophical, our centuries of thought and spirituality. We can so easily offer it generously to the people here, but must never push it down their throats, insisting that they take it. If there really is something worthwhile, it will become evident.'

This assimilation is a constant process, as Madhur Jaffrey pointed out to me, 'Think of potatoes, they came from the "New World" and now the English probably think they invented them!' Evolution will take its time, but the flavours of other cultures will naturally be absorbed as history has shown.

The important task of establishing a balance between cultures and societies is a difficult one. For young Asian women growing up in Britain there is the temptation to become an artificial rose, offering the two faces of desired beauty to the two cultures, but growing roots in neither. For others there is the temptation to be the silver paper rose, which takes the superficial gloss of both cultures, but has no possibility for growth.

Many Asians feel that the balance has often not been achieved and that the worst of both societies has been grafted on to each other to create a 'Bangra' culture. Law student Sharmishta Chakrabarti feels disappointed with the lost opportunities of her generation. 'Our parents came over, worked really hard and no one could expect them to do much more. But my generation seem not only to have opted out of political and social responsibility, but to have taken on the worst aspects of both cultures, the small-mindedness and the racism. The boys are proudly chauvinistic; sexism is almost greater in my younger brother's generation than it is in my father's. Added to this is the drinking, the drugs, the gang violence from the West. Of course, at the end of the day, they still want to marry a virgin of their own caste. But before marriage, they want to live the life of a Western pre-AIDS playboy!'

Kristine Landon-Smith, theatre producer and actress, believes that life is now seen more as a straight road to success than a journey of experience. 'At my brother's college the whole point of a degree is what you are going to do with it afterwards. They plan their whole lives in order to make money.'

Much of the responsibility for this attitude may lie with the British ethic of individualism and the new emphasis upon competition. Nevertheless, the destructive and aggressive attitudes are also induced by the junk food and the garbage of the media. The additives pumped into food make children hyperactive and the negative images projected by the TV screen make them passive and apathetic. In many respects society offers them no true sustenance. However, the Asian community must also look to its own example which is sometimes equally negative. We should be showing our children the achievements of the past and, by giving them a model for inspiration, we can hold up a new mirror of involvement and improvement which they will fulfil.

Indeed, now that the positive reflections have begun to emerge, the new generation is using the lessons of social and cultural negatives to create pictures of substance and permanence. Many Asians living in Britain who have the access to two cultures are now selecting the best of both in order to create new possibilities. This is a natural process of evolution which has always existed, as Belkis Beghani explained, 'When the Normans came to England, there was an Anglo-Saxon world and a Norman world, but that disappeared quite quickly and became England. The unique cultural form in modern Britain won't be "part British, part Asian" either, it'll be something new. There isn't even a word for it yet, but it'll come.'

Nevertheless, there are fundamental differences today in comparison to the past when peoples came to conquer and to pillage. The Asian people came to Britain to live in peace and to offer their own ways alongside their host's. This time we might choose not to have a label, as we know that names can be limiting and that the nature of something which is constantly growing and creating cannot be conveyed by a title. The children of mixed marriages are no longer called 'half' anything, they are no longer divided. They do not need to belong to 'one or the other' because the two are naturally merging. It is up to us to find the similarities within them and not force people to make false choices.

Naseem Khan, the arts critic, feels that her mixed heritage has given her a double possibility. 'I tend to reject the "half" nature of things because I never feel half-hearted about anything I do. A long time ago, when I was starting as a journalist, my father asked why I didn't make up an English pen name, "You could pass as white." I was shocked at the suggestion of giving up part of myself. "Only testing," said my father when I stopped shouting. I tend to see myself as having two parallel existences: the image is of a circus rider being carried around the ring with one foot on each horse.'

It is the skill and self-assurance of the new generation which makes them sure of their success. With their new understanding and acceptance of Western society and their ability to learn from it, they can offer their own contributions with confidence. Author Farrukh Dhondy sees this as an important development. 'You are now getting a new generation who are concentrating on their skills as professionals. They are not going to say, "Give me a job because there aren't enough blacks in your profession." They are going to say, "Give me a job because I can do this." It is a much better approach.'

As Asians we might all have the same roots, but where we are travelling to is as important as where we came from. The journey to a different land has made the path through life less clear for some who found the culture difficult to adjust to, but more defined for others who knew the goals they had travelled to fulfil. The meeting of societies and traditions has placed our children at a crossroads with many paths to choose from, but only one way forward. Some have been distracted by the bright lights and tinsel of both cultures; others by the beacon of individual success, but the wisest have seen the attraction of the rainbow in which all colours exist as a harmony and all rays lead to a single purpose.

In creating a rainbow generation and becoming a rainbow nation we are fulfilling God's promise and realising the meaning of the sign that was sent to show that the world was not forsaken. Now that our planet is dying, we have begun to understand that we do share the same world, that our actions affect each other and that we cannot isolate ourselves if we wish to survive. When Mahatma Gandhi said, 'I want to keep the window of my house open, so that the wind flows freely between my home and the world outside,' he was impressing upon us that alienation is negative, but also that the elements of the planet are shared by all and that must never be forgotten.

There is a parable which also teaches us this failing, it tells of two men, one who was lame and another who was blind. On their own neither could achieve anything, but by co-operating the lame man could climb on the back of the blind man and together they could see where they wanted to go and actually get there. The lesson of combined strength is one which we must learn in order to achieve global unity and prevent our world from suffering further injury.

National traditions and cultures are important, but if we let the past dictate our lives too rigidly then we might destroy the very future which we were preserving it for. To concentrate one's energies on the faults of the past is to weaken the urgency with which we need to respond to our future. As women and Asians, we should remember the injustices which have been enacted against us, but use the knowledge to stop history repeating itself. A global person is one who recognises all the signs of history and knows that many things are going wrong in the present, but is not bound by the problems.

We are living through a time of great change and great consequence. Politically, culturally and ecologically the globe is changing its face. As all the mystics and gurus have predicted, we are experiencing the transition between the old age and the new age; a crisis period which will either offer a new golden age or destruction. There is a dual energy at work which reflects these possibilities. On the one hand, there is a realisation that while some traditions are not enabling us to go forward, certain forms of ancient wisdom can be used to shape a better future. We have to share the world's knowledge to discover what is ultimately important, then share the world's resources to implement those beliefs. On the other hand there is a rise in fundamentalism, a rejection of this balance and unity. Such extremism is produced by a craving for security and love, a spiritual hollow which has been created by the extremes of the technological age in which human emotions are given less significance than material objects.

It is only now that we are aware of what has already been sacrificed in terms of social and ecological harmony that we are beginning to mourn its passing. However, so often simply lamenting the loss and retelling the glory of the golden age is not enough. Meera Syal, actress and author, has written a bewitching short story which tells of a land where women became so confined by their situation that they forgot that they were free and had the ability to fly. In her tale some women regain the confidence and the spirit to challenge the restrictive codes of society and begin to fly again. Nevertheless, as they are only a minority they are shunned by the others and are left with no sense of purpose. 'You massaged my wings into being but you left me no map to your land. You filled my head with dreams of soaring free, but you left me living here among the wingless ones.' Women have often been most vulnerable to oppression, but the tale offers a lesson for all.

To ensure that our world does not lose its possibility for transcendence and for meaningful life we must realise that we all share the same land and that the map which we follow is a world map. We must also remember that the purpose of flight is to convey inspiration and ideals to others. As yet few have used their wings.

In many ways humanity only discovers what is of real value when it is lost. It is only when there is no democracy that we can see its importance; only when family life breaks up that we realise its worth; only after we have neglected our culture that we feel the sense of loss; and only when we have raped our planet that we regret our actions.

There is a poem by the poetess Zehra Nigar which expresses this. In simple terms, the poem tells of a tree which appeared to be dead, it did not change with the seasons or produce leaves or fruit. The birds who had nested in this tree had flown away, but when the tree finally fell, the birds felt their own hearts give way. Only then did they realise that the old knarled roots of the tree had grown from their own hearts.

However much we want to ignore our own roots and however long we neglect them, ultimately we have to acknowledge that they are in the earth. There is a moment of reckoning when you find that you cannot run away from yourself, from your past or from your world. The birds flew away because they thought that the old tree was holding them back and they wanted freedom. It is right that the birds should be free to fly, but it was only when the tree died that they realised how important it was to their lives. Like the roots of their tree, the roots which each nation and each culture have put in the ground have grown deep into the soil, but more importantly they have reached across the land, intertwining in order to give strength to the earth.

If we are to avoid destruction and create a golden age then we too must find the golden threads which tie us each together and twist them into a chord strong enough to tie us to our natural mother, the earth. Our Eden is neither to the East nor to the West, it is before us. Only if we nurture our garden – and treasure it – can we keep the trees of knowledge and of life alive.

Short Backgrounds

Safira Afzal was born in Lahore, Punjab, the eldest of two daughters and came to Britain at the age of 5 to join her engineer father. She left a major law company to become a model and actress. Safira has since appeared in TV commercials, films, including being a Bond girl in *Octopussy* and represented India in the 'Most Beautiful Girl in the World' American pageant. She lives in London with her Australian boy-friend when she is not travelling the world on assignments. In the future, Safira intends to start her own business, importing and exporting the textiles of India and the Far East.

Rukhsana Ahmad was born in Pakistan in 1948, one of four daughters of an engineer father who had served in the British Army. After lecturing in English Literature at Karachi University, she married a dentist living in Britain. Rukhsana is a long-standing member of the Asian Women Writers' Workshop and has contributed to their first anthology of short stories and poems, *Right of Way*, as well as being commissioned to write plays for the BBC, Tara Arts Group and The Monstrous Regiment and editing anthologies. She has three children and lives in London.

Nasim Ahmed was publicity director for Muhammad Ali Jinnah, the founder and first Prime Minister of Pakistan, in the 1946 elections. When a journalist, he was the London and American correspondent for papers in Pakistan and throughout the Middle East. Nasim was the first non-white Chairman of the Commonwealth Correspondents Association (1953) and the first non-European President of the London Foreign Press Association (1962). Returning to Pakistan, he became Prime Minister Ali Bhutto's Secretary of Information and Chairman of Pakistan TV and subsequently Ambassador to Denmark until 1978, when General Zia's regime forced Nasim into exile. Nasim is now Prime Minister Benazir Bhutto's Ambassador to the UN in New York. He is married to Tina and they have one daughter.

Akhandadhi das was brought up as a church-going Presbyterian in Northern Ireland. While at Bristol University studying architecture he started wondering what was the aim of designing beautiful buildings if the people inside were crying. In 1975 he visited the Hare Krishna temple at Bhaktivedanta Manor, just outside London, and was initiated into the religion, receiving his new name. Akhandadhi das is now principal of the Manor, managing, teaching and counselling. Much of his time is spent defending the temple against those who wish to see it closed. Akhandadhi das is a member of the Central Religious Advisory Committee, advising the BBC and Independent Television on religious issues. Married to an American-born devotee, Ratnavati devi, they have a daughter, Sairandhri.

Najma Akhtar is the second of three children born to Muslim parents from central India who both came to study in Britain in the early 1950s. They founded a printing business which became the biggest Asian press in London, printing Indian film posters for cinemas as far away as New York. Najma first heard the singing of Gazals while studying for her post-graduate degree. She decided to take it up herself, and after six months of practising two songs, she won a singing competition and went to India to record an album. Now produced by two Englishmen, her biggest sales are in Japan. She has sung at the WOMAD festival, Ronnie Scott's jazz club and supported singer Nina Simone at her concert in London.

Ameera Alli was born in British Guiana, South America. Her grand-father, Mohammed Ali, was the Mulvi of its capital, Georgetown, and her father, Mohammed Inshanally, was one of the country's captains of industry. After the death of her parents, Ameera went to school in Brooklyn, New York and has never returned to what is now Guyana. She is the former Chair of the Women's India Association UK, the oldest Indian women's organisation in Britain, and her involvement with numerous charities ensured that she was recognised by the Queen at a party at the British Embassy in Bejing, China. She is married to Akbar Alli, a retired Inland Revenue officer. They have one daughter.

Arif Ali was born in British Guiana in 1935, a century after members of his family had first settled in the country. One of seven children, he came to Britain in 1957 and, after a variety of work experiences, he started publishing the monthly *Westindian Digest* in 1971. Arif founded Hansib Publishing Ltd two years later and today it is Britain's largest Third World-orientated publishing house, responsible for the weeklies *Asian Times* and *Caribbean Times*, as well as numerous books, including *Third World Impact*, the only comprehensive work of reference on Britain's visible minority communities, published biannually. Arif is currently working on his most ambitious project to date, *1992 – Five Hundred Years After Columbus*. He has five children and three grandchildren.

Jinder Aujla's family went to Kenya from the Punjab and subsequently prospered. She came to Britain to study for her A levels and afterwards had an arranged marriage to a Sikh accountant. When her two sons started school, she looked for work with flexible hours. After writing to a black woman insurance broker featured in the *Daily Mail*, she embarked on a career in insurance herself. Now an executive life underwriter with Abbey Life, she was picked as their Woman of the Year in 1988 and is a member of the Million Dollar Round Table representing the top 2% of world insurance salespeople. Through her work, she met an Asian Conservative candidate and joined the party in Margaret Thatcher's constituency, becoming a ward secretary.

Rita Austin was born in Calcutta in 1940, the only daughter of a Bengali father who rose to become India's Attorney General and a Gujarati mother who gained a Ph.D. in America. Rita's paternal grandfather was orphaned at 10, raised himself and his younger brothers and became Principal of Presidency College, Calcutta. The British awarded him one of the first honorific titles given to Indians. His three sons were sent to England to complete their educations and Rita's father studied at Cambridge in the 1930s under a tutor who was long suspected to be the 'Fourth Man' in the Philby, Burgess and Maclean affair. Rita's parents met when, finding it very difficult to get work as a barrister, her father taught at Loreto Girls' School and fell in love with his brightest pupil. He was one of the group of radical Bengali lawyers in the struggle for Indian Independence. Rita used to follow him, holding the paint, while he wrote 'QUIT INDIA' on every available surface. In 1947 Rita's mother, who had been a broadcaster on All India Radio throughout the war, introduced Nehru's 'Tryst with destiny' speech at the Independence ceremony. Rita was sent to Loreto School in Calcutta and was prepared for her first communion by Mother Teresa. Later, she went to a Loreto school in St Albans, England, for her A levels, before going on to Oxford University. Leaving Oxford after a year, Rita met her English husband while staying with a college friend. The couple moved to Swansea where both studied for a diploma, Rita going on to gain a degree at Birmingham and her Ph.D. at Cardiff. Having joined the Labour Party in 1963, she stood for Parliament in St Albans in 1983. She now lives in Cardiff and was a county councillor and Chair of the Finance Committee before internal Labour Party politics led to her deselection. Rita works for the Community Relations Council in Cardiff. She has two children.

Lisa Aziz's father, Suhail, came from Bangladesh and was a Royal Naval College-trained Officer of the Pakistan Navy. Her mother comes from Dartmouth, Devon and Lisa was born in Totnes, the eldest of two girls. After graduating from Goldsmith's college, Lisa joined Radio City in Liverpool. Eager to work in television, she wrote over 100 letters before landing a job with BBC TV West. After being 'poached' by HTV, an independent TV company, Lisa was talent spotted by TV-AM and now works with the independent breakfast television company as their main newscaster.

Aban Bana's family still runs the Bana Eau de Cologne firm established by her great-grandfather in 1876, the first in India. Her maternal grandfather combined a career as a doctor with being an actor, author and director of the famous Parsi Gujarati plays. Aban went to Vienna with her sister to study architecture, but on a trip to Switzerland, both were attracted by the educational ideas of Rudolf Steiner. Aban became a Steiner teacher while her sister became the first Eurythmist from India. At the end of her studies, Aban was invited to be a co-founder of the Steiner School in North London. She intends to return to India, to start her own Steiner school there, when the children she will have taught for all of their eight years at the school leave.

Devika Bannerjee came to Paris in 1979, aged 25, complete with twenty kilos of luggage, five words of French and 'a head full of ideas.' Educated at Loreto, Calcutta, she worked for the Indian

Embassy and helped stage Munni Kabir's Indian film festivals in Paris. When I met her, she had been in Britain for only ten days, but feels she is in Britain to stay.

Belkis Beghani came to the UK in 1971 from Uganda, where her family were established Muslims originally from Gujarat. Belkis, a television writer and media reporter, started her journalistic career with *Broadcast*, the television industry's trade magazine. She has freelanced as a writer and researcher and has worked as a TV critic for *Time Out* and *Today* newspaper. Belkis was show-biz reporter for the *Daily Mail* before becoming entertainments editor for the short-lived left-wing national newspaper, *News on Sunday*. She wrote a documentary programme for Channel Four TV, *Second Home*, which looked at Ugandan Asians settled in Britain ten years after their arrival. At the moment, she is working as a researcher for Channel Four's quiz show, *Fifteen to One*. Belkis is married to Samir Shah and they have one son, Cimran.

Suman Bhargava runs the Suman Marriage Bureau, started in 1972 as a free service. It sprang to fame in 1975 when a marriage was arranged between a Sikh woman and an Englishman. There are now about 1,000 people on its books, each paying £115 or £230 if a marriage results. Suman jokingly feels herself to be the 'thick one' of her parents' five children, having only an MA! Her husband Ramesh is the chair of the local Anglo-Asian Conservative society. The couple have two children, Parag and Purva, and live in Hanwell, West London.

Sudha Bhuchar was born in Tanzania. Her father was a teacher from the Punjab and the family 'spent much of our time crossing the Indian Ocean', moving back and forth to India before settling in Britain in the early 1970s, when Sudha was 11 years old. Her father found getting a teaching job impossible and becoming extremely depressed, he died after only eighteen months in Britain. At 16, Sudha saw a production by Tara Arts Group, then an amateur company, and was afterwards invited by the cast to come to a rehearsal. Initially shy about appearing on stage, she went along to help with artwork. Sudha's first acting rôle with Tara came three years later and she joined the now professional company after receiving her degree. In addition to her work with Tara, her rôles include the female lead in *Romeo and Juliet* at the Manchester

Contact Theatre. When she saw an advertisement asking for a presenter for BBC TV's *Network East*, Sudha applied and, much to her surprise, got the job. She is now the co-founder of the Tamasha Theatre Company with Kristine Landon-Smith.

Pushpa Bijlani won three beauty contests in India before coming to London in 1960 to study fashion design. She met her Sindhi husband when he was a navigator with Air India and turned down the chance to model for *Vogue* in order to raise a family. Their four daughters were all born in Bombay before they moved to Hong Kong and finally settled in Britain. Always encouraged to succeed, her daughters are now studying medicine, dentistry and engineering. The eldest, Natasha, is a doctor and edited the *St Bartholomew's Hospital Journal*, interviewing Princess Anne and the Duke of Gloucester among many others, during her medical training at 'Bart's'.

Rosinha 'Rose' Barreto is of Goan Catholic origin. Her father had worked as a senior cutter in Malawi before starting his own clothing business and her mother's father was a gents' tailor. Her parents met on a boat from Africa, both returning to Goa to find a spouse, and decided to marry each other. Rose, the third of five children, was one of very few non-whites at her convent school, only admitted because of her religion. She came to Britain from Malawi in 1970 to study textile design in Manchester, before moving to London, where she found that secretaries were more highly valued than designers. Rose met her husband, Narendhra Morar, when she shared a flat with one of his cousins in London.

Shakira Caine's Kashmiri great-great-grandfather took the first boat going to South America and landed in Guyana. At 5, Shakira's father died and she helped raise her three younger brothers. Surviving a terrorist bomb while working in the American Embassy, Shakira went on to win the 'Miss Guyana' beauty contest and finished third at the 'Miss World' finals in London. Actor Michael Caine spotted her in a coffee commercial; prepared to travel the world to meet her, he was told that she was living above a chemist's shop in London's Fulham Road. They have now been married for seventeen years and have a daughter, Natasha. The couple appeared in one film together, *The Man Who Would Be King*, where Shakira's character married Michael's co-star, Sean Connery. Shakira divides her time between

London and the USA, running her own international jewellery and fashion business.

Sharmishta Chakrabarti's parents are Bengalis from Calcutta who came to Britain in the 1960s. The eldest of two children, Sharmishta read Marx when she was 12 and joined the Social Democrat Party at 16. She produced the party's youth recruitment video and campaign material and served on the party's policy making body. Sharmishta is currently studying law at the London School of Economics.

Mishti Chatterji was born in Mandalay, Burma, the only daughter and youngest child of a Bengali doctor who had moved to Burma before the Second World War and served in the British Army. Mishti was educated in Burma, India and Britain before the family settled in Britain when she was 14, due to the political situation in Burma. After taking a business studies course, she became a barrister in 1973. During her Bar Final examinations she married a Bengali doctor. She worked for the Department of Health before taking a career break to be with their son, Arjun. Instead of resuming her legal work, Mishti started Mantra Publishing in 1985 with her sister-in-law, Sanjeevini, a well known Odissi dancer, producing children's books about Indian culture in Britain. In 1989, they launched MultiLink to support multi-cultural teaching in schools.

Maria Couto comes from Goa, on the west coast of India. Colonised by the Portuguese 100 years before the British arrived in India, a large percentage of the population is Catholic and Maria's family is no exception. The eldest of five daughters and two sons, Maria is recognised as an authority on the works of Graham Greene and her book, *Graham Greene: On the Frontier. Politics and Religion in the Novels*, was published in 1988. She lectured at Delhi University in English Literature and now lives in London with her husband, the Director of the Commonwealth Secretariat's Industrial Development Unit. Maria reviews books for the *Times Literary Supplement* and several Indian papers. They have three children.

Dr David Dabydeen was born in Guyana and went to university at Cambridge. He now lectures at the Department of Caribbean Studies at the University of Warwick. David's poetry includes the collection *Slave Song*, for which he won the 1984 Commonwealth Poetry Prize. He has also written and edited critical works, including *India in* *the Caribbean* and *The Black Presence in English Literature*. David appears regularly on television and lectures throughout the world.

Shirley Daniel is the first of three children born in Madras to a Christian family. Her father was a professional musician while her mother joined the Royal Navy during the Second World War, coming to Britain to earn enough money to ensure that her children didn't become musicians too! Shirley married a fellow student in India after her first year of teaching. When their daughter died after her first birthday, they moved to Scotland in 1965 to join Shirley's mother who had by then remarried a Scot. When Shirley's marriage ended in divorce, she returned to India with her son, but was unable to get a job there because of the associated stigma of being divorced. Called back to teach in London, overcoming the prejudice of her then Head, who thought Asians were only good as supply teachers, Shirley became second-in-charge of the science department and then moved schools with a series of promotions. She is now the only Asian woman to head a large comprehensive co-educational secondary school in Britain.

Geeta Dave was born in Baroda, India, the fifth of six children of a Patel family. Her father was Deputy Superintendent of Police. In 1973, Geeta married Bhupendra Dave, a Brahmin Gujarati from Tanzania, who was in Vidyanagar, Gujarat, studying engineering. His parents were by then settled in the UK and Geeta and Bhupendra joined them in Leicester after their marriage. They now run a newsagents shop in Harrow-on-the-Hill, Middlesex, and have two children. Although the business is an almost full-time occupation, Geeta's hobbies include singing and *Garbas*, Gujarati folk dancing.

Shakuntala Devi is in the *Guinness Book of Records* as the world's finest 'human computer', able to multiply two 13-digit numbers in her head in only twenty-eight seconds. Her father was a twice-widowed circus performer of 59 when he married her mother, then 14 years old. When Shakuntala's mathematical talents became evident at the age of 3, she was taken round South India performing in schools, becoming the breadwinner for the family. At 13 she went alone to Bombay where a show for the India Steam Navigation Company gained her a free ticket to Britain. Having lived in Britain since around 1950, Shakuntala has travelled the world, giving maths shows in 137 countries. She is also the author of fourteen books, including three on astrology. Shakuntala is divorced with a daughter.

Sheena Dewan was born in England. Her father, Ramesh, comes from a diplomatic family in Pathan, north west India, and now runs his own publishing house and property development company in London. Sheena's mother, Zelina, was born in Trinidad to a family originally from Utter Pradesh in India. Having achieved ten GCSEs in 1989, Sheena is staying at the North London Collegiate School to do her A levels and hopes to read Politics, Philosophy and Economics at Oxford.

Farrukh Dhondy is a Zoroastrian born in Poona, where he studied for his first degree in Physics and Maths. He came to Cambridge in 1964 as a Tata Scholar for his BA and later received his MA in English and American Literature from Leicester University. Farrukh started a career in journalism for newspapers in Britain and India while at Cambridge and wrote four of his five books during his eleven years as a teacher in London. These include *East End At Your Feet* and *Come to Mecca*, both winners of the Other Award. Farrukh is the author of many plays and television series, including *Tandoori Nights*, about the rivalry between two neighbouring Indian restaurants and *The King of the Ghetto*, about Bangladeshis in East London. He is now a commissioning editor at Channel Four Television in London.

Lally and Robin Dutt's parents came to London separately to complete their studies and met while working at the Indian High Commission, marrying in 1958. Their father comes from one of India's most remarkable families. His grandfather, Manmohan Ghose, was an eminent member of the Bramho Samaj movement, an offshoot of Hinduism and Christianity, along with his brother Aurobindo, the renowned philosopher. Manmohan went to Oxford after being educated at St Paul's and was a friend of W. B. Yeats and Oscar Wilde. Both brothers returned to India with their younger brother Barindra, where all were jailed as a result of their opposition to British occupation, Barindra saved from being hanged only by his British citizenship. Robin and Lally's mother is a Christian and a member of the Syrian Orthodox Church. Tradition states that St Thomas was shipwrecked on the southern tip of India and started a branch of the church there which still survives today. Lally, having completed an English degree at the University of London, now works for a Chelsea-based design company, while Robin is a journalist specialising in Art and Fashion and works for the BBC magazine, *The Clothes Show*.

Sadhana Ghose's Bengali grandfather came to Britain in 1911 to study law. When he returned to India, he found his Coonager royal family had mistreated his wife and so severed contact with them, moving from Bengal to Central Province. Sadhana's father became a general in the Indian Army, while Sadhana was selected as 'Best Cadet' in the Indian Cadet Corps and was commissioned into the army during the Indo-Pakistan conflict in 1965. During the next ten years Sadhana worked as an editor, advertising executive, lecturer, researcher and project officer on an information campaign to 24,000 villages, before coming to Britain almost accidentally. On her way to start a Ph.D. in America, she met a professor from the University of Kent who suggested that she come to study at Canterbury instead. Sadhana has been the National Organiser of the Black Media Workers Association and teaches part-time at Willesden College and the United States International University in addition to her work as investigative journalist and agony aunt.

Gurbans Kaur Gill's father was a Sikh officer in the British army in India. He had to leave Gurbans and her three younger sisters at the time of Partition and was thought to be dead for a time. However, the desire for a son brought him safely home to the Punjab and a son and two more daughters were duly born. He resigned while a major to look after his family, feeling his daughters' education to be of the highest priority. Gurbans left teacher-training college at 20 and had a love marriage at 21 to a fellow student. The couple followed a group of friends to Britain, where initially life was very hard. Now a wealthy businesswoman, Justice of the Peace and elected as an SDP councillor to both her district and county councils, she is the owner of a white Rolls Royce with the number plate 'SDP 1' and the proud mother of two daughters, Rippy and Reenu.

Frene Ginwala's Parsi grandparents came to South Africa as traders and prospered, owning the largest cotton gins in the southern hemisphere. While on a trip to India during the Second World War, a ship going to South Africa was torpedoed, one of Frene's relatives was killed, while others spent days on rafts in the Indian Ocean. In consequence, her family decided to stay in India for the duration of the war and sent Frene to a Catholic convent school in Bombay. Frene came to Britain, straight from India, to finish off her university entrance exams. After passing, she went to Canada, aged 14, for the first year of a degree in chemical engineering, which she finished at Columbia University in New York. Allergic to some chemicals, and aware that she wouldn't be able to work as a chemical engineer in South Africa, Frene studied law in Britain. After qualifying, she returned to South Africa and joined the African National Congress. Expecting to have her passport confiscated by the authorities there for her active opposition to apartheid, Frene first travelled around East Africa and gained valuable insight into countries there, later using it to smuggle ANC President Oliver Tambo to safety. With a break to edit Tanzania's national newspaper, she later received her Ph.D. from Oxford and now works in the ANC President's Office in London. Frene represents the ANC at international meetings with heads of state and UN representatives as well as being one of their television spokespersons.

Sir Jayvant Sinhji Gohel CBE is a barrister and banker. He first came to Britain in 1933 to finish his schooling and study law and he spent twenty-two months in English nursing homes after falling ill. Back in India, 'Jay' was a minister in one of the country's Princely states before Independence and subsequently worked for the national government for twelve years. He returned to settle in Britain in 1960. A long-standing member of the Conservative Party, Jay was National Chairman of their Anglo-Asian Association for three years. He was knighted in 1989.

Sneh Gupta was born in Kenya, one of five children. Her father was a teacher and wherever he taught, Sneh went to that school. Not wishing to get engaged, she left home aged 17 and went to Germany, spending a year learning 'German and total independence'. When her parents moved to Britain, Sneh rejoined them for a while before leaving once more to study nursing. On a night off, she entered the 'Miss Anglia TV' contest and was awarded the title when the first winner declined the necessary year working for the company. Sneh was a hostess on the TV programme *Sale of the Century*, where she gained her Equity card as an actress and went on to work on *The Far Pavilions* as Princess Sushila and the TV series *Angels*. She has now started her own television production company and was chosen to present the BBC's Hindi and Urdu television language course.

Shama Habibullah is the daughter of author Attia Hosain. She came to Britain from Lucknow in 1947, aged 6, and was educated at Cheltenham Ladies' College and Cambridge. Shama joined the Campaign Against Racial Discrimination in the early 1960s and worked on their newspaper. Her film career began with the Shell Film Unit, first as a researcher then as an assistant director and editor. Shama has also worked for the Indian Space Research Organisation on the satellite TV programme for development, as well as in the USA, Nepal and Oman, while her work in advertising in India won her an Award for Excellence. Her work on feature films in India has included *Gandhi*, *A Passage to India*, *Heat and Dust* and *Octopussy*. Shama runs Intermedia, a consultancy and production company, and divides her time between London and Bombay.

Kim Hollis' father was a Sikh from Amritsar who came to agricultural college in Cirencester in the 1930s. He met 'a nice country lass' at a college dance and the couple married after two months. After Kim was born in 1957, the family went to Calcutta for five years, her mother's first time out of Gloucestershire. Kim's parents divorced when she was 11 and she was sent to Cheltenham Ladies' College. After university, Kim was called to the Bar wearing a borrowed black sari and became the Head of her Chambers on Christmas Day, 1988, at the young age of 31. Kim is married to a property developer, Andrew. The couple have just had their first child, a boy.

Roshan Horabin was born in Bombay, the second child of four. Her Muslim parents were very pro-British and both her father and uncle were educated at Oxford. Newly-married, Roshan came to Britain in 1946 with her English husband, Ivan, the son of the Liberal Chief Whip in the House of Commons. Later, Roshan raised their three daughters and studied for a sociology degree by night. In 1954, she joined Howard League for Penal Reform and in 1960 became a voluntary associate for the New Bridge, befriending prisoners and visiting them in prison. Roshan became the first Asian woman probation officer in Britain in 1967. In 1976, she got a Cropwood Fellowship at Cambridge to study the special problems of Asian prisoners. Her work led to the Home Office inviting her to lecture at a variety of organisations related to penal reform and happily, some of her recommendations have now been implemented.

Attia Hosain was born in Lucknow in 1913, part of a privileged feudal landowning family which traces itself back to 'a mystic and saint' who came from Erzu, now in Turkey, in the twelfth century. Attia's father studied at Cambridge, one of the first Asians there, and at the Middle Temple where, in the course of studying law, he became friends with many of the other Indians there who were involved in the movement for Indian Independence. Attia grew up meeting them all. After being the first woman from amongst the Taluqdari families to obtain a degree, she came to Britain with her husband, Ali Bahadur Habibullah, when he was posted to the Indian High Commission before Independence. In 1947 Attia presented early women's programmes in Urdu for the BBC World Service and acted in their radio plays, including Desdemona in an Urdu translation of *Othello*. She is probably best known in Britain as the author of *Phoenix Fled* and *Sunlight on a Broken Column*. As an actress, Attia has appeared on the West End stage and on television. Her two children, Shama Habibullah and Waris Hussein, are both film directors. Attia, now widowed, lives in Chelsea.

Yasmin Hosain was born in 1936 in Abbottabad, in the North-West Province of India. Her father was a judge who retired in 1947 to start his own legal practice and one of her three brothers is now Pakistan's Foreign Secretary. Yasmin was perhaps the first Pathan woman to study abroad for a degree, following two of her brothers to Cambridge. On her return to Pakistan, she married Shahid, taught English Literature for twenty-five years and started a school for mentally handicapped children. Shahid became head of Pakistan's Film Development Corporation, but films he financed included *The Blood of Hussain*, directed by Jamil Dehlavi, which was seen as a piece of anti-army propaganda by General Zia. The film lead to Shahid's dismissal and voluntary exile and the couple arrived in Britain in 1979 with their two children plus four suitcases. Not wishing to start a restaurant, they instead opened a bookshop dealing in rare books and prints about the subcontinent and the Middle East. For the past six years Yasmin has also presented a weekly programme for the BBC World Service, while her husband returned to Pakistan after Zia's death and is now head of Pakistan's tourism bureau. Yasmin's ambition is to translate some of the classic British poets into Urdu.

Waris Hussein, the son of Attia Hosain, was 8 when the family came to Britain. Sent to a 'suffering all down the line' post-war English boarding school, Clifton College, he graduated from Cambridge and attended the Slade School of Art before joining the BBC as a television director. After directing episodes of a 'soap', *Compact*, he helped create *Dr Who* and directed the very first episode in 1963. He then moved on to major dramas, including *A Passage to India* in 1965, *Edward and Mrs Simpson*, *The Glittering Prizes* and the cinema version of *Henry VIII and his Six Wives*. Waris now works mostly in Hollywood although he has a home in London.

Saroja 'Saro' Hutton was the second of four children born to a Tamil property-owning family in Malaysia. Unable to train as a teacher in Malaysia, Saro saw an advertisement asking for people to become nurses in Britain and came with a group of friends. She met her English husband, Ron, a biochemist, at a hospital dance. The couple live in Bushey, Hertfordshire with their two children. Saro works as a nurse in a hospital nearby.

Gulshan Jaffer was born into an Ismaili family in Madagascar but grew up and was educated in Kenya, where she met her husband, Firoz, a partner in a chartered accountancy practice. They had two sons before he was asked to open an office in London and the couple entered the property and hotel business in Britain and America. In 1987, Firoz suddenly died after a heart attack, leaving Gulshan and the boys almost penniless, with the estate challenged by the in-laws. Within a year, she had renovated and opened a Four Crown Hotel in the heart of London with her bank's support. Today, she runs her own group of hotels and properties in Central London.

Madhur Jaffrey first came to Britain in the late 1950s as a drama student. Probably most famous in Britain as a cookery writer – the book of her TV series on Indian cookery has sold over 500,000 copies – Madhur is also a children's author and brought the celebrated film partnership of Merchant and Ivory together. She would like to be remembered as an actress, having appeared in many television plays and films in India and the West. Madhur lives in the USA with her second husband, an American, and three daughters from her first marriage to actor Sayeed Jaffrey.

Syeda Jalali's maternal grandfather worked for Scotland Yard, as a linguist helping with dialects. Her paternal grandfather once planned to run away with the English governess of his younger brothers and sisters, but instead fell in love with a Hindu Brahmin woman. After her conversion to Islam, they married and the couple went to the newly created Pakistan. As she was unable to have his children, he obtained her permission to marry a second wife who later died giving birth to their seventh child. Syeda's father, their third child, became famous for publishing a children's magazine at the age of 15 and was introduced to the then American President Eisenhower. After his marriage to Bano Khan, he came to London to study graphics. Syeda, their eldest daughter, studied pharmacology and English at London University before becoming a fashion journalist. She started her own fashion business, Aquarius Designs, in Scotland with the help of a £10,000 'Business Woman of the Year' award from the *Sunday Express* newspaper and Glenrothes Development Corporation. While in the ladies' loo at a Saudi Arabian airport, Syeda noticed that the other women wore evening dresses under their long black jhablas and her gowns and dresses are now individually designed for many of the leading ladies of the Middle East.

Sister Jayanti was born in Poona in 1949, the eldest of two children of a Bhaibundh family, the business community of the Sindhis. Her father, tired of working in Africa away from his family, brought them to settle in Britain in 1957. Wanting both to serve and be independent, Jayanti chose science subjects at school, rather than her favourite art subjects so that she could study medicine. While at London University's School of Pharmacy, her father wanted her to spend an extended period in India, to learn about her Indian heritage. After five months, Jayanti became bored with being a tourist and started to learn Indian dance. One day she visited Mount Abu, home of the Brahma Kumaris World Spiritual University, started by Dada Lekhraj (Brahma Baba), a relation of her father. There she 'fell in love with God' and joined the movement. Returning to London in 1969, she found that people were 'not really ready' for their ideas, especially from a 19-year-old girl. Since then, Sister Jayanti has taken her message of peace, love and healthy living to seventy countries through conferences, lectures

and seminars, helped organise activities for the UN International
Year of Peace and conducted meditation at the House of Lords.
She believes that 'meditation is of far greater importance to good
health than medication.'

Bidge Jugnauth was the only daughter born to a low-caste family in
Mauritius. Leaving behind the restrictions of caste and sex, she came
to Britain to train as a nurse. Bidge soon fell ill and discovered that
her body occasionally produces an excess of red blood cells which
causes internal haemorrhaging and prevents her walking. Accepting
her disability, she met her husband, the brother of Mauritius' Prime
Minister, and the couple now have three children. Bidge is a personal
counsellor, runs assertiveness courses for women and is a presenter
of Channel Four's TV programme, *Same Difference*, one of the rare
series by and for people with disabilities. She is a founder of the
Asian People with Disabilities Alliance.

Dr Hoshang Jungalwalla was born in Bombay, but spent the first
few years of his life in Indonesia, where his father worked with the
World Health Organisation. His mother is the educationalist and
author Piloo Nanavutty. After a period as Assistant Director-General
of Health Services in India, Hoshang's father moved to take up
the post of Director of Public Health at WHO's headquarters in
Geneva. Hoshang originally came to Britain to study A levels at
Epsom College, returning for his medical training at the London
Hospital. He is now a Consultant Psychiatrist at Ealing Hospital,
London.

Nasreen 'Munni' Kabir is the fifth of six daughters born into a
Muslim family in Hyderabad. The family moved to Britain in the
early 1950s where all the children were sent to a mixed boarding
school and Munni spent many hours in the school holidays in the
Scala cinema in London's Charlotte Street watching Indian films.
Arriving in Paris after leaving school, she worked as an assistant to
director Robert Bresson and later studied for her MA in Cinema at
Vincennes University, Paris. Munni went back to India several times
where she researched Indian films at the National Film Archive in
Poona and as a result, organised major festivals of Indian film at
the Georges Pompidou Centre, Paris. In 1982, she moved back to
Britain and became Channel Four TV's Consultant on Indian cinema. Channel Four is based in the same Charlotte Street building

as the old Scala cinema and Munni recalls Alfred Hitchcock's saying that 'you always return to the scene of the crime.' Since 1986 she has directed and produced forty-nine programmes of *Movie Mahal* in two series on Hindi cinema.

Daksha Kenney's father, T. A. Bhatt, came to East Africa from Bombay in an Arab dhow during the 1930s. In the Second World War he supplied paper and printing for the British government and became the largest publisher in Kenya, with seventeen publications including an underground newspaper for the Kenyan Independence movement which led to British raids on their home. Daksha's father looked after President-to-be Kenyatta's daughter during his exile. Daksha came to London to do her A levels and then studied journalism. As part of her training, she worked in Parliament for Hansard in 1967. She joined the National Council for Commonwealth Immigrants, but left it in 1972, disillusioned with the path the race relations industry was taking, to start her own stationery business, trading with Africa and the Middle East. Returning to Africa after a divorce from her English husband, Daksha started a public relations firm. Back in Britain, she became an impresario, promoting Indian classical music.

Dr Roeinton Khambatta's Parsi great-grandfather came to Sindh in the wake of Sir Charles Napier's conquest. His paternal grandfather laid out the horticultural gardens of Hyderabad and Karachi. His father, a doctor, served in the public health department of the government and was responsible for keeping yellow fever out of India during the Second World War. Both his sons became doctors and graduated from Grant Medical College, Bombay. Roeinton has been active in Lions International and was the first International Director from south-west Asia and Africa. He was also District Grand Master for Pakistan in the United Grand Lodge of England. Now retired from active hospital work, he still consults at the Royal Masonic Hospital and in private practice. Roeinton came to Britain in 1974 with his wife, Rhodabe, and two daughters, Rowena and Ramona.

The arts critic **Naseem Khan**'s father came from a family of hereditary dewans in a small central Indian state. He came to England for additional medical qualifications in the 1930s, where he met Naseem's mother, sent out of Germany by her Trade Unionist father who foresaw the results of Hitler's ambitions. Naseem was born in Birmingham in 1939, went to Roedean school and to Oxford to read English. After graduating, she spent a year teaching in Finland, before becoming a journalist almost accidentally, unable to resume a career in publishing after a six month visit to India. In time, her career developed into arts policy development and Naseem has done considerable work to ensure that the arts of different cultures are recognised, valued and funded by British society. In 1976, her book, *The Arts Britain Ignores*, was published as the first study of these arts, commissioned by the Arts Council, Gulbenkian Foundation and Community Relations Commission. To prevent the book falling prey to the 'Dusty Shelf Syndrome', Naseem's advisory committee, all black and Asian artists, set up regional conferences that brought artists from various cultures and communities together for the first time. That led on to the creation of MAAS (Minorities' Arts Advisory Service) of which she was the first Director/Co-Ordinator. In 1984, Naseem co-ordinated the 'Festival of India-in-Britain' which promoted Asian arts in Britain and was a response to the official Festival of India whose performers were flown from India. Her second book, *Ocean of Milk*, reflects her interest in Indian classical dance, which also led to her attending the first Indian dance school in London in the 1960s, 'before the paint had dried'. Married to John Torode, the chief leader writer at the *Independent*, they have two children.

Barrister **Naseem Khan**'s father was the most successful insurance agent in Pakistan and went on to become a member of The Million Dollar Round Table Club. She came to Britain to study for the Bar in 1968, then returned to Pakistan for eighteen months. Suffering from amoebic dysentery in warm climates, she now lives in London in a kind of 'medical exile'. After six years in chambers, Naseem joined a neighbourhood law centre in Newham, London, directly helping women with their legal problems. Specialising in immigration, she now works at Paddington Law Centre and is actively involved in campaigning against unjust British immigration laws.

Tara Kothari is the eldest daughter of a Gujarati family from Ahmedabad. She came to England in 1958 with her husband who had been appointed the first Indian manager of the Bank of India in London. In 1967, Tara organised *Sangam*, 'meeting together', of Asian women and later founded the UK Asian Women's Conference in 1977. She has recently been awarded the OBE for her services to the community. Tara has three daughters, all settled in Britain.

Kiran Kumar was born in Kenya in 1948. Her grandfather had brought his three sons from the Punjab to start a soap factory, only to be killed by an English drunk-driver who was never prosecuted. The eldest son started working on the railway as a ticket collector, supporting his brothers through their legal studies in Britain. In return, Kiran's father insisted his elder brother qualify in Britain too and supported his brother's family during his absence. On his return, they started the law firm of Bhandari and Bhandari. Her parents had six daughters – Veena, Kiran, Rekha, Sureta, Ashwini, Supriya – four of whom are now lawyers, before a long-awaited son. Kiran came to Britain for her master's degree in mammalian reproduction. Not wishing to marry any of her parent's suggestions, she started a Ph.D. in prostaglandins before leaving to work for the Wellcome Foundation in the same field. Her parents then introduced her to Harsh, an Indian from West Africa, 'the only one both my parents and I liked.' Now married with three children, Kiran supported her husband for 18 months after he resigned from a commodity broking firm in disgust at being denied a promotion because of his race. Harsh now runs his own successful commodity firm.

Kristine Landon-Smith's Australian father, a doctor, married a Punjabi artist, Lalita Bhandari, in Britain, but feeling homesick, took the family to Australia when Kristine was 3. The second of three girls, she only fully realised her mother was Indian when she started speaking Hindi on a holiday in India. In fact, her mother's father had been Mahatma Gandhi's physician for a time. Kristine returned to Britain at 20 to go to drama school and then went on to teach at India's only drama school in Delhi. At one stage, she had two separate acting careers, one Asian, one European. Tired of people asking why a white actress was taking Asian parts, she started using her Indian grandmother's name as well. Kristine was invited to play a part in a Tara Arts Group production, where she met Sudha Bhuchar. The two have now formed their own theatre company, Tamasha, in London and recently put on the play *Untouchable*.

Pramila Le Hunte's father was an Anglophile Punjabi engineer, himself a graduate of Bristol University, while her mother had a degree in Philosophy and Politics. An only child, she was brought up in the midst of a large number of English 'ex-pats' in copper mining towns in north-east India. Pramila's determination to come to England led her to read English at Cambridge, where she married another undergraduate, Bill Le Hunte. After they had finished their degrees and Pramila had their son, Arjun, Bill got a job with IBM in India. Three daughters, twins Anjali and Ashika, and Abha, were all born there. Pramila taught at Loreto School, among many other activities. Returning to Britain, Pramila became Head of English at North London Collegiate School. After her own children had grown up, she joined the Conservative Party and became a Parliamentary candidate, standing in Birmingham Ladywood in 1983. Pramila is now divorced and, in her usual resourceful way, has started her own business, In Touch Services.

Sharon Lutchman was born in South Africa. Her father's Sikh family originally came from the Punjab and her mother from South India. Theirs was a love marriage between two Indian communities, at that time causing quite a stir. Her parents made a political decision to leave South Africa in 1965 and came to Leicester because of the shoe industry there, her father having worked as a shoe designer. Sharon went to St Martin's School of Art in London and has already presented a one-woman show of her paintings at the Barbican Centre. She teaches part-time at an art college in London.

Lata McWatt was brought up in a Hindu Brahmin family in Allahabad, Northern India, one of five children of a government doctor. She taught at the University of Allahabad for one year before taking up a postgraduate scholarship at the Queen's University, Belfast, in 1972. Lata's first job in Britain was with the Commission for Racial Equality and she now works as a Corporate Planner for race relations in the London Borough of Croydon. Her husband is from Guyana and they have one son.

Ira Mathur's grandfather was the Nawab of Bhopal; her grandmother was Princess of Savanoor, a small South Indian state, until she divorced her husband for gambling away the family wealth. Her great-grandmother, 'not known for her generosity,' put all her money into Swiss numbered bank accounts, dying without telling anyone the numbers. The money is still there, truly untouchable! Her great-great-grandfather, Sir Afsar Ulmulk, served in the British

Army and was knighted by Queen Victoria. Her mother was raised as a strict Muslim, but eloped with Ira's father, a Hindu in the Indian Army. After eleven years of moving around India, due to Ira's father's postings, he left the army, going to Trinidad and Tobago where he built the first highway on Tobago. Ira was first sent to Britain for her education at the age of 13, returning for a post-graduate degree in journalism after obtaining a degree in Philosophy and Literature in Canada. She now works for the *Trinidad Guardian* and the BBC South Asia and Caribbean services.

Farida Mazhar's Muslim parents went from India to Aden, where her father was one of the first doctors. Born in Aden, the youngest of five children, Farida was sent to a Diocesan boarding school in Pakistan, returning to Aden to study for her A levels. She then went to London University for a degree in economics and was joined in London by her mother after the death of her father. Her first job was at the Bank of England. After two years, Farida left to join *The Banker* magazine, a division of the *Financial Times*. Progressing to Lloyds Bank, she was the director responsible for the Middle East and North African business of their Trade and Project Finance department. Farida is now at the French Banque Paribas in the City of London.

Meera Mehta was born in Britain, while her mother, a sculptor, was born in Africa and her father in India. Her parents met in New York and came to Britain in 1961. Meera's maternal grandfather was M. P. Shah, a highly respected philanthropist. Meera was sent to a 'progressive' co-educational school in London and works in her father's aeronautical spare-parts business when she is not riding her horse, George. Their relationship had an uncomfortable start, for Meera at least. On one occasion, George suddenly changed his mind about entering his trailer and she ended up concussed, lying on the grass, while he happily ate the greenery in the next field. As Meera was being taken away in an ambulance, she was only worried about him, asking that he be given some hay. In another incident, the pair ended up in a position usually reserved for cats: stuck in a tree. He now behaves 'quite well' and they have won over 100 rosettes together in dressage competitions up and down Britain. Meera is as well known in equestrian circles as she is in the casualty departments of her local hospitals and has been featured in *Your Horse* magazine for her ability in reforming

George. Meera's ambition is to start a shelter for animals. Her parents, after initial misgivings, now support and encourage her love for her dumb friends.

Janaki Menon's father is from a landed family in Kerela, South India and her mother came from St Kitts in the West Indies. They met at a party in London and married soon afterwards in 1966. Janaki went to North London Collegiate School on a bursary. Before reading law at Cambridge, she spent three months with her father's family in India. Presently, she is working for a new charity, the Citizenship Foundation, whose aim is to promote effective citizenship among young people, before she trains as a solicitor in London.

Katy Mirza was born in Aden where her father was an income tax commissioner. Her family was given safe conduct out of the country to Britain when civil war broke out in 1967. At 17, Katy was noticed by a *Sun* news photographer while shopping in Oxford Street and he immediately offered her a career in modelling. At the same time, she studied Graphic Design during the day and worked as a receptionist at the London Hilton in the evenings, where she was discovered by the Public Relations Officer for the Playboy Club and offered the opportunity to become the first Asian 'Bunny Girl'. Within no time, Katy's good looks and outstanding personality earned her the status of a 'VIP Bunny', where she was called upon to do a great deal of charity and social work. Soon after, she met with the veteran Indian actor Raj Kapoor who was smitten with her charm and offered her a career in Indian movies. Unfortunately, Katy was offered more of the sexy and glamorous rôles accompanied by adverse journalistic publicity, instead of serious acting rôles. Disappointed by the Indian movie scene, she returned to Britain and did many TV shows of which the most popular was the soap opera *Crossroads*. Katy now pursues her TV career and is a fashion designer.

Narendhra Morar was born in Southern Rhodesia and was involved in the struggle for Zimbabwe's independence. He came to Britain in 1974 to study politics at Birmingham before writing his thesis on Asians in Kenya for London University. Wanting a job as a lecturer, he started applying for many other jobs to get interview experience. One of those, for a researcher on *Eastern Eye*, was so successful that he was offered the job. Narendhra went on to produce the music programme *Club Mix* before becoming the editor of the BBC's *Network East*. He is married to Rose Barreto.

Hena Mukherjee's father was one of the many Indian students repeatedly imprisoned for their opposition to the British presence in India. After graduating in philosophy, he married another Bengali before he left East Bengal for Malaya on the advice of his mother. Hena was their third and youngest child, born in 1942 during the Japanese occupation of Malaya, now Malaysia, where the family supported Bose's Indian National Army which fought with the Japanese. Raised by Chinese baby-sitters, Hena grew up speaking more Cantonese and Malay, than English and Bengali. After the war, the Partition of India at Independence meant that her parents' families lost all of their lands in what is now Bangladesh. The family moved instead to Singapore, where, during the final year of a degree in English Literature, Hena married a Bengali doctor going to Britain to continue his studies. In 1964, she joined him in London for a year in which she studied German and French. Hena has spent most of her life working in universities, including gaining her Ph.D. as a Fulbright scholar at Harvard studying the philosophy of education. She has also found time to 'script and voice' educational radio programmes and write many published papers and articles. Hena is now Chief Project Officer of the Commonwealth Secretariat Education Programme, one of the few senior-level Asian women there.

Varsha Mulchandani was born in Hong Kong, where her parents had moved to start an exporting business. Varsha came to Britain to start her degree in French Studies at Durham, finishing it at Pau, south-west France. She married Girdhar, a chartered accountant, in London in 1987. Varsha works as a sales executive for the Hyatt Carlton Tower Hotel and is also a correspondent for *Bharat Ratna*, a Hong Kong based Indian colour magazine.

Jyoti Munsiff's great-grandfather was the first Indian to be made a magistrate. Her parents married after her father attended one of her mother's lectures on the Baha'i Faith. Jyoti was born in 1947, an only child. The family came to London nine months later where her father set up the Indian Tourist Office. A diplomatic posting to Washington DC followed five years later. While in America, Jyoti's mother was given an award by the Red Cross for exceptional services to the poor and was the first woman to be made an honorary member of the Lion's Club International on Capitol Hill. Offered the Consul Generalship in Hong Kong, her father instead returned to London after four years, much to India's Prime Minister Nehru's disappointment. Jyoti passed her A levels at 15 and had to wait until she was 21, then the age of majority, before she could enrol as Britain's youngest ever solicitor. Within a year, she was the only woman in Shell's legal department, at least twenty years younger than anyone else there. Twenty years later, as a Senior Legal Adviser, Jyoti is the highest placed woman in Shell's world-wide organisation and threatens to 'take my career seriously now.'

Piloo Nanavutty (Mrs Jungalwalla) is the eldest of four daughters. Her Parsi father was the Chief Justice of Lucknow and, as a child, Piloo had plays written for her by Attia Hosain. Piloo's mother formed a sporting club in Lucknow, to break the purdah system. Before they could join, men had to bring a woman relative, not in purdah, who also became a member. When all of the city's professional classes were members, the club was wound up as it had served its purpose. Piloo was educated at a Loreto convent school and in 1933 became one of the first Asian women to go to Cambridge, where she stayed to do her doctorate on the Eastern influences in Blake's poetry. Returning to India, Piloo lectured in English Literature at the universities of Bombay and Delhi, then became the Principal of Janki Devi College. Today she is well known for her histories of the Parsis and her children's books on Zoroastrianism. Piloo is married with one son, Dr Hoshang Jungalwalla.

Sita Narasimhan's great-great-uncle founded *The Hindu* newspaper. Both her grandfathers entered the Indian Civil Service, quite a feat when only one Indian, with the highest exam result, was admitted from an area the size of England and Wales each year. Both served as Chief Ministers for Princely States, one in Kashmir, the other in Vijayanagar, Baroda (resigning in protest at the ruler's bigamy) and then Jaipur. After Independence, they both served in Prime Minister Pandit Nehru's cabinet, one as Defence Minister, the other responsible for the first two Five Year Plans. Sita's father, V. K. Thiruvenkatachari was a lawyer in Madras and helped to draft the Indian Constitution, becoming Chairman of the Indian Bar Council.

The eldest daughter, at 13, Sita had the best Senior Cambridge exam results in South Asia. After attending Presidency College, Madras, Sita came to Cambridge in 1947, where she studied English Literature as well as economics. Returning to India, she lectured first at Delhi University and then for ten years at Presidency College as Professor of English, before going to the universities of Yale, Paris and Utrecht on a UNESCO senior fellowship in 1960. Married to the designer of the first Indian computer, Sita took up a long-standing offer of a fellowship at Newnham, her old Cambridge college, in 1966. A patron of the British Association of Tamil Schools, Sita is one of the few women to study the Hindu tradition in Sanskrit and Tamil. As a member of the Divinity Fellowship at Cambridge, she also lectures in comparative religion. In her spare time, Sita is a designer and composer of the dance drama *Fiercer Kind of Being – Tales of Indian Women* and another, based on the classic Sanskrit poem by Kalidasa combined with a medieval Tamil epic, which was created to enhance the mutual understanding of the different cultures in Britain. A single parent, she has one daughter, Tanjam 'Jinny', who works in publishing in the USA.

Saadia Nasiri's parents were born in India, but moved to Pakistan at Partition. She was born in 1964, the third of four children, and was brought to Britain three years later by her father, who had tired of the corruption he found in his job as an engineer in Pakistan. They emigrated again in 1976, going to Canada for three years before returning to Britain. After her A levels, Saadia gained a diploma in advertising, public relations and business studies before trying to enter the advertising industry. Saadia's local BBC radio station, Radio Bedfordshire, was just about to open and was interested in having an Asian programme; having heard of her interest in the media through the local Community Relations Council, the producer rang Saadia and asked if she would like to be a presenter. After two months, she was offered a full time job at the station, 'you name it and I did it.' After a year, Saadia and another young Asian woman, Smita Barcha, were given their own programme, *Smit' Petite and the Karachi Kid*, which Saadia produced. As 'The Karachi Kid', she was heard across London on Saturday evenings. Saadia has just married a fellow Muslim and now lives in Wales.

Zehra Nigar was born in Hetroval, South India, the fourth of ten children of Muslim parents who would move to Karachi, Pakistan at Partition. She started writing poetry when she was 10 years old, her first poem being about an arranged marriage between two of her sister's dolls. Her grandfather, also a poet, disapproved strongly when he found out, as women poets were associated with low-caste singers and dancers. But her parents both encouraged her to continue and Zehra is now one of Pakistan's top poets, receiving invitations to read her poetry from America, the Middle East and India.

Namita Panjabi is the younger of two daughters of a Sindi family. Her paternal grandfather lived in the style of a Nawab in his home state of Hyderabad, while her maternal grandfather was a Karachi lawyer who believed in simple living and education. Namita's mother was engaged to be married at 6, but Namita's grandfather had a dream which told him to break the engagement, a breach of promise which shocked the whole community. Namita's mother went on to become the first Sindi woman doctor. Namita's father studied at the London School of Economics and returned to India to become a banker, in charge of safeguarding India's gold reserves during the Second World War. After schooling in Bombay, Namita read economics at Cambridge before becoming the first woman hired as an executive by the Midland Bank. During her period there, she advised on Britain's entry into the European Economic Community. Returning to India she worked in a merchant bank in Bombay before a conversation at a party led to a career in fashion. Namita is married to another international banker and she now designs and manufactures a line of jewellery and silk leisure garments for top international stores including Harrods and Bloomingdales. Her newest business enterprise is a cross-cultural restaurant in London's King's Road.

Shruti Pankaj's grandfather emigrated after the First World War to Kenya, where Shruti was born in 1966. The family left Kenya in the 1970s, coming to Britain largely because of the better educational opportunities. Shruti, though, was frustrated that her girls' school didn't teach such 'masculine' subjects as economics and so studied for her politics A level at a boys' school. She started writing poetry aged 5 and her first book of poetry was published in 1982. A TV feature on her followed and led to her being asked to write and present pieces for *Crying Out Loud*, *Here to Stay* and a documentary on Lord Fenner Brockway. Before her degree in South Asian

Studies at the University of London, Shruti started writing for *New Life*, establishing herself as a regular columnist. Entrusted with the rôle of press officer, she helped promote the world-wide publicity for the inauguration of the London Peace Pagoda in 1985, as well as being the youngest participant on the preceding week-long pilgrimage from Canterbury. Shruti also helped organise the 'Peace Bus' from London to Moscow for the World Conference on Religion and Peace in 1987 and was one of the fifty young people on it. Returning from a long holiday after graduating, she is now working as the Asian Arts Development Officer for Watermans Arts Centre in London.

Arunbhai Patel was born in India and brought up in Uganda. When General Amin expelled the country's Asian population, Arunbhai's family came to Britain. Originally intending to study to be an aeronautical engineer at Imperial College, he instead qualified as a Chartered Accountant. In 1987, he persuaded two banks to lend him the £17,000,000 needed to buy the Finlays chain of newsagents, Britain's oldest. Arunbhai quickly transformed a £2,000,000 loss into a £4,000,000 profit by using his accounting skills to discover that such traditions as the sale of tobacco were commercially unviable. Realising that the future lay in electronic publishing and information technology, he was engaged in turning a 'very outdated' company into one which would flourish into the next century when a cash-flow problem in October 1989 led to the receivers being called in. Finlays' future is now unsure, but Arunbhai, genuinely popular with his employees and fellow businessmen, is sure to re-enter the *Sunday Times*' list of the 200 wealthiest people in Britain. Married to Mina, the couple have two sons, Anish and Alkesh.

Dr Chandra Patel was born in a small village, Amalsad, in Gujarat. Her father, a philanthropist who built many schools, water stations and roads in the area, died when she was 10. Just before his death, he was made Raosaheb by King George VI. As a woman, Chandra found it difficult to obtain an education, but successfully crammed a five-year course at Kervi, a women's university, into nine months before studying at an Indian medical school. In 1954 she married a lawyer from Kenya who had studied law with her brother in Gujarat. After two years living in Nairobi, the couple came to Britain only to find that getting legal work was difficult so her husband bought some property and started a hotel business instead. Determined to study medicine, Chandra was only admitted to medical school after a long struggle, but proved one of the best students and six years of hospital work were followed by seventeen as a GP. Medical school had taught that stress definitely was not the cause of high blood pressure, but her paper in *The Lancet* on the use of relaxation and biofeedback as a means of lowering blood pressure attracted 1,200 letters from forty countries around the world. Chandra gave lectures across Europe and America and has written two books. The first, *Fighting Heart Disease*, proved so popular that it was translated into many languages. Chandra is now a Senior Lecturer on Community Medicine at University College London and a founder member of the British Holistic Medical Association. Chandra's son is a consultant working in a hospital in America and her daughter, who was born in her final year of medical studies, is also in America. Chandra is thinking of joining them when she retires to write a book on Indian herbal remedies.

Anjali Paul is the eldest of five children of a family originally from the Punjab. Her father, who is in the oil business, took the family to Australia, Libya and the Far East over a period of six years, before coming to Britain in 1971, when she was 10. Anjali has a degree in English Literature from Aberystwyth and did a course in film making at Croydon. She presently works in advertising as a copy-writer. Writing is the first thing she remembers doing and she is currently writing a humorous science fiction novel.

Aruna Paul is married to Swraj Paul, an international Indian industrialist. Aruna was born into the Vij family, a Suryavanshi, the ancient rulers of Hindustan decesended from Ram. The Pauls first came to Britain to obtain medical treatment for their youngest daughter, Ambika, who later died but is remembered in the name of the family's home and a hostel for children in Calcutta. Aruna was educated at the Loreto school in Calcutta, where she gained her BA and teaching degree, then taught at Mother Teresa's Shisha Bhawan before marrying. Aruna has acted in and produced plays, worked in family planning and is now actively involved with many children's charities and the Women's India Association UK. Aruna and Swraj were close friends of Mrs Gandhi. They have three sons, one daughter and five grandchildren.

Shyama Perera was born in Moscow in 1958, where her father was Junior Trade Attaché with the Sri Lankan Embassy. They came to Britain in 1963, where her parents divorced. Shyama left home at 16 and spent two years as a 'Temp' before getting a job as a reporter with a news agency, rising to work on the *Guardian*. A happy turning point in her life occurred when Shyama returned a book to the hostess of a party attended by the Head of Features at London Weekend Television. Six months later, when looking for a presenter for *Eastern Eye*, he remembered the young Asian woman with pink hair and hired Shyama. While at LWT, she became 'the prat' on the *Six O'clock Show*, a typical assignment being to run a nose-blowing contest. She remembers her year there as being well paid and fun, but soon also unbearable. After an attempt to start a PR company failed when their main client went bust, Shyama returned to the *Guardian* as a general reporter and is now a presenter on BBC's *Network East*. She is married to a fellow journalist.

Asha Phillips was born and brought up in France where her father, Padmashri Jehangir Bhownagary, worked for UNESCO at their Paris headquarters. In India, he was Chief Producer of UNESCO's film division and later became Chief Adviser (Films) to Mrs Indira Gandhi. Asha's mother was brought up very strictly and regarded marriage as a liberation, a chance to do anything, 'which came as a bit of a shock to my father!' Her mother went on to write for radio and reviewed films. Asha, an avid Beatles lover, first had her interest in India aroused by the group, especially by George Harrison's discovery of Indian spirituality. Asha came to Britain for her degree in psychology at Sussex University, where she met her husband, Trevor Phillips. He became the first black president of the National Union of Students and is now a broadcaster. Asha trained to be a teacher in London, before doing an MA in psychology back at Sussex University and Child Psychotherapy training at the Tavistock Institute. She now works as a child psychotherapist in London. The couple have two daughters.

Navin Ramgoolam's maternal grandfather came to Mauritius as an indentured labourer to work on the island's sugar-cane plantations. Hard work enabled him to eventually buy half of the land he was working on. Navin's father was the first Prime Minister of Mauritius and died as Governor General, aged 85. Navin is married to Veena Brizmohun. When they first met, at the races, they didn't realise that her grandfather had also come as an indentured labourer and had bought the land next to Navin's grandfather. Navin studied medicine in London and Yorkshire and is now studying law at the London School of Economics.

Usha Devi Rathore's maternal grandfather was the last Maharaja of Burdwan, a 6,000 square mile kingdom stretching from near Calcutta to the borders of Bihar. Usha's grandmother, the daughter of Rai Bhadur Doonichand Mehera of Amritsar, was asked by the Congress Party in the 1960s to stand for Parliament and won a landslide victory. The Maharaja of Kashmir wanted to marry Usha's mother, but she fell in love with, and married, an officer guest of her father. After going to the 'frightfully proper' Walsingham House School For Girls, Usha came to Britain to study television production and 'to party'. Back in India, Usha worked at the Satellite Instructional TV Experiment, surrounded by people who wanted to make 'art', while she wanted to make educational programmes. During her year in London she had met a Scottish rock musician. He came to ask Usha's father for her hand in marriage, but when her father emphatically refused, the couple married anyway. After some time in India, they returned to Britain, where their son, Nikhil Shravan Kenneth Kristyan McAndrew, was born. Now separated, the couple are still best friends. A keen practitioner of Yoga, Usha did her teacher's training at the Bihar School of Yoga, founded by Swami Satyananda Saraswati. She is a patron of the South Asia Council of the English Speaking Union and now divides her time between writing the screenplay for a film about deforestation in India and teaching people to stand on their heads.

Nasreen Rehman was born in 1951 in Rawalpindi, Pakistan, as the second of two daughters. Her military father was involved in the 1958 coup and became Director of the National Construction Bureau and Secretary of Information and Broadcasting, but later resigned in protest against government policies. Nasreen came to Britain for her teaching degree and married a Pakistani settled in Britain. Her father became Pakistan's ambassador to Britain in 1978, just before President Zia's execution of his predecessor, Ali Bhutto. Both his daughters joined the protests outside the embassy and Nasreen feels their protests probably eased her father's conscience. Nasreen's marriage ended in 1983 and, although her two daughters live with her, they are wards of court and cannot leave Britain. She has worked as a research economist for an international bank, studied Urdu and Musicology at London University's School of Oriental and African Studies and is now working on a research project with her guru, Pandit Ravi Shankar.

Siromi Rodrigo's Oxford-educated Sinhalese father was Education Officer at the Sri Lankan High Commission in London in the early 1960s. The fourth of five children, Siromi returned to Britain alone in 1970. She had become involved with the Girl Guides movement in Columbo and was asked by the Chairwoman of the Asia/Pacific region if she was interested in applying for a job at the Guides' International Headquarters in London. Initially employed for two years, Siromi has been in the job for eighteen, travelling all over the world for the Guiding movement. Siromi is now their Deputy Director (Training and Development), effectively the second highest placed professional in the movement.

Amit Roy's father, Benoy Roy, edited many Indian newspapers, including *Indian Nation*. Born in Assam, Amit was sent to St Xavier's, a Jesuit private school in Patna, where cricket was considered 'frightfully important.' The family came to Britain in 1961 when Amit's father joined the BBC's World Service as a producer in their Bengali service. Amit, then 14, was very surprised to find that 'playing with a straight bat' was not considered all that important in his new school. When his father left Britain in 1966, Amit stayed on, winning a scholarship to Cambridge to read mechanical sciences. Having started writing seriously at 16, he began a career in journalism working for the North London Press Group, but after only eight months moved to the Fleet Street offices of the *Glasgow Herald*. In 1973, Amit joined the *Daily Telegraph*, one of 'hardly any' Asian journalists then working for Britain's national newspapers. In November 1979, he was covering events in Iran for the *Telegraph* when the American Embassy was seized. The only foreign newspaper correspondent in Tehran, Amit approached the gates in a bad temper. He told the revolutionary students that he didn't have all day and if they wanted to say something, they'd better get on with it. Amit's message to his editor read, 'This is a typical student sit-in. It won't last more than two hours. Suggest you ignore story. . . .' He was still in Iran when the American Embassy hostages were released, 444 days later! He accepted this 'slight misjudgement' in his typically humorous way and was 'head-hunted' by the *Daily Mail* in 1982. Amit is now a feature writer with the *Sunday Times*.

Gita Saghal is the youngest child of three, her parents having divorced when she was 10, something very unusual in late 1960s India. Gita was brought up by her mother, a political journalist and author who had been to an 'Ivy League' college in America, and her step-father, an unusual man in that his wife's career took priority over his own in the civil service. Always expected to achieve academically, she first went abroad at 16 when she got a scholarship to Atlantic College, a pioneering sixth form college in Wales committed to international understanding. A degree in history at London University followed. Returning to India for several years, Gita became involved with Indian feminism. Then married to an English diplomat, she came back to London, where she uses the lessons learnt in India in the campaigning work of the Southall Black Sisters. Gita was a presenter on the black current affairs TV programme, *Bandung File*.

Sehri Saklatvala's father, Shapurji, was the third Asian MP, first as a Labour MP and then as a Communist in the 1920s. He married an Englishwoman from Derbyshire and said he wanted each of his five children to marry a different nationality, to make a nice hodge-podge and help end nationalism. Sehri, their youngest child, started her career as an actress and during the Second World War toured with a theatre company. After Indian Independence, she worked at the Indian High Commissions in London and Switzerland before a period with the Greater London Council. Now retired, she uses her vocal training to record audio tapes of books for blind people and is researching the life of her father.

Mohini Samtani's father, Paramanand Anand, started the family business exporting Indian films in the 1940s. The second of seven children, Mohini was born in Hyderabad, but brought up in Poona. She went to Trinidad with her husband in 1965 because of the demand there for Indian films. As she explains, Indians arrived in the West Indies over 150 years ago as indentured labourers. Today, they have a mix of old Indian and modern Western customs, meaning that the interest in Indian cinema is high, but as Indian languages have been dropped in favour of English, the films have to be subtitled. The film business was also the reason for Mohini coming to London, as the family owned the Liberty chain of sixteen cinemas running Indian movies in the 1960s. All have now closed, due to the boom in video recorders and the resulting film piracy. In turn, the family has adapted to the video age, owning tape duplicating plants in Nigeria, the West Indies and Dubai. Mohini has two daughters, the eldest, Anita, now runs the family business in Trinidad. Mohini is secretary of Sangam and an exective member of the Sindhi Nari Sabha and runs their charity section. Her famous chutneys and pickles were initially sold for charity and her own brand is now sold to outlets throughout the world, including Fortnum & Masons.

Samir Shah was born in India and went to school in London before reading for a geography degree at Hull University and being awarded a doctorate from Oxford for a thesis on the nature of explanation in urban sociology. After a period working in the Home Office's research department, in 1979 Samir applied to be a researcher on London Weekend Television's *The London Programme*. Failing to get that job, he was called a few days later and offered the post of reporter on their black affairs programme, *Skin*. From there, he went on to *Weekend World*, *Eastern Eye*, *Credo* and became Editor of *The London Programme*. In 1987, the BBC appointed him their Deputy Editor of News and Current Affairs, with particular responsibility for network current affairs programmes. He is married to Belkis Beghani.

Vasuben Shah was born in Kenya, where her father still works in his hardware business in Nairobi. Her grandfather came to Africa at the end of the nineteenth century because of a famine in India, selling his wife's jewellery to pay for his passage. When he arrived the only work he could find was helping build a mosque, which he took on, although a Jain. With the money he earned, he built up a trading business. The third of five children and the eldest daughter, Vasuben was one of the first women in her family to go to college, in Bombay. She shocked her father by wanting to work on her return to Nairobi and so was sent to live with an uncle for a few months, in the hope that she would forget the idea. Instead, she used the time to secure a teaching job. Vasuben had a love marriage within the community four years later and came to Britain with her husband so that he could study economics at London University. The couple travelled the world before returning to Kenya where their three children were born. Maya, her second, was born deaf, blind in one eye and with a hole in her heart, caused by the rubella Vasuben caught from a visitor during her pregnancy. Maya learnt to walk by holding on to the family dog's tail, 'she would look after him, he would look after her!' Unhappy with the standard of deaf schools in Kenya, Vasuben offered to start one herself, but her offer was not taken up by the Shah community, so Maya was sent to a school in Britain. The whole family came to London in 1982, where Vasuben's husband had a fatal heart attack within six months. Courageously rebuilding her life, Vasuben started teaching English as a Second Language, before joining the Citizens Advice Bureau as a voluntary worker and becoming the headmistress of a Saturday school for Gujarati children. She uses her skills in sign language as a specialist social worker for hearing-impaired people and is studying to become a personal counsellor.

Rani Sharma was born in Leeds, England, the eldest child of a Hindu family from the Punjab. Her father came to Britain just after Partition and started his own business. When Rani was 5, her grandfather, a landowner in the Punjab, asked the family to come back to India. The family returned to Leeds six years later and she had an arranged marriage at 17, moving to Reading. Rani is one of the founder members of the Asian women's centre *Sahara*, 'support', and has presented her own magazine programme *Sangeet*, 'music', on Reading's Independent Local Radio station, Radio 210, for over five years. She is the co-ordinator for the 'Video Project' for Berkshire Education Department, producing films for Asian and black parents and children. Her most well-known video, *In Their Own Words*, was made to disprove the suggestion from a secondary school Head that education was wasted on Asian and black girls and features the lives, work and experiences of Asian women living in Britain today. Rani has remarried and has one daughter, Meerja, from her first marriage.

Sarah Sheriff's father was a Radio Officer with the British Merchant Navy. When his wife was expecting Sarah, the first of two children, she asked him to stay on land and he became a radio engineer with the British Forces Broadcasting Service (BFBS). Sarah was born in Malta and lived in Kenya, Libya and Cyprus as her father was posted around the world. She was 11 years old when she came to Britain; her parents were quite happy in Cyprus, but everyone in the BFBS had to do a tour of duty in Britain. Sarah studied the politics and history of the Middle East at London University and Library and Information Science at the Polytechnic of North London. While her brother was at Imperial College. While there, he found 'true Islam' and gradually involved the rest of the family. Sarah started wearing Islamic dress after a conference of Islamic students in Derbyshire and now works for the Islamia Schools Trust where she occasionally represents a Muslim point of view in articles and to the media. She has two books to her name and is acting Co-Director for the Muslim Women's Helpline project.

Thrity Shroff was born in London in 1952, the only child of Zoroastrian parents. Her mother's family is known for the title of Nekhsathkhan Khansaheb which they received from the Moghul emperors in India. Her father, a consultant engineer, together with the family, returned to Bombay when she was 1 year old. Brought up in a traditional family in India, she is proud of her roots in the community. Eight years later, the family moved to Iran. After studying for a degree in psychology and English at Bombay University, Thrity worked as a librarian for the British Council in Iran. Eager to see the country of her birth, she came on a visit, but ended up staying in Britain. In 1986 she was elected on to Harrow Council, having served the local community for ten years in a voluntary capacity. She is currently working with the Prince's Youth Business Trust as a National Co-ordinator, helping to build a bridge between the Trust and the minority communities.

Vina Shukla was born in Bihar State, in India, the second of five children. Her father came to Britain ahead of his family and studied for degrees in English at London and Cardiff. The family was reunited in Walsall in 1974, when Vina was 6. For her law degree at Cambridge, Vina studied the Dewsbury dispute which raised many issues concerning multi-cultural life in Britain. She is now at Oxford studying for her post-graduate degree.

Nahid Siddiqui was born in Pakistan, an eldest child. When her father was jailed under martial law for printing posters, her mother, Tallat, became a successful actress, working on radio, stage and screen. Travelling with her mother, Nahid became attracted to dancing, while her younger sister, Arifa, is now a singer, actress and TV personality in Pakistan. Nahid's formal dance training began relatively late at 15, but her talent at *Kathak* ('A story teller', a Moghul court dance performed with strings of bells around the ankles) meant that she was asked to appear on Pakistani television by her future husband, international actor and producer Zia Mohyeddin. Nahid joined a dance company which took her around the world, before moving to Britain in 1978 when women dancing on TV was declared to be indecent by the newly appointed Minister of Culture, producing headlines such as 'Nahid Siddiqui is ruining the younger generation!' Now based in Birmingham, where Zia Mohyeddin produces and hosts his own programmes *Here and Now* and *Spice*, Nahid still 'weaves golden spells' dancing to audiences worldwide. The couple have one son.

Bapsi Sidhwa was born in Karachi in 1939 and brought up in Lahore, Pakistan. Her maternal grandfather was Mayor of Karachi, while both her father and her brother have been elected to the Pakistan parliament, her brother serving as Federal Minister for Minority Affairs. Bapsi was married at 19, three children quickly following, before a divorce at 23. She became a writer after hearing the story of a woman being murdered for running away from her husband. The first of her three novels, *The Bride*, was the result. All three have been internationally published, the others being *The Crow Eaters*, about a Parsi family in Lahore, and *Ice-Candy-Man*, set at the time of Partition. Now remarried, Bapsi teaches creative writing at various American universities and has won several awards, including the Pakistan Academy's National Award for English Literature and the prestigious Bunting Fellowship at Harvard. She represented the Punjab during the United Nations 'Women's Year' of 1975.

Mani Sidhwa was born in Bombay, where her father was a stock broker and astrologer, and her mother a teacher. After gaining her BA in Economics and Geography from Bombay University, she worked for Tata Fisons for six years, leaving to marry her husband who had settled in Britain. Mani worked with a local Community Relations Council before leaving to be with one of Britain's largest marketing consultancy, research and training firms. The couple have one son.

Sister Joseann is from a large Catholic family in Kerela, South India. Inspired by Mother Teresa of Calcutta and feeling drawn to God, she joined the Missionaries of Charity and is now the regional superior for Britain and Europe. In her Order, even the non-Indian nuns proudly wear saris.

Devinia Sookia's real name is Trivedita Devi. Born to a Hindu family in Mauritius, she came to Britain in 1974 after four years in France studying French Law and Political Science. Devinia was called to the English Bar by the Honourable Society of Lincoln's Inn in 1979. After having completed a three-year journalism course in eight months, she returned to Mauritius to practise, but is now in Britain as the group advertising manager at Hansib Publishing and their women's page editor. Devinia is married to Bashir and they have one daughter.

Pireeni Sundaralingam was born in Ceylon to Tamil parents, the eldest of three children. Her father trained to be a surgeon in Britain, although he now works as a General Practitioner. Her mother fulfils the equally life-sustaining rôle of 'domestic engineer'. The family came to Britain in 1970, when Pireeni was 2, and returned to Sri Lanka for a year when she was 6. After attending many primary schools, as her father moved from hospital to hospital, she went to a 'very minor' private school for the whole of her secondary education. There, Pireeni faced resentment and harassment from her predominantly male peer group. However, refusing to conform, she proudly retained her own identity. After finishing her BA in Experimental Psychology at Oxford, Pireeni is now involved in research at London University in Child Psychology.

Meera Syal came with her parents to Britain from India as a young girl. Brought up in the Midlands, she graduated in English and Drama from Manchester University. Her one-woman show, written with a fellow student, appeared in Bombay and the Edinburgh Festival Fringe, before being filmed by the BBC. Now a professional actress and author, Meera has appeared in several productions at London's Royal Court Theatre, including *Serious Money*, as well as on television (for example, *The Secret Diary of Adrian Mole*, *The Bill* and *Black Silk*) and in films (*Sammy and Rosie Get Laid*). As a writer, she is a member of the Asian Women Writers' Workshop and is the author of episodes of *Black Silk* and *Tandoori Nights*, plus another one-woman show, *The Leather Mongoose*. Meera is a third of the Bhangra group Saffron and sings with a jazz band. She is married to Shekhar Bhatia, a journalist.

Freni Talati was born in Peking, China. Her uncle came to China prior to the Boxer Rebellion to trade and was soon followed by her father, Jamshed. After a brief stay, he went back to India to marry Freni's mother, Najan Neckoo, and returned with her to Peking. The owners of the Talati House Hotel and Grand Theatre in Tientsin, the family were the only Parsis in Peking. Freni was the second of three daughters and became an expert in Mandarin Chinese, meeting Princess Der Ling, the principal Lady-in-Waiting to the Empress Dowager, while researching for her book on Chinese court costumes. When Japan attacked the USA and Britain in December 1941, the family were celebrating Freni's mother's birthday. Their celebrations were interrupted by the Japanese who took her father for questioning 'for a few minutes', but did not return him. The women were interned some months later; told they were being taken to a holiday centre, they could only take what they could carry. They were actually taken to the horrific Weihsien camp, about a quarter of a square mile shared with 1,000 English, Dutch, French and American nationals, where they were reunited with Freni's father. After the Japanese surrender in 1945, Weihsien camp was the last to be liberated. Freni's eldest sister, Shireen, had studied music in London and was repatriated immediately after the war to Britain, where she married and invited the rest of the family to join her. Both of Freni's parents died soon after arriving in Britain, the direct cause of their deaths being the extreme hardship suffered during the war.

Kusoom Vadgama's father enlisted in East Africa during the First World War, but the family's direct links with Britain go back to 1921 when he came to London to study automobile engineering, later moving to Paris and Berlin. He admired the British education system, but at the same time hated the British rule in India. His clothes were always made from Indian material and there was a family boycott of all South African goods. Kusoom was born in Kenya and, not surprisingly, politics and patriotism were major interests and influences on Kusoom's life. At the height of the 'Quit India' movement in the 1940s, she was a prominent member of the Indian Voluntary Force in Nairobi. While studying the history and glory of the British Empire at the Government Indian Girls' High School, her spare time was spent leading anti-British processions and attending 'Free India' rallies. Kusoom came to Britain in 1953, where her main interest has been the study of the very special relationship that exists between India and Britain, in particular the influence and activities of Indians in Britain before India's Independence. She went to the USA in the early 1960s for further studies at the Illinois College of Optometry in Chicago and later moved to New York where she studied drama at the American Academy of Dramatic Arts. However, after returning to London, Kusoom decided to be an optometrist rather than take up a thespian profession. Her present efforts to put on record *all* Indian contributions in Britain can only be described as a 'magnificent obsession'. Kusoom is the author of *India in Britain*, a pictorial record covering the period from 1852 to 1947, and now chairs the Centre for Research into Asian Migration at Warwick University.

Ella Vala's paternal grandfather came to East Africa in 1901 from Gujarat to trade. Ella left Uganda at 14 with her mother and four brothers and sisters in the enforced Asian exodus when President Amin expelled the Asian population. After landing at Stansted airport and a period in a Haverhill refugee camp, the family joined her uncle in Maidstone, eleven people sharing two bedrooms. Because Ella's father didn't have a British passport, he had been placed in a refugee camp in Italy for eight months. After having studied as a trainee accountant, Ella now works as a consultant in legal accountancy and is married to a lawyer, Ramesh.

Rozina Visram's Ismaili grandparents came from Kutch to Zanzibar to run a grocer's store. The fifth child of six, Rozina was educated in Zanzibar, Nairobi and Makerere University College in Uganda. She came to Britain in 1969 to do her master's degree at Edinburgh on Scots explorer David Livingstone's links with India. She went on to start a Ph.D. as a part-time student. Unable to teach in Scotland, she came to London where she taught history and politics in a large London comprehensive school and abandoned the Ph.D. as she became more involved in her teaching. The impetus to write about the history of Indians in Britain came from the realisation that blacks were invisible in school textbooks. Her first book was researched when she was an Inner London Education Authority Teacher Fellow at the Centre for Multicultural Education. Originally concentrating on the nineteenth and early twentieth centuries, she then discovered that Indians have been coming to Britain since the eighteenth century. Her research was published as the book *Ayahs*,

Lascars and Princes, with a version for schools, *Indians in Britain*. Rozina is currently Deputy Director of the Community Division at ILEA's Centre for Urban Educational Studies.

Iqbal Wahhab's academic parents came to Britain when he was 8 months old, as his father started studying for his Philosophy Ph.D. at London University. Expecting to return to East Pakistan after its completion, his mother bought an enormous trunk to fill with 'goodies' to take back with them. Twenty-five years later, the family still has the trunk in London and Iqbal's mother, now a headmistress, still occasionally puts things in it. After studying politics at the London School of Economics, where he edited the Student Union newspaper, Iqbal joined the *Asian Times* as a trainee reporter. He rapidly rose to become the paper's deputy editor before leaving to be appointed the editor of the *Asian Herald*. The co-founder of the Black Journalists' Association, he now works as a freelance journalist for the *Independent*, *Sunday Times* and *Daily Telegraph* newspapers.

Koki Wasani's father travelled to Uganda from India's Saurashtra state, now part of Gujarat, at the turn of the century. Starting as a coffee broker, he became the owner of many cotton ginneries. Koki was the ninth of ten children and travelled to India to study with an elder sister. After finishing her studies, 'as is usual in Hindu families', her father started looking for a husband for her. After two years' 'negotiations', Koki married. Their son was born in Uganda before the family moved to Kenya, then on to Britain in 1976. Koki started work at the photographic counter at Boots, where she was forbidden to wear a sari, before working in her husband's photographic business. In 1987 she became the first woman president of the Lohana community in Britain.

Amrit Wilson was born in Calcutta in 1941. Her father was in the Indian civil service and the family moved around Bengal and North India. The second child of three, Amrit was 20 when she came to London for postgraduate study in physical chemistry at Imperial College. One firm she worked for before becoming a journalist manufactured dangerous explosives, dangerously! Amrit married an Englishman and the couple ended up staying in Britain when he couldn't find a job in India. Her book, *Finding a Voice*, about Asian working-class women in Britain, was published in 1978 and won the Martin Luther King award. Amrit teaches part-time in an access course for black students and is writing a book on Eritrea.

Jeya Wilson was born in Ceylon on Bastille Day, the eldest of two daughters to a Tamil father who unusually wanted girls. Her parents took her to England when she was 8 so her father could complete his post-graduate degree. The next eight years saw Jeya moving around the world, back to Sri Lanka, to the USA as an American Field Service scholar, to Western Samoa, finally ending up in New Zealand. After receiving her first degree in political science, she worked as a civil servant, a researcher/journalist and an actress, including a rôle on a New Zealand TV soap opera, *Close to Home*, before gaining another degree. An accomplished debater, Jeya was the reigning Australasian champion when she went to Oxford University as a Commonwealth scholar and became the second Asian woman President of the world famous Oxford Union debating society in 1985; the first had been Benazir Bhutto. She is married to a New Zealander, Professor Peter Utting. In 1981, the couple visited South Africa and wrote a book, *Babes in Verwoerds*, a play on the name of the architect of apartheid, Afrikaner President Hendrick Verwoerd, revealing their misadventures as a mixed-race couple.

Renoo Zaiwalla is the eldest daughter of three. Her father qualified as a doctor in Britain and stayed for five years, returning to India in the mid-1950s where he died when Renoo was 12 years old. She stopped studying for her Chartered Accountancy exams to get married to Sarosh in 1976. He came to Britain to qualify as a solicitor specialising in marine law and the couple 'gradually' stayed on ever since. They have two children.

Marc Zuber was born Zubair Ahmed Siddiqi in Lucknow. His father came to Britain in 1949 as a BBC radio producer and Marc followed two years later with the rest of the family. After school, Marc went to Harrow Technical College and then chose to go to a drama school, the Webber-Douglas Academy of Dramatic Arts, rather than university. He left in 1968 when signed on by the theatrical agent, Jimmy Fraser. Marc changed his name after Jimmy's first piece of advice, 'Well, I don't think this name's gonna get you very far.' In his years as an actor, only two-fifths of his rôles have been 'Asian' and he is adamant that he is not an 'Indian actor', but an actor who happens to be Indian. Marc is proudest of his two years at the Royal Shakespeare Company, during which he had to turn down the chance to appear in Vinod Pande's first film. Many years later, he went to India for Vinod's second film and rapidly became a major star in Hindi cinema, appearing in 'forty-seven or so' films.

Index